T0209186

A present for your present.

TO: _____

I am always thinking of you and how you are developing into a good and exemplary human being. I will always want the very best for you.

I realize that living a good and productive life in "today's" environment is far from being an easy task. However, the more we all know about "life" and its human inhabitants, ourselves, the better we can make the decisions we need to make to give us the best chance for a good life.

Please use the REMINDERS you will discover in this book to assist you in ALL you PLAN.

_____

Date:

Balboa Press books may be ordered through booksellers or by contacting:

Balboa Press
A Division of Hay House
1663 Liberty Drive
Bloomington, IN 47403
www.balboapress.com
1 (877) 407-4847

Print information available on the last page.

ISBN: 978-1-9822-1210-0 (sc)
ISBN: 978-1-9822-1211-7 (e)

Library of Congress Control Number: 2018910903

Balboa Press rev. date: 10/17/2018

Uncovering A Non-Mystifying Way To Understand
And Benefit From Positive Human Relations And
The Resultant Individual Self-Realization

REMINDER!

When We Discover How "Life" Will Behave
Toward Us, When We Behave Properly Toward
"Life," Smooth "Sailing" Is On The Horizon

The
TIT 4 TAT
SOLUTION

"I Give You Like For Like"

A NON-FRICTION Writing, Not Intended
To Have a "TEFLON EFFECT"

Bengt Olov Danielsson

BALBOA.
PRESS
A DIVISION OF HAY HOUSE

The
TIT 4 TAT
SOLUTION

< Beneficial Things to Remember >

and

DO

Bengt Olov Danielsson

**IN LIFE, THERE IS TOO
MUCH TO GAIN TO LOSE!**

Awaken your intellect, your reasoning power. This is a time of preparations for what is expected of ALL HUMAN BEINGS to enable a good life to be lived.

LEARNING is guided SELF-DEVELOPMENT.

Book Review

"This stunning, remarkable, well-intended self-realization book – demands a wide audience."

Grandfather's Own Thoughts

WARNING!!!

What you are about to be reminded of is non-controversial.

It may be non-offensive and non-disturbing to ALL audiences.

Reader attention can be highly beneficial.

KNOW THIS!

This book is FOR YOU and about you. It is about answering the one very important question that is "COMMON" to All Human Beings and which you <u>NEED</u> a helpful answer to.

This is the question!

> "What do I need to do for myself to live the
> best and most positive life I can?"

WELCOME TO A DEGREE
OF ENLIGHTENMENT

Let me start out by saying – Learning how to be living a good life is not going to be all that easy. But it can be a very interesting and potentially very positive undertaking that is "doable" and well worth all our time on this earth.

All you will need are some good common sense directions and a clear realistic "picture," in your mind, of all the good and meaningful things you would like for yourself and your family. Then start "moving mountains."

Remember, as one human being you cannot be expected to, nor will you be able to, change the world and all its citizens. But you may be able to benefit greatly from "looking" at yourself and consider changing yourself in all ways that you would deem beneficial to you based on your personal goals for living a good life.

This book, *TIT4TAT*, will provide you with much good insight on how to do it for your considerations and benefit.

Look for "Eye Openers"

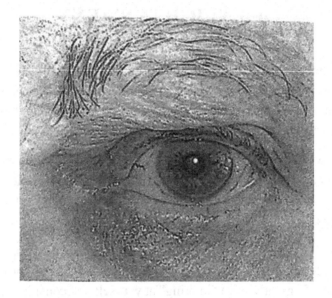

Something that causes your "mind's eye" to see an opening to enlightenment or startling disclosure or experience. It is always the mind that sees. The eyes are merely receptors that translate light rays into signals to the brain.

Is

The Human Factor Involved

With All That We Do?

YES!

You Are CAPABLE!

To PLAN your life's direction is to believe in tomorrow.

Learning what to do and how to do it, <u>AND</u> accepting full responsibility for getting it done, - <u>THIS</u> is a good cause for success.

You should consider reading this book **IF** you are at all curious about and desirous of learning how the life you are currently living can be made better for you (by you). Is there any doubt in your mind that any current situation(s) of yours cannot be made better?

CONTENTS

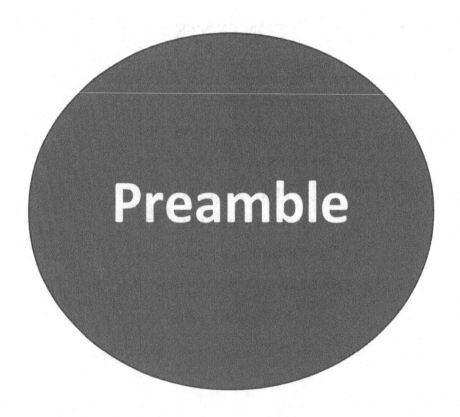

Preamble

AN INTRODUCTION TO
SELF-REALIZATION

GRANDFATHER'S LEGACY OF HOPE

"Yesterday I was <u>clever</u>, so I wanted to change the world.
Today I am <u>wise</u>, so I am changing myself."

(Rumi, Persian Poet – 1207-1273)

"To be or not to be,
That is your decision."
(Your Teachers)

PERHAPS?

When you pick up a book that has peaked your interest, it is a pretty good bet that you had good reasons in mind. Anytime you decide to peruse the contents of a book, it is most likely because your curiosity and your desire to know more about a specific subject overruled other thoughts.

This book is formatted somewhat different than other books you have read. When you read a "story," true story or fiction, you have the beginning, the middle, and the ending, and everything is correlated. When reading this book, you will find that just about every paragraph or page contains these three parts. Therefore, it is suggested that you read this book in a perhaps more meticulous fashion since, to the writer's intent, each paragraph or page will or may contain both a question and answer in order to most clearly and timely make "the point."

Slow, thoughtful reading while mindfully putting the pieces of this "puzzle" together will benefit you the most.

Your personal THINKING TIME when reading here should be on the side of generosity.

About This Book

It is suggested by the experts, the very knowledgeable book publishing "gurus," that you "present" your book on the first few pages with some very "mind-catching" words to entice all potential readers to want to read the entire book immediately.

Well, I tried putting some very positive and important "mind-catching" words on a "one page" presentation, and believe me there are many. But when I completed my attempt, I realized I had completed this entire book.

"Big point" here – Everything in this book can be very "mind catching" and, I believe, will have the potential of being extremely helpful to all who undertake reading this book. After all, I cannot think of any human being who does not want to have a good life, and if they are already living a good life – to make it better. Better is better!

This book is an introduction to "REMINDERS" of knowledge that many of us already know, but do not necessarily use or practice as much as we should to earn, for ourselves, the most benefits available.

When you want or need to do something, it has already been decided, in your mind, what it is. What you now have to do is also learn and decide what you have to do, what steps or "moves" you need to take in order to get done what is on your mind.

Your mind does not automatically fill itself with ideas of pleasant and profitable opportunities for you to pursue and complete. You have to WANT something first, and that something, I trust, will always be things that will add to and continue to build a good life for you and your family.

This book is full of "common sense" insight to the functioning of the human mind. It suggests how the human mind can respond when it is fed certain input. The content of this book is not intended to tell you what you should do; that is your decision to make. But it does suggest what your results can or will be if you use this knowledge in a positive way.

Remember this, and please always keep it in the forefront of the THINKING part of your mind. "Your present will be determined by your past. Therefore, in the future you should be very careful what you do in your past." (Ziggy cartoon)

When planning for the rest of your life, THINK ABOUT IT this way. Your life will always consist of the PAST, the PRESENT, and the FUTURE.

The past is the past. You can THINK about it, you can LEARN from it, and, hopefully, be happy about what you accomplish. Other than that, you cannot go back and do things differently or undo things you did.

The present is now, "TODAY." What have you planned for "today" that can and will make you feel good and proud at the end of "TODAY?" Remember, once "TODAY" is over, it becomes the past. Do not let TODAY go by in vain.

The Future – ah! The future. This is where everything will happen for you that has not yet happened. Are you prepared? Your future is all yours to do with whatever you want. The only thing you FIRST have to do is decide "What do you want?"

Question! Why would you not want to make your every future "move" count toward something, anything that could be to your personal benefit?

I am hoping that you are a person who wants good and pleasant things to happen to you and be forever a part of a good life for you. Listen! We all have opportunities to make things better for ourselves; it will just depend on how much we want to make things better.

This book is intended to be educational, informational, and inspirational.

Always keep this in mind – "Tomorrow's comforts require today's preparations." Don't sell yourself "short." Live for "today," but also prepare yourself for "tomorrow."

"The 'MO' you know" should be part of your daily thinking about yourself.

This book is not written as the "traditional story" where the plot evolves and ends up with a "big bang."

However, each section of this book will remind you of many different things, all positive. And each section will demonstrate the "point" that the writer wants to share with you. So each section can stand on its own validity. But when you complete your reading of this book and you put all the sections together, it will, hopefully, represent to you a very usable "eye opener" and positive guide to how best you can live and foster a good life for yourself.

You will notice, when reading, that many thoughts are being repeated several times in the various sections. The reason for this, in the author's mind, is the importance to you of "getting it!"

What Else is This Book All About?

It is about figuring out for ourselves the potential value we can create for ourselves, personally, with each "step" we take as we "walk" through our respective lives. Because of all the circumstances that we are constantly surrounded by, and the indisputable fact that we have an absolute limit of 24 hours each day to make the most of everything positive, each positive step we take can add to our "coffer," and each negative step we take can reduce what is already in our coffer.

Well, you may question, "Does that mean every minute we are awake and walking around we have to be "tip toeing" around, carefully, so we don't 'trip' and hurt ourselves?" Metaphorically speaking, Yes!

It is, to my way of thinking, humanly impossible to be your most productive self if you try to "walk around" each and every day without being able to tell yourself, with reasonable accuracy, which direction "your feet" should be facing as you walk. Telling yourself which direction "your feet" should be facing as you walk through each day, week, and month of your lifetime is not going to be all that difficult. It is not going to be difficult because you are already doing it, to an extent. You are essentially giving "your feet" direction each time you make a decision to do something, i.e., driving to work, driving to go shopping, perhaps picking the children up from school, going with your family to church, etc. These are simple examples. But the effort to create a direction for "your feet" to take you wherever you decide you need and want to go with your "life" will involve a little more thinking on your part. Thinking about positive things into your future is usually filled with much pleasure and anticipation, thereby making it a lot easier to accomplish. And, of course, the only basic human resource you will need to start the ball rolling, as it were, is you. Yes, you are and will be the "producer and director" of your own life. Perhaps a good motto could be, "Life is a do-it-yourself job, which I will nurture into a good life."

The intent of this writing is to help you with some good reasons and reminders of how we can accomplish creating the most beneficial directives for ourselves.

The potential values that can be created for ourselves, that I alluded to in the first sentence above, can be about nurturing our health, adding to our knowledge base, adding to our group of friends, adding to and protecting our personal finances, etc.

Please keep the intent of this writing on the "front burner" as you read and think about what is being suggested.

About the Author

You may wonder who is this "Grandfather" who is writing this book, *Tit4Tat*?

Well, I would love to be in a position to outline here all my writing accomplishments by noting all of the various awards that I have collected in my lifetime, but Alas! I cannot. Besides an occasional very long letter, a short speech, a subjective short lecture, this book is my very first attempt at influential authorship. However, in my humble opinion, one does not need to be a well-known, highly accomplished writer to share helpful knowledge gained from 80 years of living a good and productive life.

Having learned and acquired the knowledge, the ideas of how you can produce for yourself a good and productive life should be of interest to all. It is knowing how to develop an accurate answer to the proverbial question whenever anything happens in your life, good or bad, "Why did this happen?"

Remember that there are always reasons that "back up" everything that happens in our lives. It is commonly referred to as the "Cause and Effect" phenomenon.

That is what this book is all about. And my personal experiences that I have enjoyed up until now (and it does continue) is based on "REMEMBERING" and exercising what, in a highly positive sense, is total "common sense moves" on my human brothers and sisters.

When you are in a position, as a human being, and you realize that you can only progress your life with the help and assistance of other human beings, you cannot function effectively if you do not, at least, have a good basic knowledge of what makes you and what makes all others "Tick."

This book, *Tit4Tat* has many good basic REMINDERS of how to deal with Human Relations, Personal Health, and Personal Finance, and what I believe are valuable ideas of how we should consider thinking about just about everything meaningful.

Author's Objective!

To remind us ALL of an "END" toward which our efforts should be directed, should be aimed at.

This "END" will represent the attainment of our purpose on this earth, the fulfillment of living a good life, and being able to "shout" with sincerity;

EUREKA!

(An exclamation of triumph at having discovered early in our lives God's intent for living our life when creating humanity in His own image.)

Just think of the author as the MESSENGER.

My thought is – "Helping" one human being will not change the world. But surely for that one human being the world will change forever. I will attempt to help someone in need to be reminded of and recognize advantageous "tools" to use to enable the best possible life to be lived.

My Opening Suggestion

I suggest to all of us with all my sincere affections for Humanity

"NO EXCUSES"

Making excuses for yourself for not doing "right" by yourself is MOST NEGATIVE.

To all of us who may feel that we did not "get the breaks" as we were growing up, for those who feel they were "short changed" by their upbringing – LISTEN!

Are you "looking back" on your past to try to figure out why you are not doing <u>now</u> what you <u>now</u> know you should be doing for yourself?

Other human beings do not "owe" us (individually) anything unless and until we have first given them a reason to feel indebted. However, we owe ourselves <u>a lot</u>. How? By learning how to get along, in a positive way, with "others," and by learning what is required from each of us to live a good life for ourselves. Know that there are reasons for everything that ever happened or will happen to each of us in our lives. Learn what works well and what does not work well. And then choose "which" directions you want to proceed with your life.

It is a Do-It-Yourself Life!

If you have any doubts about this heading, "Don't!" It is definitely a "Do-It-Yourself-Life," so whatever you do TO yourself and FOR yourself, you have to live with it. Therefore, make doubly certain that you only do good things for yourself and let some of the good stuff you do flow over to others who may always be able to use a "helping hand."

That is what the "Tit4Tat" concept has always meant (except for the original usage, which involved "WARS").

IS IT RELEVANT?

What we **think** should be relevant. What we **say** should be relevant. What we **do** should be relevant.

BUT, relevant to what?

RELEVANT to our acknowledged PURPOSE for living our lives.

RELEVANCE is important to each of us in "TODAY'S WORLD." Living a good life demands a continuing process of matching our positive thoughts with our positive actions.

From the initial stage of **visualizing** how we want our life to "play out," relevance will be a major factor in allowing us to adjust our available time to perform the essentials for living a good life.

This book has **many** pages, and to many readers "of today" who are looking for ways to learn in smaller slices of time, do consider this:

- In addition to the opening "Salvo" and the Summary sections, this writing has six (6) distinctly separate sections of reminders of "good stuff." It is almost like six (6) separate smaller books that can be read separately at any time.
- When you complete your reading of the six (6) separate sections, these reminders will no doubt flow together in your mind and give you a clear and pleasant "picture" of how a human being's life can be arranged (by you) in the most pleasant and fruitful manner.

This book is intended to help us better understand how to BUILD a good life for ourselves and what we need to do to SUSTAIN a good life.

Remember that all the "building blocks" that you will need for a good life emanate from human beings.

Salute

Here is to ALL of us who live and work for satisfaction and security.

Knowing how "Life" is meant to work will give us an advantage that can help ALL of us.

Knowing the existence of the cause and effect phenomenon can move us ALL a little closer to perfection.

May we ALL do, for ourselves, what we know we should do, without delay.

May we never, ever have an opportunity to think to ourselves, "I wish I had done that!"

Knowledge is what gives human beings abilities. "Abilities" are what gives a human being value. Remember, a human being without knowledge has no abilities and, therefore, it would suggest has no value.

"New" Formula Based on Old Formula, Dusted Off

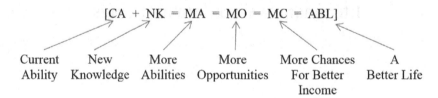

$$[CA + NK = MA = MO = MC = ABL]$$

| Current Ability | New Knowledge | More Abilities | More Opportunities | More Chances For Better Income | A Better Life |

Your "Ability" inventory, the larger the better, is what will allow you to become more successful.

Does this "Formula" give you some "food for thought"?

I am hoping it will.

Focus on the Following as You Keep on Reading

"Continuous effort, not strength or intelligence, is key to unlocking our potential" (Winston Churchill).

Meaning: You can possess all the knowledge in the world, but if you put NO EFFORT into applying it to gain results for yourself – it is of little or no value.

"Creating a spending plan and envisioning what you want down the line actually stimulates the same part of the brain that the Lottery does. It is emotions, it is that vision, that is what motivates people, not lectures" (Brad Klontz, Financial Psychologist).

Meaning: A spending plan, in this quote, means a "Plan," by you, as to how you want to spend your TIME and your MONEY to create and live a good life for yourself and your family.

"THINK ABOUT IT!"

If I have used this saying, "Think About It," once, I must have used it a "million" times in this book.

I want to explain why. To my way of thinking, the expressions "Think About It" means the same as the warning shout, "WATCH IT." It is meant for your benefit.

You understand when someone hollers "WATCH IT." It is usually to prevent another person from being injured by a potential dangerous happening. Writing or saying "THINK ABOUT IT" is intended to entice people to "STOP" and consider the "pros and cons" of what is being said or read, and evaluate how it could or may affect you personally. The saying is meant for you to give the subject matter enough "thinking time" to fully understand it, and gain from it everything that could be beneficial for you.

Let's Have a Good Talk

This is grandfather's unsolicited, prudent advice for living a good life, for his off-springs and all human brothers and sisters who would like self-sustaining good counsel.

To my own family, I realized some time ago that it would be both mentally and physically impossible for all of you to "lend me your ears" long enough to allow me sufficient time to tell you, to <u>REMIND</u> you of the many proper, good, an simple ways to live a good life. Things that us "old timers" learned years ago and which are still in vogue today, and will be "tomorrow" and "forever."

Over the years as you all grew and matured, there were times when I put on your table some "food for thought," which at the time I felt would be good for you to be aware of. I realized that as young little humans you only "ate" what you wanted to "eat" and your "vegetables" always seemed to be the "losers."

Well, hopefully at this point in your life your mind's "appetite" will be more wanting for nourishment and that you will be willing to try to rationalize and more easily and clearly understand, in your own way, what can be good for you. Not only good for your physical health, but that your maturity and more clear understanding of all things, in general, will allow you to digest more of the same kind of "food for thought."

Although this time it will serve you even better since now you are, and some of you will soon be, "on your own." When it comes to guiding your own life, it will be advantageous to have learned how to rationalize what will be truly most beneficial for you and your present and future families.

This "menu" of REMINDERS, and they really are reminders of very meaningful thoughts and human behaviors that has always been an integral part of what is still today a very sensitive and extremely important subject called Human Relations. To your grandfather's way of thinking, a good dose of knowledge and understanding of how effective positive human relations works is paramount to giving everyone the opportunity to living a good and successful life.

Why not consider this book as another "pocket dictionary" that you can use over and over again, at your convenience, to refresh your memory on what human beings need to always be keenly aware of when trying to "get along" and work together for <u>mutual benefits</u>.

A great ending begins with you. Your rewards from living your life is and will always be a direct consequence of what you do. Without knowledge, a human being is not worth much. THINK ABOUT IT!

Greetings

You will now be REMINDED to REMEMBER!

You will never reach an age beyond which you can no longer do good for yourself and for others. Use your every living moment to your advantage. "Time" is a most valuable resource, <u>BUT</u> only if you do something <u>VALUABLE</u> with it.

The use of common sense, of being practical, judicious, sensible, and of having an instinct of self-preservation should prevail in all our activities to move our lives forward.

It will be clear in your mind, as you read on, that all the challenges you will face will always, and <u>ONLY</u>, involve other human beings as well as "Mother Nature."

When you learn and you act on what you have learned, you will come to realize that the **WORDS** you use when communicating with others and the **ACTIONS** you display (your attitude/behavior) with others will give you specific results that will define how effective living your life can be. In other words, how you decide to deal with other human beings will help define the quality of your own life.

The content of this book will help you to have a **"conversation" with your future** and it will begin now. Since the author has not had any formal introduction to the techniques of writing, "what you see is what you get." However, will it really matter how useful knowledge is being conveyed as long as it is in a clear and reasonably complete manner? The knowledge the author wishes to share with you is as important to our overall well-being "Today" and "Tomorrow" as it was "centuries" ago.

Your journey through life will benefit by your basic knowledge and adherence to four essential subjects:

- ✓ Your workable knowledge of human relations
- ✓ Your personal finances

- ✓ Your personal health
- ✓ Your relationship with your Maker

Having good basic knowledge and understanding of these subjects will definitely facilitate living your life in the most positive and best way possible. This book will attempt to give you that good basic understanding.

If "a picture is worth 1,000 words," can you imagine what an **UNDERSTANDING** can be worth, to you, as it concerns knowing how "life" will treat you in return for how you treat "life?" Living a good life has to do (all the time) with communicating with, working with, and accomplishing positive things with other people. Nothing will affect our lives more than our mode of action toward each other.

"REMINDERS"

Are you "looking" favorably on "REMINDERS"?

If not, do remember "that a reminder" is just as valuable as "remembering," especially if you have temporarily "forgotten." WOW! That is a pretty "catchy" statement.

The word "REMINDER" is on the cover of this book. It is there to remind us that "REMINDERS" can be healthy happenings for everyone. Except, of course, for those human beings who will never forget anything.

You may be a person with many "TALENTS" and that can be very good for you. But! Make certain that you become the "MASTER" of the "things" that will be most helpful and productive for you.

"THINK ABOUT THIS ONE!"

When we need or want to really accomplish something good, beneficial, and productive for ourselves, we need to "FIRST" have a good, firm understanding of what that should be. We need to really get to know ourselves. Not that we don't know who we are, but rather what we need, what we would like to do for ourselves to help us exist in a reasonably comfortable setting. And what we as a human being can offer to others that will prompt others to help us, to assist us to succeed.

To be able to provide a good life for yourself and your family, you will need "KNOWLEDGE" and "ABILITY" that is in high demand in a consumer-oriented society. Remember that in a consumer economy, demand for product and services is what "drives" our economy.

However, although KNOWLEDGE and ABILITY, by itself, is an extremely important "ingredient" – the understanding of what is needed, by all of us, to cause the application of our knowledge and abilities to be more effective for us is as important. It is to learn how to be amicably interdependent with other human beings. This, too, is a talent that should be carefully "honed" to as near perfection as is possible. The section of this book covering "human relations" should give you a good "basic handle" on this subject.

Now with accomplishments comes the need for the ability to be able to properly and effectively deal with your personal finances. The section covering this subject will also give you a good "basic" understanding.

And now the "frosting on the cake," as it were, for having a good life would have to be our personal health. Don't sell this requirement "short." Without good health you probably may not be able to effectively use your knowledge and abilities to accomplish what you need and want. The personal health comments, reminders you will read about in this book, may, hopefully, encourage you to do the right things for yourselves. This book does focus on delivering a basic understanding of "human relations" actions, "personal finance" actions, and the "pièce de résistance," your personal health need requirements.

Your VERBAL Journey!

Let's begin with a philosophical thought.

Sometimes we need to take a realistic "looksee" at how our daily actions affect our lives and think about what is important to our personal overall well-being. Things that we may not initially attach too much credence to until the "point of no return" has passed. But, as we know, we can, of course, sometimes "back track" and correct certain oversights to give us the benefits we will need to live our lives better. Having a thought process in your mind that will help you to direct yourself in meaningful, positive ways is what this REMINDER writing is intended to assist you with.

The "thought!" "If we start our daily activities with a clear perspective of our goals for living a good life – would living our lives feel easier to contend with?"

Well, having goals definitely give us a direction and knowing what we need to do will give us a sense of control. We can develop our own answers to this thought after we try it.

Do realize that there are three things we will always need to feel good about living our lives. THINK ABOUT IT!

The three things we will need to allow us to feel good and positive about living our lives are:

1. Our personal IDEAL for living. (Ideal = is our own PLAN of the level of perfection we wish to attain from living our lives on a daily basis.)
2. A steady, reliable source of personal income needed to pay for the opportunities of living an ideal life.
3. Knowing from where the "INVISIBLE SUPPORT" comes when we need and ask for it.

Now, when you commence your verbal journey, consider the fact that "knowledge is power" that will offer you clarity of mind to help you "smooth out" your "road" for travel.

IT IS YOUR LIFE – LOVE IT!

"De-Weed Your Life"

IF your life, as you are living it now, feels cluttered and full of "things" that may make you uncomfortable and perhaps even afraid – THINK ABOUT IT!

This could be likened to a once beautiful, well-kept garden now being "choked" by troublesome weeds. "Weeds" occurring obtrusively in your life to the exclusion or injury to your positive goals. To free your life from "weeds" or troublesome situations, you need to find ways to root out and, as much as possible, remove unfavorable happenings to you.

This book, "*The Tit4Tat Solution*" will offer much positive "food for thought" for your consideration when searching for credible, common sense corrective thinking and action.

Let us <u>ALL</u> learn from EXPERIENCE, the range of human experience, and let us <u>prevent</u> CATASTROPHE from being our teacher.

HOPE!

When we have HOPE, when we are hopeful, it gives us the impetus to overcome any resistance inherent in living our lives successfully.

HOPE is to have expectations of something desired. HOPE is to be able to look forward, with confidence, to good future happenings that can lead to our success. HOPE is a feeling that is not subject to change. It is an eternal feeling. Never lose it. Never lose HOPE.

Also, never lose sight of the <u>fact</u> that feelings of HOPE are created by human beings, <u>but sustained</u> by an unshakeable BELIEF in our "MAKER."

So let us begin by acknowledging some irrefutable logic:

"Success begins when PREPAREDNESS meets OPPORTUNITY."

I wish you "NURTURED" reading.

KNOW!

That if you are in "LOVE" with being alive and you are in "LOVE" with your "DESTINY," the way you have personally PLANNED it, and you "LOVE" to help and please others – you will have every opportunity to become the beneficiary of all you will ever need.

VENI, VIDI, VICI

I came to this earth, I saw what is happening, and
I conquered all negativism with positivism.

How is that for your "life plan"?

"The Pen (<u>The Word</u>) is Mightier Than the Sword."

Forget guns and missiles, language may be the most powerful weapon in the human repertoire. It can be found in music and art, in politics and prayer, and <u>NOW</u> as the focal point for an exciting <u>TALE</u> of what is needed to live a good life for each individual human being.

Words are like actions; they never go without consequences. Things happen because of words. Language is a weapon for GOOD and EVIL. Choose your words well.

Look! and See
Listen! and Hear

Make certain you fully understand the effect your own words and deeds can have on your good life. Be guided by good common sense.

UNIVERSAL GOOD ADVICE!

"Seek and Ye Shall Find."

To write it in a less mystifying way – when you decide what you want from living your life, then you start working for it by learning what you need to do to put yourself in a position to attain it. Then put your heart and soul into your positive action.

REMEMBER! Who and what will always be the "driving force" behind all that you want to accomplish? IT IS YOU!

MEMBERSHIP FEE!?

We cannot get away from it. Everything that will constitute a good life for each and every human being requires a "payment," a "fee" for the privilege to be a RECEIVER.

From birth we became indebted to each other. We are placed under obligation for benefits, favors, assistance, etc. by becoming a member of HUMANITY, the absolute largest and most diversified entity known in the universe.

The "fees," as they become due, are never negotiable. It will be a fixed "fee" for the duration of mortal life. The "Doors" to benefits, favors, assistance, etc. needed for a good life will not open until the "Fee" has been paid, with sincerity, and receipt has been acknowledged.

The "Fee" paid to each other, with no exceptions, when due, is a non-monetary substance referred to as "human relations building blocks." The essence of this "fee" is representing the "FOUNDATION" on to which you build your good life.

The Fee: "RESPECT AND KINDNESS"

NOTE: Non-compliance or "late payments" will
compromise your quest of a good life.

LOVE GROWS FROM RESPECT AND KINDNESS

My Reverence for "You" is Undeniable

Sometimes all a parent, grandparent are able to give their offspring are some sound advice that can lead to their self-satisfaction. It is based on adopted knowledge which, when activated, turns out to be very positive, such as how to live a good life following some specific common-sense requirements that is a factor which is judged necessary, according to the nature of things, or to the circumstance of the situation.

Sound advice could be likened to an old proverb—"Give a man a fish and you feed him for a day. Teach a man to fish and you feed him for a lifetime."

If a "man" knows and applies what actions by him causes the human race to respond in a humane and positive way, then his path toward success, peace of mind, a good life, is moving forward.

Know that CHANGE REPRESENTS PROGRESS. And "progress is impossible without change; and those who cannot change their minds cannot change anything" (George Bernard Shaw).

An Important Requirement!

If we want meaningful results from living our lives, we must first acquire certain positives.

We must have healthy <u>DESIRES</u> which should impel us to <u>LEARN</u> and attain relevant <u>KNOWLEDGE</u> and then add our personal <u>ACTION</u> – This will provide us with hope and give us our best opportunity for gaining what we <u>NEED</u> and <u>WANT</u>.

Positive Inspirations!

<u>Learning</u> – is knowledge acquired by systematic study.

<u>Inspired</u> – is to produce or arouse a feeling or thought in the human mind. Like being inspired by a belief in a better future.

<u>Learning</u> is really the only way you can be <u>inspired</u> to work for a better future for yourself.

<u>Learning</u> helps you to get to know and understand many things not now known to you. This gives you additional "POWER."

"KNOWLEDGE IS POWER"

The Power of
Time, Knowledge, Understanding,
and Positive Action

To provide someone a CAUSE to believe in the truth of what is alleged, to convince a "man" of his errors can be a most valuable challenge to overcome.

What is the significance of "POWER"? Knowledge is power, but only if you realize and understand how you should use it for "good" and for your benefit.

What good is knowledge if you do not focus on the significance of what it can do for you, how it can help you? There is a lot of knowledge out there in our world. Some knowledge has little or no effect on you and me personally. But for sure, no knowledge will be any good to anyone if we do not act on it. That is if you have not learned how to use it to your positive advantage.

When you possess something that is powerful, you need to fully understand why it is powerful, and then accept that unless you use it, by your actions, it is of no value to you.

Just like your "TIME." TIME is a very valuable commodity. But say – you have a "block" of time "sitting" on your shelf and you let it just sit and do not touch it. Then it really has no value to you. TIME has no "shelf life." You use it or lose it. That is the unfortunate situation with time.

So what should you do to get the full benefit from your "block of time?" Well, think of it this way – time is only valuable to you IF you use it to create something valuable for yourself or someone else. This is where the concept of "PLANNING" enters the solution. If you properly plan your use of each hour in that "block of time," you will collect the most benefit.

I wonder sometimes when you write something and use words that connote powerful meanings, how many readers say to themselves

– "Why read this again? I already know these things" – "Why can't someone write something <u>NEW</u>?" And then, the reader continues to think about what he just told himself and what he read, and takes a look at his own personal situation. Do an honest self-examination. What do you come up with?

If you already know all of the things you are now reading, how is it, or how has it affected your personal life? How are you living your life? On a scale of 1 to 10 (10 being the best), how close to a 10 are you?

If you realize or sense that there may be room for some positive improvement to living your life, why do you think that is? Could it be because, although you feel you have known about this type of "self-development" writing all along, you have never realized or felt the significance of the "power" to you contained in knowledge?

You ask yourself - "How could this be?" "I know about these things and I feel I am still missing out on some very valuable benefits. Why?"

Once you have developed, in your mind, an honest and complete response to your question "Why," you will have your answer. However, I will give you a strong hint as to what your answer will probably be. You will come to the realization that you have never fully put your knowledge into your own actions. You have not done for yourself what you have known all along will be highly beneficial for you.

This is the something new I am trying to "germinate" with this writing. I sincerely hope it will be helpful.

What Does Being "FAIR" Mean?

Are you a "FAIR" person to yourself when it comes to your decision-making on matters that could be positive/good for you?

In other words, do you do for yourself what you should realize could be positive/good for you?

The meaning of the word "FAIR" is:

> "A person who is free from bias and dishonesty, a person who will remain unprejudicial of his/her feelings, opinions, or judgments of any matter until first acquiring adequate knowledge, thinking, and reason."

Fair implies the treating of all sides alike, justly, and equitably.

Being unprejudicial means not influenced or swayed by bias, or by prejudice caused by irrelevant considerations.

What I am hoping for in this section is "Fairness" to yourself by making certain that you fully understand the intent of the messages in this book and that you will "TRY IT" and then be guided by your own results.

Think About It!

"Time is only valuable if you do something valuable with it" (Author).

"Consider knowledge a recipe for potential good things" (Author).

"You cannot do a KINDNESS too soon because you never know how soon it will be too late" (Ralph Waldo Emerson).

"I can't do everything for everybody all the time, but I can do something for somebody some of the time" (Author Unknown).

"Life begins when a person first realizes how soon it can end" (Columnist Marceline Cox).

For Starters

Thank you for helping me prove that we can all build a good life for ourselves as long as we find the correct "recipe" and we do not skimp on the "ingredients."

Let us all "play it straight" with each other.

If you believe there is any human being in this world of ours that "owes you a living," think again. Anything you will need or want will be strictly up to your own positive ingenuity and cunningness to achieve. You are definitely like all the rest of us human beings in a "do-it-yourself" world when living your life.

Do realize that you have the possibility to be friends and/or "partners" with anyone you choose as long as you do not give them a good reason not to want you.

To feel we have HOPE is very important to all of us.

To my way of thinking, to have HOPE is to be able to visualize in our minds what we will need and want to live a realistic good life. And to know and accept that we are in control of all of our actions needed to achieve our needs. And, of course, we must possess an unfailing strong desire to help ourselves.

As you will read throughout this book many times, there is no getting away from the fact that we are all "life members" of the "Do-It-Yourself" world family.

THINK about it! What gives you good feelings of satisfaction and progress? Do you like feeling satisfied and that you have made or are making progress? Listen! These two kinds of human feelings are "universal." They are just noted in several different languages.

As you read this book, you will be reminded of how the "Tit4Tat" concept, when used, will help you achieve these feelings. It is not a "Free Lunch" concept – it is a "Road Map" for each of us to travel by while we are taking action in our "Do-It-Yourself Life."

What is this book about? Well, have you ever had to question yourself Why? and How?, about anything very significant and important to you personally?

If your concerns are about your own life and how it is progressing – do you ask yourself, at times, Why are the results from living my life so inconsistent? Or perhaps you ask yourself, How can I live my life differently to help foster a more consistently good life? This book is intended to help you answer these questions.

Remember! Have you ever felt, or do you always feel a strong need for being the "First" person in line where they were giving out valuable "Free Stuff" so you could make certain you got "one"? And by doing this, trying to get to be "first in line," you exhibited assertiveness and perhaps, at times, a somewhat bold aggressiveness so the people around you might "TAG" you as a "selfish" person and may not like you because of that? Well, as you read this book you will or you should get a "firm handle" on how and why you should always be following the "*Tit4Tat*" concept, be the <u>first</u> in line to do meaningful things, and as a result reap lots of benefits. And for this "me first" reaction, you will never be looked upon as a selfish person, but rather as a positive, generous, kind, and likeable person.

As you read this book, please accept that it is written with one, and only one, very serious intent, which is to give the reader plenty of "food for thought" on how to live a good life.

Do not try to look for and create in your mind negatives from this writing that may lead you to not "work" with this concept. If you do, you will, no doubt, miss out on a lot of good stuff.

Reality for you, the reader, will be what you make it. If you consider and do "hang on" to a concept, a long respected opinion, view, and belief that if you "do good" you will "receive good"; you will be heading into "calm waters" with enough wind in your "sails" to move you steadily forward.

We should always remember and we should accept that for us EVERYTHING IS POSSIBLE! But it is up to each of us how far we want to "go" with our lives. If we ask ourselves, "How far can I 'go' with my life?," an answer must be another question; "How far do I, very much, want to 'go'?"

Wanting to do something, anything, and willing to "move mountains" to get there is the <u>TEST</u> we must all meet.

We must learn from our past. We must plan for our future, and we must live in the moment.

Begin the Beginning

I have arbitrarily picked the following "thought" to be the first of many that I wish to convey to your "mind" as you start reading this book.

This book should help us to understand and accept why we all need to be knowledgeable and conscious of how:

- Good, positive Human Relations is important to us.
- Consistent, basic Personal Financial control is important to us.
- Persistent, good Personal Health is important to us.
- Spiritual Nourishment is important to us.

Begin at the beginning is always a wise and intelligent move by anyone who is being challenged to a contest of skill and strength to live a good life in the best possible way. When you understand what you will be "up against," in preparing yourself for this type of challenge, you will do much better as you start to collect the positive results for yourself. REMBEMBER, you are the DETERMINATOR of the results you want.

While reading this book, I feel certain that you may realize that you are already somewhat or perhaps very knowledgeable of the above subject matter. However, like so many of us human beings, we think about and do so many things, every day, and these four (4) subjects that can and will "define" how well our daily lives will evolve, it seems, many times are not given enough attention and action by each of us.

Knowing about and committing yourself to use the knowledge of these four (4) subjects in a positive manner in your daily life will help you to create and live a very good life for yourself. We should all realize that this is "knowledge" that has been in existence for longer than two (2) millenniums, and that will serve all of us (who decide to use it) well. The positive effect of applying this knowledge to ourselves will be "proof positive" to you that it "works" the "minute" you avail yourself of its positive intention.

Being "REMINDED" of good things and finding solid reasons to explore, identify, and employ ideals that will truly work for us in creating and helping us to live a good life is "PRICELESS."

READ, QUESTION, UNDERSTAND!

I am hopeful that the content of this book will serve as a powerful PROPELLANT for your good life as you keep on reading and acting out this knowledge for your personal benefits.

Yours truly,
Grandfather

"The Start of the Beginning"

Every day we work we look for and listen for "things" we can use to create a better life for ourselves.

Living a life that is filled with "Happiness and little or no suffering" – HOW DO WE DO IT?

We will need clear and concise knowledge and understanding of how each human being must behave toward each other in order to maximize mutual benefits. Benefits that encompass everything that is meaningful to each human being in their efforts to "build" and live a good life.

Everyone's life needs a direction.

Getting the most out of living our lives need clear directions, solid focus, and strong motivation. Your directions will come from identifying your PURPOSE, your reasons for your existence on this earth.

"A human being without a PURPOSE is like a ship without a rudder – a nothing, a no man."

(Thomas Carlyle)

"A human being without knowledge, relevant to life's purpose, is not worth much." (Author)

Knowing our purpose for living our lives gives us direction and meaning. It simplifies for us how we need to go about creating a good life for ourselves. It gives us a focus on what we need and want. And this knowledge turns into motivations, our incentive for doing what we need to do.

Everything we do on a daily basis should have a purpose, a reason attached to our decisions to do it. If there is no reason for doing something, why do it? True! So let us make certain that we all have good, positive reasons for starting something and completing it.

When you give yourself this kind of directive, to have good positive reasons for doing something, anything, it would be most meaningful, to you, if the "thing" you decided to do became an integral part, albeit perhaps a small part, of a larger focus in your mind. This larger focus, I am suggesting, should be your overall MAIN FOCUS on your ultimate reason for living your life. Everything we do should be on PURPOSE.

Every day in our lives we perform multiple tasks required of us to live a good life. We try to do things that please us, which expresses our love, caring, and respect for our family, friends, and co-workers. And what gives our family food and shelter and protection of our health. That's pretty much it in a "nutshell: Is it not?"

Well, if we try to condense the above brief paragraph to a few words that could represent our "TOTAL" purpose, our absolute main reason for existing on this earth, could it be to achieve:

"Happiness and little or no suffering."

Begin!

This book is pretty much all about understanding why better is better for you.

The "KEY" to "understand" is to be a person with curiosity and inquisitiveness.

A person who understands has developed the ability to recognize the "truth" and the common sense in what is being said or done. And one who has the mutual comprehension of each other's meaning, thoughts, etc. And who is thoroughly familiar with and apprehends clearly the character or nature of the subject at hand. This is an understanding human being. It also signifies a state of good or friendly relations between persons.

A person who, in the context of this book, displays "curiosity" is a person who has the desire to learn or know about anything that may turn out to be positive for him/her.

A person who is "inquisitive" is a person who is desirous of, or eager for, knowledge and given to inquiry or research.

We should all dream "LOFTY" dreams about the positiveness we strive to have in our personal lives. We should "dream" of our success with all of our future endeavors, and we should always feel very strong about a "Yes I Can" attitude every single day of our lives. However, one thing, one concept we must always incorporate into our decisions to proceed with any endeavor intended to help us to live a good and productive life is the concept of <u>REALITY</u>.

Reality is a state of fact of being real. It is something that is existing or occurring as fact. It is actual (rather than imaginary, ideal, or fiction). The reality we are referring to here is very obvious. How <u>REAL</u> are your complete "ABILITIES" to PLAN, finance (with money or knowledge or both), and execute to completion your "projects?"

The objective that I will try to make "flower" in this book – "What can we do, how should we behave (as individuals) with our lives in order to make living our lives better?"

Every day can be the beginning of something positively wonderful for you. But do not just sit and wait for it – start creating it.

This writing is full of valuable "REMINDERS" of how to do, for yourself, what will count toward living a good life. These reminders represent "APPLICATIONS" that have withstood the test of TIME (centuries).

Think of the following as an unalterable fact that cannot and will not ever change.

As a person of "one," we will not be able to change the direction our "world" is heading. We simply have to live with what happens and with the consequences that may follow. However, we can decide to change, improve ourselves individually in order to help minimize any "bad" consequences that could happen to us in our world. We can change ourselves or improve ourselves because we have complete control over how we think about all matters, on how we decide on our choices to move forward, on how we behave in our daily lives to gain positive help where we need it.

Be aware that you do not have to compete with anyone other than yourself. Meaning, the only one you should be in fierce competition with is yourself by making yourself better and more valuable "TODAY" than you were "yesterday," etc., and that way you put yourself in a good competitive position with your peers.

This book is written with the sole intentions of providing solid good REMINDERS of what each of us can do, for ourselves, in our daily lives to help foster a more positive, more healthy and productive life for ourselves.

Be your own AGENT for change!

Remember, better is better

THINK ABOUT IT!

"Think About It!" This is something I say a lot in this book. Why? Well, I believe that if you do not thoroughly think about, important to you, subject matters you usually cannot "catch" the full significance of what it is trying to tell you. By catching the full significance, what I mean is simply this. You may not fully understand a particular situation and then the whole thing would really be meaningless to you. And by it being meaningless to you, you will not know if this particular situation could have been good or bad for you. Good or bad? I think you would want to know.

"TODAY"

The world we live in "today" is full of uncertainty for our individual and collective freedom and well-being.

Uncertainty – is, for certain, a very insecure feeling about our future. Our future is lacking in predictability as it concerns all of us living our lives with a healthy freedom, peace of mind, and our NEEDS satisfied.

There is only one "entity," the human entity, which <u>MUST</u> assume the full responsibility for placating these strong feelings and the reality that causes this uncertainty to exist. And that "entity" is represented by our world's constituency and our elected LEADERS.

There are human reasons for all human dissatisfaction. Whatever happened to our feelings for "too much NO GOOD, but plenty alright?" And the concept of sharing and compromise?

Where do we start when looking to accomplish a change for mutual betterment?

There can only be one indisputable place to start, and it is with us, all of us, every single world constituent.

This "food for thought" suggestion will probably "choke a horse," but where else could there be a better, potentially workable, place to start?

Why don't we all keep this thought in mind as we keep on trying to live our lives in an "epic-like" manner and let's see where it takes us into our future. I think we can agree on one thing – any positive changes we make for ourselves can immediately make things better for us as individuals.

HEADS UP!

Listen carefully to some sage advice from one human being to another human being.

It very much matters to <u>you</u> which <u>plan</u> <u>you</u> put in motion for living <u>your</u> life to <u>your</u> liking. Think about and sort out all the options you feel and believe you have when deciding on your <u>plan</u>. Test your options, one by one, by truly getting a good feel what each will be about and mean to you. Then pick the one that strikes you in the most positive and enjoyable manner. Outline the steps that will be necessary for you to take, each and every day, to fulfill your plan and walk proudly forward.

Remember, you can reach your "stars," your objective, as long as each step you take, as outlined by <u>you</u>, in <u>your</u> <u>plan</u> is taken with <u>your</u> intent and purpose clearly on your mind. And accepting that your life is a journey that is intended to take time and will each day bring you enjoyment and feelings of accomplishments on your way. All of this effort by <u>you</u> will represent a good life for you.

"The *Tit4Tat* Solution," I believe, should give you very good <u>HINTS</u> which, when followed, will make it easier for you to build a good future life for yourself and your family.

NOTE!

Living our lives in the best way possible is based on a positive "give and receive" concept. No matter how you look at this sentence common sense dictates that <u>giving first</u> and <u>receiving second</u> is the way living a life will provide you the most benefits and satisfaction.

Someone will now suggest here, "Okay," I am willing to "give" before I "receive" – but what about the "other guy?" Should not "he" do the same thing? Of course "he" should, and when that happens we move closer to living an ideal life together. Think about it!

Thinking in Certain Ways
Can be Very Beneficial

Here is something I received on my e-mail account. The author is unknown.

"My body sometimes feels sore, but it works. I don't sleep well most nights, but I do wake up to 'fight' another day. My wallet is not full, but my stomach is. I don't have all the things I ever wanted, but I do have everything I will ever need.

I am thankful because although my life is by no means perfect, it is my life and I am happy."

To me, this is a human being who is thinking about the current status in his life and feels comfortable and, as a result, has everything good to look forward to every new day. And by not feeling that, you have to struggle to "catch up" every new day you awake – your feeling is that what you have now is good and what positive things you can add to your life today will make it better. And you know that better is better. All you need to do is make it better.

Think of Self and Do For Others and Your Life Will Start "Effervescing" With Added Meaningful Results

Self-development tools for a better life have always been available to us. It is just that, for some of us, we never really thought it through what it really could mean for us.

We always knew that we had to know something; we had to have some ability to do something of "value" in order to get ourselves a "job" to earn a living. However, for many of us our self-development activities slowed down when we got a job. We worked at our jobs and we put forth our best efforts at all times, but we gave little thought to other aspects of self-development. What I mean by this statement is this. Many of us allowed our "on-the-job training" and learning to be sufficient for our needs. We really did not think and focus on our future. We became comfortable and felt satisfied.

We were always a little confused and we may have felt a little anger when we saw some of our colleagues on the job receive promotions to better jobs and more pay and we did not. This is my way of suggesting that we can become too comfortable with what we are doing and, consequently, not give much thought to our future life.

This book, it is hoped, will REMIND you of a few more things which, when learned, accepted and practiced will cause your self-development to be more complete and your opportunities more plentiful to do things of more value in return for higher rewards.

Remember that tomorrow's comforts require today's preparation.

"Find a Need and Fill It" – Good Idea!

"Ability is of little account without opportunity."

"A human being without knowledge is not worth much."

"Knowledge provides you with ability, and ability allows you to 'work' opportunities to your personal advantage."

How do you find "opportunities" to pursue for personal gains? Look for them! An "opportunity" will be anything that will represent a "human" NEED OR WANT that has yet to be satisfied. Or KNOWN NEEDS OR WANTS that can be satisfied in a "better" way than in its present manner.

"Do You Hear Me Now?"

Listen to this one! To truly benefit from an intended positive "input" given to you, you must "<u>Hear</u>" it and also "<u>understand</u>" it. If you do, and you act on it, it may help you a lot.

When someone, anyone, in a knowledgeable position and in a position to help you suggests that you act or believe and do certain things in a certain way or manner, listen and absorb. <u>IF</u> you decide to do it without first really understanding the benefits that can accrue to you by your actions, it may not always work in the way it was intended. Why? Because you may not be fully committed. However, what is being suggested to you, really THINK ABOUT IT, make sure you <u>understand</u> and can sense, the benefits this can have on or for you. And, as a result of this, you decide to comply, the positive results for you personally, I believe you can "take to the bank."

In other words, if you understand how you, by doing certain "things," can improve your own situations by a lot, is there anything that should stop you from trying it?

The reason for writing this way is that so many times during our lifetime, we may hear suggestions on how we can do better for ourselves and without giving the suggestion enough THINKING TIME" we simply "poo poo" it and forget about it. How many times do you think we may have "lost out" on something very beneficial because we did not "THINK" long enough to understand the full gist of a suggestion?

What Can "Sharing" Do For Us?

Listen! Can someone else effectively do your thinking for you? Of course not!

But what "others" can do is share with you how they think about certain "subjects." By listening to "others" talk or "think out loud" on different subjects (perhaps problems), it may help "trigger" in your mind different approaches to solving your own "problems." There are many times, I am certain of it, that you may have "quietly" said to yourself, "I never thought of it that way," as you heard someone speak on a subject that could or would be of concern to you.

You can take full advantage of opportunities like that by making certain you understand what was said and intended. And then by you continuing the same line of thinking, it is very possible that it would be helpful to you if or when you realize it "touches" closely on your own problem.

If you think POSITIVE THOUGHTS to yourself and for yourself, you should find this book very interesting and possibly very beneficial.

The door to our "Tool shed" (our brain) has always been open to us when we were looking for ways to help ourselves improve our ways of living a good life. However, sometimes for all of us the "door" may not have been "open wide" so we may not have noticed all the various "tools" available to us.

With this writing, we shall try to give ourselves more opportunities to do more for ourselves and others.

When you hear someone holler, "WATCH IT," in your direction, you will probably take notice to see if you need to do something to protect yourself. – That's Good!

This time you will hear (see) the words, <u>THINK ABOUT IT</u> a lot. What I will try to do with this "outburst" is call your attention to meaningful statements which, if you allow yourself sufficient time to fully understand the meaning and its intent, you can benefit. – That's Good!

Do You Ever Question Yourself?

I sometimes question myself. "Do I know what is good for me?" If I do, why don't I do more of that for myself? Am I focusing only on things that give me instant satisfaction, like the 'instant gratification society' does?

I believe all of us should pose questions to ourselves periodically about "what can I do for myself" that will be more positive for my well-being.

We should remind ourselves that if we don't think about and "discuss" with ourselves, periodically, what is good and less good for ourselves and make decisions for our own betterment, we can truly miss out on living a better life.

We have to accept that we are the "DETERMINATOR" of what our lives will be like. We must accept that challenge and consistently "work it" to our own benefit.

Additional Preparation

From a positive viewpoint, with all the wondrous things that are happening all around our world (wars and terrorism not included), through human beings from so many different cultures, we should feel blessed, and we should, at the same time, not forget what we human beings need to do to further the production of the "CAUSES" that can help continue the positive ways to a good life for all of us.

Evil is still hanging around in our world, but hopefully not for long. We may never totally be able to eradicate evil, but we should, with the right leaders, be able to substantially reduce it.

Learning the "basics" of how "things" work and what makes human beings "tick" in harmony with each other is how you prepare yourself for building a good life.

Once you learn how various human needs are met and what makes a human being "tick," you will know yourself and feel more confident, and you will also know every human being you make contact with throughout your lifetime. What follows is your ability to better understand what you need to consider doing to reach your own objectives (goals) and how to make other human beings "tick" in harmony with your own "ticking." This ability will help you to create opportunities for productive communication and activity with our earthly brothers and sisters.

My intent of this writing, *Tit4Tat,* is to share with you (or if you will – Remind you) of some of the proven knowledge available, and that if it is used properly can help prepare you for creating very beneficial results for yourself and your family. My reasons are not to try to stimulate you and suggest that you can become a multimillionaire in "5 short steps" if you apply this knowledge. But it is to help you prepare to do yourself a lot of good. Although the end results for you if you engage your life activities in the various ways outlined here, you may be pleasantly surprised at what you can accomplish for yourself.

Remember – If you are properly and adequately prepared for most eventualities that may cross your life's path, you can move in any direction you wish, or if along the way you decide to change direction, you are prepared.

Think About It!

As we grow from birth to adolescence and beyond, at some appropriate time in our lives we, no doubt, need to <u>ADD</u> something to our lives in order to make it easier for each of us to continue our efforts to become better and better human beings.

We could, and perhaps we should, ALL liken ourselves, our lives, to a "work in progress," which is sometimes in need of repairs, remodeling, expansion, etc. We should "tailor" our "modus operandi" to the way we <u>need to think</u> and <u>work</u> to reach our predetermined objectives.

Remember, "By failing to prepare, you are preparing to fail" (Benjamin Franklin).

Our education is a never-ending challenge. You do not just read a book, pass an examination, and then convince yourself that you have completed your education. Your entire life is a process of learning that you should never deny yourself. Educate yourself for what <u>you want</u> to accomplish.

Certain words can be very invigorating to our minds. The words <u>curiosity</u>, <u>opportunities</u>, and <u>possibilities</u> are some of these words. "THINK ABOUT THIS ONE!"

If you exercise your <u>curiosity</u> about something that is new to you, you can create <u>opportunities</u> for yourself and then if you "open the door" to the new opportunity you are creating <u>possibilities</u> for yourself. You may have discovered a "new" NEED that you can now have the opportunity to fill. I am sure you have read the sign, "FIND A NEED AND FILL IT." A potentially rich motto.

"If you want to do really 'important' things in life and big things in life, <u>you can't do everything by yourself</u>. And your best teams are your friends and your siblings" (Deepak Chopra). I am interpreting Mr. Chopra's use of the word *siblings* as referring to our brothers and sisters in the entire world. I feel it may be appropriate since we are all so interdependent on each other, and the things we need to get done requires an interdependency on all human beings in the world as we know it. And, besides, positive basic human relations is what this book is primarily about.

"We live in a wonderful world that is full of beauty, charm, and adventure. There is no end to the adventures that we can have if only we seek them with our eyes open" (J. Nehru).

Everything in Your Life is Staged!

It is staged by you or for you. Do you want "another" to stage your life? If you do, you will subject yourself to the "whims" of someone who does not know you and what you want from your life. Is this what you want?

If you "stage" your own life, you have the opportunity to build your own "road" to travel on. You will have the opportunity to "mix and match all your NEEDS and WANTS in such fashion or manner that you will always know where you stand and what you need to do to make yourself Happier and more satisfied.

The <u>one</u> thing you must always be aware of is that you <u>must</u> remain <u>REALISTIC</u> toward everything you wish to accomplish, and you must always know the <u>LEVEL</u> of your own <u>ABILITIES</u>. That way you should not, on your own, create any disappointment for yourself.

"I intend to"

Do we have good intentions?

Are we human beings of Action?

I have heard it said, and in many cases I believe, it is a fact that many of us, if not most of us, judge ourselves by our intentions to do good and positive things rather than by our actions to get it done. Others judge us by our actions.

No one has ever been successful with good intentions alone. There must be action.

You can learn more from <u>listening</u> than from talking. "Listen" to what this writing is suggesting. And if what you "hear" spells out, in your mind, <u>POSITIVENESS</u>, in large neon letters, why not embrace the various concepts for your own benefits.

When it comes to improving ourselves, the following quote (taken from the Internet) I believe will be beneficial to remember.

> "Employ your time in improving yourself by other 'men's' writings, so that you shall gain easily what others have labored hard for."

It is suggested that this is a quote attributed to SOCRATES, Athenian Philosopher, around 400 BC. Think about it! This is a piece of advice that has been around for about 2,400 years and still has "no dust" on its meaning.

What is a Fact?

To my way of thinking, <u>A FACT</u> is what is <u>accurately</u> described as having happened.

NOTHING VENTURED!
NOTHING GAINED!

How True Is This?

If the readers will have a new meaningful life because of what they will be REMINDED of with this writing, I will be very pleased.

I know that writing this book has helped me become more organized, in my mind, about important things that matter the most when it comes to living the best life possible for yourself.

There are "NO GUARANTEES" in life, but many, many opportunities.

One thing that I have found to be a certainty a large percentage of the time is that when you exercise, in a positive way, the concept of "Tit4Tat" it works. That is when your attitude calls for "Like for Like," meaning that when you behave in an exemplary manner toward others, you receive the same in return. It may not happen 100% of the time, but when it does happen it feels great, and that should be good enough for all of us.

Try!?

The word "Try" <u>is not</u> a dirty word.

The word "Try" should be considered a word filled with curiosity (the desire to learn or know about anything).

The dictionary meaning of the word "Try" is "to test the quality, value, fitness, accuracy of a thing" or of a piece of knowledge newly learned or recently brought to light.

Think about it! Everything you do for the first time, or anything that you have already done before but now will do again, but this time you will do it differently, lends itself to the use of the word "Try" or "Trying."

If you are going to do something new for the first time, or repeat something you have already done but now will do it in a different way or manner, you are, in effect, exercising your curiosity. You are trying something that you believe and hope will give you a degree of personal benefits. It could be something, anything, which will have a positive effect on your overall well-being. It could be for your personal health, your personal finances, and your personal relationships.

Your "lifeline" is being sustained by curiosity, whether you ever thought about it that way or not. By being a curious individual, you are a person who is desirous of learning and knowing. You are inquisitive, meaning you are eager for knowledge.

It is my opinion that we cannot live our daily lives in the best possible way without the positive effect of being curious. If we were not curious, would we ever learn and know about many things that could be, undeniably, helpful to our quest for living a good and progressively better life?

This book, with the title, *Tit4Tat*, is "loaded" with good old knowledge that we are being reminded of. As you keep reading, you will, no doubt, develop a level of curiosity within you that cannot be properly satisfied unless and until you test it for accuracy. And <u>trying</u> the suggested various approaches to living a good and better life is, to my way of thinking, the only way you can test the VALUE to you of the "Tit4Tat" concept. Trying anything to prove a point necessitates a degree of consistency, from a time viewpoint, sufficiently long to allow the intended positive effect to germinate.

Proof

PROOF is evidence sufficient to establish a thing as true, or to produce belief in its truth.

When you read this book and if you find that you have any doubts about the validity of what is being written, I suppose you would want proof.

Well, there is plenty of proof all around us. Where, you say, is all this proof?

Well, since what we have suggested from the early pages, the "back bone" of this writing has to do with our "Common Sense" that all of us possess in varying degrees. Open your eyes, think about what you are observing wherever you witness the "Tit4Tat" concept at work – there is your proof. The unalterable facts of how human beings react to the cause and effect phenomenon.

Do not ever sell this phenomenon "short." If you live by it, in a sincere way, it can help you do so much good for yourself and others.

Proof that "something" works is not a guarantee that it will automatically continue to work. The guarantee that the "Tit4Tat" concept for "living a good life" will continue is totally up to each of us individually. We have to maintain a continuing forward movement. If you do not "feed it," it will not grow.

Common sense is alive and well. Let us make certain we use it as much as we use our lungs to breathe.

Common sense is a basic ability derived from experience to perceive, understand, and judge things which is shared by ("common to") nearly all people, and can be reasonably expected of nearly all people without any need for debate.

Common sense, as we use it here, refers to – practical matters that affect human being's feelings and attitudes on a daily basis. It involves the inherent human feelings common to all – the desire for "happiness and no suffering."

Strategy for Living?

"Dr. Phil" writes very helpful books and articles about increasing our abilities to live a better life for ourselves. "Dr. Phil," in an article in the *O Magazine* (September 2014), made it quite clear, and I have always agreed with this, that we all need "a philosophy of our own" to guide us through life. And "the way to get started is to recognize what is really important to you. Who are you and what is your strategy for living?" The word *strategy*, as a reminder here, simply means your own method of conducting the operations of your life. "Dr. Phil" further suggests that we "sit down and have a real talk with ourselves because we need to be able to clearly articulate our own guiding principle." And once we have identified our strategy, we should make certain that every choice, decision, and move we make in our lives will be guided by our own strategy. And to get this strategy down pat, apply the three Ps—Practice, Practice, Practice.

What Should be My Strategy
for Living My Life?

How do you start and where do you start when it comes to building a good and better life for yourself? This is a very serious question that each of us needs a clear answer to. Would we want to live a life that is not very good and does not seem to want to get better with each new day? I do not think so!

My suggestion is this – you start at the beginning. Where else?

You have to <u>prepare yourself</u>. What does that mean? It means you have to <u>positon yourself</u>; you have to put yourself "on the road" that will lead you to the "things" you have planned and want to accomplish. This also means – really think about this – it should be considered the most important transformation any and all human beings can do for themselves. You must make an honest, real life presentation of yourself as a human being <u>KNOWN</u> for his/her <u>sincerity</u> and <u>integrity</u>. And also as a person whose purpose (strategy) for living is <u>KNOWN</u> to be <u>useful</u>, <u>responsible</u>, <u>honorable</u>, and <u>compassionate</u>. This is the kind of human being all other human beings seek to be associated with.

Then you have to carefully formulate, in detail, your plans (goals) that you want to reach and then <u>add</u> the "steps" you will need to take to reach your objectives. Sounds like a lot? Well, it is not really a lot when you consider it will represent your living a good life. After all – if you are anything like most human beings, you have to stay active in order to affect your own good life. So why not be active on your own terms and with your own plans?

Words to Meditate On

WORDS – Are a sign of conception (feelings)

FEELINGS – Are mood generators (pleasurable or painful, sensation experienced, when one is stirred to sympathy, anger, fear, love, grief, etc.)

MOOD – Is a frame of mind, fits of uncertainty, spirit (attitude)

ATTITUDE – Is your position, disposition, or manner with regard to any anticipated action to a person or thing.

The words you use when talking to another human being generate specific feelings in that human being, which creates a certain mood that is directly coupled to the attitude reactions displayed and which helps decide the "fate of the day" of those involved.

Carefully choosing your words to fit your purpose is what all human beings can do for themselves to create a life that is more pleasant, more endurable, and more successful.

CHOOSE YOUR WORDS WELL

Preparedness

To be prepared means to be ready, willing, and able to immediately confront all positive opportunities and to do something with them that will help you to build and sustain a good life for yourself.

How prepared are we, individually, to make ourselves and our lives better in meaningful ways?

Every day is filled with opportunities to make our personal situations better. How focused are we in our lives? Are we in a position, from a strong desire, to recognize opportunities as they appear?

When we do recognize opportunity, do we have our "TOOLS" ready to employ? Is our "TOOL SHED" sufficiently well-organized so we do not waste any time and we do not lose the opportunity?

What we mean here is "Who we are," do we really have the "mind set" to do good things for ourselves? Do we keep our eyes and ears open for the purpose of finding new knowledge that can help us to move forward in a positive way with our lives? Or do we believe that if we wait long enough some "happening" will come our way that will do some good for us? Do not ever forget for a moment that you are in a "do-it-yourself life" situation. Meaning, that if you don't do what you need to do to obtain what you want to obtain – you may never get it.

FAVORABLE TIMES

Here you are – facing opportunities which, if you can handle, will help provide you with what you will need to live a good life. However, you may be somewhat "hesitant" to "strike" because you are not sure exactly how you should get started.

All you need to get going in building a good life for yourself are some clear and easy-to-understand directions and you can be on your way.

This book will clarify, in your mind, what each of us should consider doing and the direction we should be heading in to give us the best possible chances of being successful in all our endeavors.

Never underestimate the "power" of good "common sense." Do not allow prudent advice to pass you by without grabbing a large dose of it for yourself.

A Fact of Life

There are many "facts" of life!

However, this one fact is a fact you should always remember:

> "No other human being will ever 'owe you a living' unless or until you have first given him/her a good reason to be indebted to you."

Anything you will need or want will be strictly up to your own positive ingenuity and cunningness to get. You are like all the rest of us human beings when living your life in a "do-it-yourself" world.

Discovering SELF-REALIZATION is also very important to us. This means that we come to realize, within ourselves, how much more we are capable of accomplishing than we have. We learn that all we need to do is understand and apply the reasons of success and Try! Try! Try!

This book can help you a lot to more fully comprehend how to live a good life for yourself and your family.

Stay With Me!

This writing represents a lot of good and useful "REMINDERS" to all of us that when we do good and helpful things, honorable things to others, we expect and usually receive the like in return.

There are things we do <u>TO</u> and <u>FOR</u> each other that provide a positive return for all concerned. There are things we do <u>TO</u> and <u>FOR</u> each other that can wreak havoc with our respective good lives.

Knowing which things to choose to do will be good and comforting to realize. And by making the correct choice should substantially shorten our journey to reach our respective state of living a good life.

This will not be an "END ALL" information-gathering coup. But hopefully it will "engage" our "THINKING engine" to a point that will enable all of us to live our lives in the best way possible.

There is a lot more to living a good life than to <u>just know</u> what and how to do something. We have to actually put the meaning of the word "ACTION" into living our daily lives and do what is correct and expected <u>of and from</u> every living human being.

THINK ABOUT IT!

"I will give you 'Like for Like' so we can ALL live a good life."

The beginning, the middle, and the end of this writing is intended to be a <u>NON-FRICTION COMMUNICATION</u>, but not intended to have a <u>TEFLON (nonstick) EFFECT</u>. This writing is about us as individuals; it is about your life and my life. We are not going to try to change the world. Although the causes and effects we decide to set in motion for ourselves could have a positive effect on the entire world, would that not be a "humdinger?" But we shall try to prepare ourselves to have the best life possible regardless of the adversities lingering throughout our entire world.

With each year that passes, we may find our reasons for doing certain things and thinking about certain matters changing. Your reasons for wanting to accomplish certain things will be different. Things that used to be on your mind and be important to you are no longer relevant, and things that were still in your thoughts but did not receive much attention will now become more important to you. I believe this is a natural evolution of life in this age. Your mind and your body matures and your appreciation for health, knowledge, and good friends become stronger and you want more of the same.

I believe many persons who live a responsible life or who, after a fling of perhaps a less responsible life during their period of adolescence and then turn to a more responsible life, will agree with the following assumption.

It may not be too clear to us during our early years what will be our destiny, but one thing is 100% certain – and that is whatever our destiny we, individually, will be the <u>only one</u> responsible for determining it. So remember this advice now and forever: "Your <u>present</u> will be determined by your <u>past</u>. Therefore, in the <u>future</u> you should be very careful what you do in your <u>past</u>." (from a Ziggy cartoon)

There seems to be a feeling among many people today that even though our future can be based on history, a pleasure to look forward to, there is an even stronger uncertainty now if that will be the case. For each of us to feel stronger about dealing with our respective futures in the most positive way, we have to learn "new" things and be REMINDED about "Old" things that will work for us as we keep on building a good life for ourselves.

There are many people in our world who are living a good life "today," and there are many more people who are trying very diligently to build a good life for themselves. Both of these categories of people are facing the same uncertainties about our future. There will be people who will be more successful than others in dealing with these uncertainties as they become real because they will be more prepared to handle surprises. I cannot know of specific uncertainties that will or may come to fruition, but categorically speaking they could be about human health, financial difficulties, peace amongst ourselves, human food and water supplies, and perhaps others. So, if we accept our individual situation, whatever it is "TODAY," we need and should do more for ourselves to be properly prepared to effectively deal with our future. We should strive to make it better. Always remember that better is better.

We need to clarify to ourselves what the things are that could prevent us from continuing living a good life if strange and tough to control "things" start to happen. If life gets really tough to deal with negative events, many of us may have to temporarily return to trying to satisfy our basic needs, which will be to having a roof over our head, food on the table, and clothing to wear. If you can continue to provide these basic needs for yourself and your family, you will have the opportunity to start again, as things improve to create reasons for hope.

So then, what can we do as individuals to try to prepare ourselves to effectively handle potential difficulties which may be facing all of us to varying degrees? Well, some of the obvious things that can have, or will have, a negative effect on each of us if they are not "up to par" will be our personal health, our personal finances, and perhaps most important, our relationships with other human brothers and sisters.

I refer here to our human brothers and sisters as our best "security" for helping protect our good ways of living our lives when help is really needed.

You may say and wonder – how is that?

Well, the answer to that question is what I am hoping that this "REMINDER" writing will bring to you with sufficient clarity for it to be helpful. However, think about this! If you found yourself and your family "outnumbered" in a "do or die" situation, and all of a sudden you look over your shoulder and you see a large group of your "brothers and sisters" ready and willing to "have your back." Good relationships are extremely important. And how you can build them and keep them will hopefully "hit home" as you continue to read this book.

I hope these REMINDERS will be inspiring to all who read this. When you are trying to inspire someone, you are trying to influence someone's thinking, to try to arouse a feeling, a thought of positiveness, as it may concern a person's way to living a good life.

I hope you are all INSPIRABLE!

SPOILER ALERT!

Your life will be what you make it!

Now, tell yourself to create an image in your mind with specificity of what you really want from living your life and what you are willing to do to achieve it.

With this image clear in your mind, you will have the DIRECTIONS needed for positive results.

THIS IS ALL "FAMILY BUSINESS" ON A GRAND SCALE

Do some people, sometimes, forget to help themselves? Yes! I think we ALL do that at times. So what?! Well, whenever we do forget to help ourselves, we may be putting ourselves at much disadvantage and perhaps losses.

This book is intended to REMIND us of the appropriate "common sense" things we need to do in our daily lives in order for our lives to return, to each of us, full and uncompromised benefits.

"Tit4Tat"

Who can benefit from reading this book?

Any human being who wants to live a good life by using a common sense means of understanding of how the human mind and body reacts to specific <u>causes</u>. And what <u>effects</u> are generated by the human mind, in kind, as a direct result of the <u>causes</u>.

This is not "rocket science," but simply a REMINDER of what makes a human being "tick." You will be pleasantly surprised at how much you already know about this conundrum. You may, perhaps, also ask yourself, "Why am I not using this knowledge more?" This is always a good question to ask yourself about all positive knowledge.

Read everything in this book, understand what is being suggested, follow good logic, common sense – reap a better life.

Happy Reading

The poor scribe

Tit for Tat

(Do like for like)

Only positive things

The title of this book could be your motto.

Always remember this. The "Tit4Tat" concept, when employed, will give you lots of choices. It will give you more choices than you can "shake a stick at."

You will have so many choices to feel GOOD! You will have an equal number of choices to feel BAD! It is unbelievable!

This is how you do it!

If you want someone, anyone (friend or foe) to be nice, pleasant, and helpful to you, <u>BE THIS</u> to them <u>FIRST</u>.

If you want someone to be nasty, unpleasant, violent, and do you wrong, <u>DO THIS</u> to them <u>FIRST</u>.

You can be your own best coach for your <u>success</u>, or you can be your own worst enemy for your <u>failures</u>. Which one do you want to be?

What does all of this mean? It is very simple! It means you are responsible for what you do <u>FOR</u> or <u>TO</u> yourself.

You can thank! yourself for the good life you can live.

You can Boo! yourself for the less than good life you can live.

This book is dedicated to ALL HUMAN BEINGS OF GOOD WILL.

Religious beliefs of <u>ALL</u> religions embracing, with cheerful acquiescence, as a CAUSE – "GOOD WILL TO <u>ALL</u> Human Beings" – are <u>ALL</u> included. And if the "shoe does not fit," consider getting a new pair and walk with the rest of the greatest multitude now emerging with clarity of mind.

Think About It!

FIND A NEED AND FILL IT

A Potentially "Rich" Motto

- But how do you do this?
- Well, it will take your imagination, a strong desire to be useful and helpful, vigilance and watchfulness over what exists, what is happening around us, and what may be of a troubling nature needing corrective attention. And, of course, ingenuity and personal action.
- REMEMBER! In order to be personally rewarded for their efforts, human beings must FIRST provide positive benefits to each other. A need is satisfied, is filled, when the recipient derives satisfaction which will add to living a good life.
- To our brothers and sisters who find ways to properly satisfy the needs of MANY others, this will cause their own lives to become successful and satisfying.

Think About It!

Stay Alert

HOPE AND REALITY

(should be considered together)

"Living a good life" for yourself must begin with your mind "picturing" what living a good life means to you. "HOPE" – Having Hope is having expectations of something desired. It is having confidence in future events. "REALITY" – for you, the Reader, is what you make it.

If you consider "Hanging On" to a concept, a long respected opinion, view, and belief, that if you "do good," you will "receive good," your life will be heading into "calm waters" with always enough "wind in your sails" to move you steadfastly forward in a positive manner.

The *Tit4Tat* concept, I give you "like for like," when adhered to in a positive manner will represent a "pre-emptive strike" to eradicate, to pull up by the roots, negativism and negativistic tendencies that cannot sustain living a good life.

I wish you constructive reading.

Change for Your Progress

This book, *Tit4Tat*, is intended to be all about an individual "human being" who has decided to practice individualism concerning many important aspects of living a good life in a highly uncertain world that is becoming more and more interdependent. Practicing individualism is the habit of independent thoughts or actions. It is the pursuit of individual, rather than common or collective, interests that will greatly assist in creating a good life.

Positive change will mean better improvement for the "changer."

"Change" is not something that is just waiting to happen. There is no automatic "start" button to press. Change must, and usually is, started by one "thought" in the mind of one human being with the hope that other human beings will share the same thought, and then together start to implement the necessary actions to accomplish "change."

To "change" is to make a material difference so that the "thing" (to be changed) is distinctly other than it was.

How about a positive "slight change" to our lives' *'modus operandi'* to cause enormous progress for our individual self?

How do we begin?

As one human being, what do we need to do for ourselves?

If we, as individuals, want to live a good life and feel successful, we need to accomplish and maintain the following:

- We must "build" and maintain a healthy body and soul.
- We must build good relationships and learn how to get along with people.
- We must develop, for ourselves, a positive attitude about all aspects of living.
- We must learn to hold ourselves together and not be torn apart by negativism that can disrupt your living a good life.
- We must clearly define, for ourselves, our PURPOSE for existing on our earth. A purpose will give each of us a direction for living our lives. Without directions, where will you be heading? We are all put on this earth to accomplish something. And that "something," by each of us, should be a personal effort that will add "value" to your life and to the lives of other human beings. This is a purpose.

Did you know?!

"We find in life exactly what we put into it"

- Emerson

"Life is not a problem to be solved, but reality to be experienced."

- Kierkegaard

"To live your life in your own way …
To reach for the goals you …
Have set for yourself …
To be the <u>you</u> that you want to be …
THAT IS SUCCESS"

REMEMBER – ALL IT TAKES IS ALL YOU GOT!

God is <u>LIMITLESS</u>
Human beings are <u>LIMITED</u>

Do <u>all</u> you believe and feel you can do for yourself and others, then do a little more. And then be satisfied with your accomplishments. And find ways to live your life, honestly, within your means, financial and otherwise.

This may be very difficult for some human beings to do – if they have a wild imagination – but do find a way to do it – you will be the beneficiary.

Please do! For your personal benefit, <u>ALWAYS</u> reflect, honestly, on <u>ALL</u> that you already have in your life and a lot less on what you do not have. Remember, feeling gratitude is more important to having a good life than the feelings of a constant longing for more "wants."

Human Relations
Personal Finance
Personal Health

"Human Relations is the study and understanding of human behavior for the purpose of improving interpersonal relationships." Our mutual responsibility to each other as human beings is to seek out each other's needs and wants and to try to make a "fair trade-off" for mutual benefits. In other words, create a "win-win" situation for all involved. Accept the fact that the "human factor" is involved with all that we do.

Personal Finance is a learned "Art" that focuses on a common sense attitude toward the positive handling of what "money" we possess now and into our future.

Personal Health is our "ticket" to a good, happy, and productive life if we LEARN and PROVIDE for ourselves the proper, continuous MAINTENANCE.

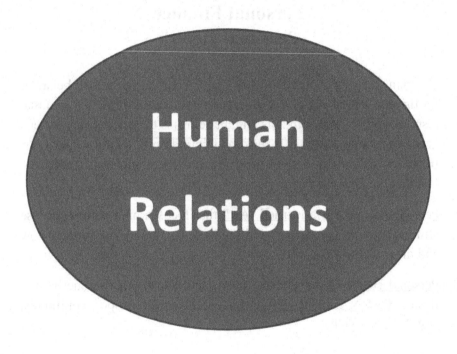

Human
Relations

Good Personal

Human Relations
Finance
Health
Spirituality

These are the four (4) subjects that need to be clearly understood and exist together, as one, to bring you <u>ALL</u> the potential benefits of a good life.

In a Manner of Speaking

Our biggest reason, our only purpose for living our lives is to be HAPPY and to experience as <u>little</u> suffering as possible. And to "help" as many other human beings as we can to reach the same feelings.

Where and how do we start our journey to accomplish this for ourselves? Well, let us first get on the "same page" as to the meaning of the words <u>HAPPINESS</u> and <u>SUFFERING</u>.

"<u>Happiness</u> – is the result from the possession or attainment of what one considers 'good.' Contentment is a peaceful kind of happiness in which one rests without desires, even though every wish may not have been gratified, i.e., Contentment in one's surroundings."

"<u>Suffering</u> – is to undergo experience, or be subjected to pain, distress, injury, loss, or anything else unpleasant."

Now back to the question, "How do we go about starting and accomplishing this for ourselves?

<u>First</u>, let me emphasize very clearly and with no misunderstanding and with no compromise on the meaning of this statement; "The human factor is involved in everything that we will do and try to do. And there will always be one or more human beings involved in any and all meaningful accomplishment we need and want to attain for ourselves and others."

Now we need to understand how we build our "road" to our personal success in life. We can build a "road" that is very straight, very strong, and that will provide the smoothest ride ever. Or, we can build a "road" that will be very curvy (slows down our speed to success), less strong and less stable (you cut corners on your "specifications"), and, consequently, will give you a very rough ride through life.

You will be using with all other human beings the exact same "road-building" equipment when building your "road" to a successful, good life. Your end results, however, will be strictly determined by how you use the "equipment" at every moment you are in the position of adding "roadway" to your life.

The "equipment" that will totally dominate your worksite (your life) while on this earth will be your personal health, your personal finances, and the pièce de résistance, a good understanding of how positive Human Relations efforts on our respective parts works to everyone's benefit.

As you continue to read this book, please allow yourself sufficient THINKING TIME to give yourself a very clear VISION of how these suggested activities, on your part, can help give yourself inspiration, a cause, a reason for improving your present situations.

Point of Fact

When you think about yourself as well as all the other human beings that we "live" and "exist" together with every day of our lives, what are we all looking to accomplish each day? We are all working toward, and looking forward to, being and feeling satisfied and secure.

The way we interact with each other, the way we act and behave toward each other, the way we create reciprocal reactions with each other, all play a pivotal role in all of our future successes in our respective lives.

In other words, good, proper, and positive Human Relations activities on our respective parts is the absolute best and most potent "antibiotic" to help cure human malfunctions.

We have never received any promises or guarantees that life would be fair and equally rewarding to all of us. Life is not fair, life's rewards are not equally distributed to all, life is very competitive, and life is very difficult and demanding. However, life and its opportunities for "wealth" is up for "grabs." It is there for all of us to achieve.

Those who achieve the most "wealth," or rewards, from life are those whose "values" are realized over and over again.

"Wealth" is having things of "value" to you in great quantity.

Life's "wealth" is up for "grabs." It is there. But we as mere mortals must first devise a PLAN, which, when adhered to, will allow us to "grab" a fair share of the available "wealth."

We cannot achieve "wealth" simply by expecting it to come to us. We shall acknowledge and accept that we must be prepared and willing to do the right things in order to receive our fair share.

Humanity's "Laws" of Life

"The most important thing in human life is to seek and do the will of God" (Norman Vincent Peale).

To understand and benefit from the "laws" of life, and to properly interpret these "Laws" for our personal benefit, we will not need a Law Degree nor do we have to be admitted to the "Bar" of the practicing members of the legal profession. All we have to do is become keenly aware of what the "laws" are and use them to our benefit every day for the rest of our long, beautiful lives.

God's Ten Commandments I believe can be referred to as the first general rules, or "Law of Life," intended by God to regulate Humanity's behavior or thoughts. From the point of issue and for centuries upon centuries, humanity's experience and diligent observation of mankind's behavior toward each other has produced a solid understanding of which words and actions used by human beings toward each other produces the most and the best adhesion, respect, and love among all of us.

This was God's very simple way of giving us all a very clear, easy to "read" road map exclusively for our personal benefit.

This book, *Tit4Tat*, in all respects is intended to represent what the "Law" of Life can mean to all of us. The "Laws of Life," when adhered to simply represent human mannerisms that have proven to work positive results for humanity for centuries. I suggest there will be no end in sight and unless human beings in our future turn out to be "inhuman," the feelings and desires for good, happiness, and peace of mind will always be in "Vogue."

So let us all identify the "Laws" of life as being the "things" we do to and for each other that make each of us feel safe, blessed, useful, helpful, compassionate, and loved.

Let us not have any "lawbreakers" among us.

P.S. There are many times during our daily life when we may "throw up our hands" in frustration and wonder "what is wrong with my life." Well, when we do the right things that we know how to do, and we "follow the 'laws,'" we usually come out on "top." "Try it – you will love it!" And this will be doing God's will.

"To do better for yourself, you need to understand why things happen to you. Good or bad."

Positive Basic Human Relations
Is Not "Rocket Science"

It is pure "common sense" knowledge developed (by human beings) over centuries of observations made of human beings' reactions to human beings' behavior toward each other. Our behavior toward each other is <u>always</u> an important factor in deciding our responses of "Like or Dislike" to happenings created by human beings. Do you see? Human beings, and only human beings, are involved in creating <u>everything</u> from good to bad except, of course, for whatever "mother nature" contributes.

Can we agree? All of us? That our basic knowledge of and our use of positive human behavior toward each other is probably the most important "tool" we can possess that will help us to make the quality of our respective lives the best ever.

Remember that knowledge is power. And the power is in knowing what to do and how to behave in all situations so that it will create an "outcome" beneficial to all concerned.

Know that a human being without knowledge is not worth much as a contributor to building a good life.

Note: If a certain, specific human behavior, when exercised, will help make living a life better for many, many human beings, is it possible that that human behavior will work positive things for you?

If in doubt – try it out, and you will find the proof you need if it will work for you. And the cost to you for this "Try Out," if needed, is $0.00 and the prudent use of your intelligence.

"Human Relations 101"

What is human relations? Simply put, it is how we, as an individual human being, decide to relate to other human beings in such manner that will result in something positive for all involved. I think we can say that the basic knowledge of human relations, developed over centuries, is a potpourri of human behavior observations. It is knowing or anticipating a certain behavioral response from one human being to another human being based on some activity that occurs, be it "verbal" or "deed."

Learning about and knowing how behavioral responses from human beings can affect our personal goals and aspirations is of paramount importance to our peace of mind and future prosperity.

Learn what is the best way to relate, and then do lots of it. Also, learn what is not good to do, and do not ever forget it, and do not do it.

Human Relations – "101"

Good, positive human relations goes hand-in-hand with common sense.

Life is full of good and wonderful things just waiting for us to experience. However, intertwined with the many good things there are many "strange" things happening that we have to overcome and deal with to give ourselves a good life. Living a good life takes consistent positive work on our respective parts. However, it is all "work" that is doable if we know and use the basic knowledge of "what to do" and "how to do it."

Only those who learn to THINK, ACT, and BEHAVE in certain ways will reap the full benefits from the opportunities that will become available when we live our lives in the "light" of positive human relations.

"HR" stands for Human Relations and for you it can also stand for HOME RUN. It will, of course, depend on your aptitude to engage life.

This subject will teach you what you need to do to EARN RESPECT from others, and to cause others to LIKE you and to WANT to help you to get the important things done for you to have a good life.

This section represents but a small part of the available knowledge on the subject of HR. However, I believe this part will give you all you will need to begin the "construction" of or continue the betterment of a very good life for yourself.

The subject matter of this section is HR, which I like to refer to as Common Sense. This subject, in my opinion, will be helpful and positive for all human beings, young and old, "well off" and less "well of" alike. If you are blessed with good health or reasonably good health, you are, to my way of thinking, a human being who is "well off." However, in reality, being "well off" is also represented, in varying degrees, by the spiritual values and material things each of us possess.

In order to put all the readers on the "same page," this is what we are talking about.

<u>Human Relations</u> (HR) is the study of human behavior for the purpose of improving interpersonal relationships. Our mutual responsibility to each other as human beings is to seek out each other's needs and wants and to try to make a fair "trade off" for mutual spiritual as well as material benefits. In other words, create a "win-win" situation for all involved to allow for an individual's attainment of "Happiness" with as little suffering as possible. Know that the human factor is involved with all that we do and want to do.

<u>Common Sense</u> is a basic inherent ability to perceive, understand, and judge things, which is shared by (common to) nearly all people, and can be reasonably expected of nearly all people without any need for debate. It is used to describe the natural human sensitivity for other humans.

Our good health is something we all must guard and protect with love and caring for ourselves. We must work at maintaining good health <u>DAILY</u>. We must continue to grow our spiritual wealth within us. We must fully understand what affects our abilities to create VALUE and why our actions work <u>for</u> and sometimes <u>against</u> us in our efforts to create value. We should all realize and remember that we must become very efficient in creating value <u>before</u> we can expect to receive value – in that order. "Value" here is referring to spiritual wealth and material wealth, which together will give you what it takes to live a good life.

There is so much helpful knowledge just laying around waiting to be used, which I feel will be very worth our time to be REMINDED of. It is true that you have probably heard much of this before and accept that this is the way it works. But for some reason, we do not always follow up and act on what we already know. Is it because we, for that moment, had stored this knowledge so far back on the "back burner" that we simply did not have it handy? Well, <u>words</u> can be inspirational to all of us, at times, and can get us started on THINKING again. But the thing that will make the biggest positive difference in our lives is when <u>INSPIRATION</u> turns to <u>REAL ACTION</u> on our part.

Throughout your entire life you will be meeting so many different people. The kind of people you will meet, have contact with, develop relationships with, and rely on for many different services make it very important for each of us to know and understand as much as possible about the subject called HUMAN RELATIONS. Consider the policeman for protection, fireman for protection, doctors for health, mechanics for your car, teachers for knowledge, employers for earning a living, spouse for a more pleasant life, children and friends for an even more pleasant life, ministers for your spiritual nourishment, etc.

The first thought that should come to mind IMMEDIATELY when you have contact with any human being is how should you treat each and every one of them? Depending on the kind of human being you meet, would you treat them differently from each other? Yes? _____ or No? _____

Well, your answer, of course, in your mind should be a resounding NO. You should treat all of them in exactly the same way – WITH RESPECT AND KINDNESS.

Why? Because from a human relations viewpoint, these people in the United States and in all other countries throughout our world are all the same. We, they, are all members of one very large human family. And all our family members are entitled to and deserve RESPECT and KINDNESS.

My personal motto has always been:

"I like everyone I meet until they give me a good reason not to."

The Dalai Lama identifies One Human Family in this way:

> "Whether we like it or not, we have all been born on this earth as part of one great human family, rich or poor, educated or uneducated, belonging to one nation or another, to one religion or another, adhering to this ideology or that, ultimately each of us is just a human being like everyone else: We all desire happiness and do not want suffering. Furthermore, each of us has an equal right to pursue these goals."

Happiness and no suffering should be our personal goal for living a good life.

If we all agree that creating Happiness and No Suffering for ourselves is a goal, we want to achieve because it will allow us to live a good life, then all we have to do now is figure out what we must do, individually, to earn this reward from life.

We must realize and agree that creating the ability to live a good life for ourselves will not be an automatic adjustment and it will not become real without work and understanding on our part.

The question is, "What do we need to do to make this goal a reality?" That is the answer that I will try to help all of us reach and understand. Remember that really understanding what is what, is a very important point, I believe, in allowing us to move forward on every front toward our goal.

How to achieve Happiness – Here, again, the Dalai Lama offers the following insight:

> "For a start, it is possible to divide every kind of happiness and suffering into two main categories: mental and physical. Of the two, it is the mind that exerts the greatest influence on most of us. Unless we are gravely ill or deprived of basic necessities, our physical condition plays a secondary role in life. If the body is content, we virtually ignore it. The mind, however, registers every event, no matter how small. Hence, we should devote our most serious efforts to bringing about mental peace."

From my own limited experience, I have found that the greatest degree of inner tranquility comes from the development of love and compassion.

The more we care for the happiness of others, the greater our own sense of well-being becomes.

Since from the moment of birth, every human being wants happiness and does not want suffering. I believe it will be appropriate for all of us to believe and accept that our purpose for living our lives is to acquire what every human being wants.

The question in our minds should now be. "How do we start to understand how to accomplish this purpose?"

The idea behind this writing started out as a thought of writing a letter to my children and grandchildren. As a parent and grandparent, I feel an even stronger sense of responsibility to share what I believe is important for all of us to be reminded of and understand, hence the "letter" to my family.

After a while, it also became evident, in my mind, that this is the kind of knowledge, information that could be useful and meaningful to anyone reading it, especially since this writing deals with, in my opinion, essentially with the Common Sense Approach to each other's senses. Meaning, we will be reminded of what it takes to make others "tick" in harmony with us and vice versa.

There is a positive side of life. And there is a negative side of life. Guess which side is the best side to be on? Watch out! It is a "trick" question.

Writing anything in hopes that others will read it and find some benefits in reading it is, in my opinion, tantamount to assuming much responsibility. What you write should represent credible data on the subject matter.

Well, when you write on the subject of living a good human life to its fullest and in the most positive manner, you are going to be dealing with your own personal experiences and the personal experiences of others that you have read or heard about. And also the ongoing observations that many have made of how and why people act and react to each other the way they do, and their opinions as represented in their writings.

So much has been written about the positive and negative effects people have and have had on each other over the years. The cause and effect phenomenon deal with people exclusively and once we thoroughly understand how causes and effects are created by people I suspect we will have learned how to build the most positive and productive relationships which, in the end, should always show satisfactory results for all involved.

There is so much "down-to-earth thinking," "common sense thinking," "one-liners," etc. that have been brought to us in the form of writing that if we all understood and accepted their intended meaning and we referred to them periodically during our own lives, we may remind ourselves how and why we are in the position in life we are. And perhaps acknowledge to ourselves with gratitude for being in a very favorable position in life, or acknowledge to ourselves that certain adjustments may be called for in our own way of acting and living that in turn would give us, personally, more benefits and perhaps even improve the lives of others.

When you read about subjects like this, it requires, I believe, several readings. And in between each reading some serious thinking about what you have read. Understanding what you have read and picturing in your mind what positive impact the ideas represented can have on your personal life is the objective you must reach in order to make the changes in your life that could benefit you personally.

Also, if there are children in the home of the reader of this book that are not yet old enough to understand the potentially favorable impact this type of understanding of how to live your life in a most positive way can have on children as they grow and mature, you may wish to coach them as their lives progress!

When you sit down to write something, anything, that is intended and hoped to be helpful to others, you try to develop thought patterns in the reader's mind that the reader can build on to help himself/herself to think more clearly and positively about matters important to him/her. And to motivate him/her to move forward accomplishing things that will make him/her feel very content and bring much happiness and value into their life.

Let us understand this up front; that a person's thought pattern, from the moment they wake up each morning until they go to sleep at night, can "make or break" a person's opportunities to make himself/herself what he/she really wants to be. I think it is safe to say that a person's thought patterns become their Attitude. Check out the meaning of the word "Attitude." "Your position, disposition, or manner with regard to a person or thing."

The most important single factor that guarantees good results, day in, day out, all the months and years of our lives, is a HEALTHY ATTITUDE. ATTITUDE is the magic word. Here is a little different definition of the meaning of the word *Attitude*: "The position or bearing as indicating action, feeling, or mood." And it is our actions, feelings, or moods that determine the actions, feelings, or moods of others toward us. Our attitude tells the world what we expect in return. If it is a cheerful, expectant Attitude, it says to everyone with whom we come in contact that we expect the best in our dealings with our world.

Our attitude is something we can control. We can establish our attitude each morning when we start our day. In fact, we do just that whether or not we realize it, and the people in our family – all the people in our world – will reflect back to us the attitude we present to them.

It is then, our attitude toward life, which determines life's attitude toward us – Cause and Effect. Everything we say or do will cause a corresponding effect. If we are cheerful, glad to be experiencing this miracle of life, others will reflect that good cheer back to us. We are the kind of people others enjoy being around.

You and I are each responsible for our own lives. You and I produce causes all day long, every day of our lives. The human environment can return to us only a corresponding effect. That is why, it is a fact, that each of us determines the quality of our own life. We get back what we put out.

Each of us shape our own life.

Most people never think about their attitude at all. For most of them, it is a matter of beginning each day in NEUTRAL. Their attitudes are neither good nor bad. They are poised to react to whatever stimuli they encounter. If the stimulus is good, they will reflect it; if it is bad, they will reflect that too. They are going through their days reacting to whatever confronts them. And these are the people of our environment. That is why it is so important for us to control our attitudes to make sure they are excellent.

If we take the attitude that we cannot do something, we generally will not do it. With an attitude of failure, we are whipped before we start.

William James of Harvard University, the Father of Psychology in America said, "Human beings can alter their lives by altering their attitude of mind."

Sometimes it is hard to convince people that the world they experience is a reflection of their attitude. They take the attitude that if only people would be nice to them, they could be nice in return. They are like the person sitting in front of the cold stove waiting for heat. Until he/she puts in the fuel, there will not be any heat. It is up to him/her to act first. It has to start somewhere. Let it begin with us.

Our personal life is a mirror of our attitudes and expectations. The world plays no favorites. It is impersonal. The world does not care who succeeds or who fails. Nor does it care if we change. Our attitude toward life does not affect the world and the people in it nearly as much as it affects us personally.

The following little tidbit is going to be very worthwhile remembering 24/7.

NOTE: Everything in the entire world we want to do or get done, we must do with and through people. Every dollar we will ever earn must come from people.

Keep the above-noted little tidbit in mind and do this:

Treat every person with whom you come in contact as the most important person on earth. Do this for three (3) excellent reasons:

1. As far as every person is concerned, he/she is the most important person on earth.
2. That is the way human beings ought to treat each other.

3. And by treating everyone this way, we begin to form an important habit.

There is nothing in the world that men, women, and children want and need more than self-esteem – the feeling that they are important, that they are recognized, that they are needed, that they count and are respected. <u>They will give their love, their respect, and their business to the person who fills this need</u>.

Act toward others in exactly the same manner that you want them to act toward you. Is there any other way?

<u>Here is my prognosis</u> – If your attitude is in check, to be highly favorable to others, the personal results of your endeavors will be – VERY NICE. If your attitude is the opposite of highly favorable to others, your results will be NOT SO NICE.

Part of living a good life is to master your problem-solving skills. Why? Well, have you ever heard of anyone living a good life that never has problems that "pop up" now and then? When they do "pop up," you need to address all problems in a very positive and expeditious way with the absolute correct attitude. You need the attitude that tells you that you have the ability to correct the problem.

Remember – It is our attitude at the <u>beginning</u> of a difficult task that more than anything else will bring about its successful outcome.

Also part of living a good life, perhaps, no not perhaps, the absolute most important part now is understanding, believing, and accepting beyond a shadow of doubt (now that is heavy, but real) that everything ever fashioned successfully by a human being is a direct result of goal setting, and a complete clear, detailed plan to achieve the goals set. No one has ever made a purposeful accomplishment without a clear goal toward which to work. Establish a clear goal, think about it frequently every day – to impress it into your mind. Particularly, your remarkable subconscious where, I have been told, forces greater than we can imagine can come to our aid.

Look at it this way: Your goal is in the future. Your problem or challenge is to bridge the gap that exists between where you are now and the goal you intend to reach. This is the problem to solve, the challenge to overcome.

Successful people are not people without problems; they are simply people who have learned to solve their problems.

Living successfully, getting the things we want from life is a matter of solving the problems that stand between where we are now and the point we wish to reach. No one is without problems; problems are a part of living. But we waste much time worrying about the wrong problems.

Building and living a good life for yourself will take a great deal of commitment from yourself to yourself. Unless commitment is made, there are only promises and hopes, but no plans. Always remember – You are responsible for creating your life by every thought, action, and choice – SO PLEASE CHOOSE WELL!

Problems and worry will, to a degree, follow you throughout your very long and good life. Remember when you are facing a problem that simply cannot be overlooked; it must be solved before you can move forward with your plans. Solutions to problems can sometimes be very hard to find, but know that there is a solution to every problem. Consider this fact – If you can determine the Why? As in, "Why did this problem happen?" you will be looking at the possible solutions.

When something goes wrong – determine Why it went wrong. Correct it if you can; if you cannot, let it be and move on.

We do worry – often we worry about things that do not materialize. But there are also times when we become lost in worry about real-life problems, either personal or global. The following is a reflection suggested by the Dalai Lama. "If you have some fear of pain or suffering, you should examine whether there is anything you can do about it. If you can, there is no need to worry about it. If you cannot, then there is also no need to worry."

I know from personal experience that it is not easy to not worry about certain matters, but I think you may agree that the Dalai Lama's reflection on this subject is "spot on."

Why? Why? Why?

I would wager all my good thoughts on that the word "Why" is mentioned or asked billions of times each day throughout the world without many pursuing an accurate and verified response.

Let us look at the word *"Why."* Why do you think that the word "Why" is so important to us? Because when you understand what the true response to the word "Why" represent, you will have all the answers you will ever need to proceed successfully to achieve happiness with a lot less suffering. Think about it this way. When something "good" happens to us, we usually do not stop to think of <u>why</u> it happened. We just accept it. Perhaps if we stopped to determine the "Why" (as in, Why did this happen?) we may be able to create more "good" happenings for ourselves. Know that everything in life happens for a reason and a purpose, and it serves us. <u>AND</u> when something "Bad" happens to us, we immediately feel sadness, anger, unfair treatment. We tell ourselves that we did not do anything to deserve this "Bad" happening. That is the proverbial answer, "We did not do anything." Remember, if you believe everything happens for a reason and a purpose, you need to stop and determine the "Why" (as in, Why did this happen?). You may not like the answer, but without the real and honest answers to the "Why" you cannot effectively deal with the "Bad" happening.

When something good happens to us, we can just accept it and go on with our lives and we will be okay. But when something bad happens to us and we do not try to understand <u>why</u> it happened, <u>we cannot</u> simply accept it and expect our lives to continue to be okay.

If we do not learn quickly to determine "why" the things that happens to us do happen, we may inadvertently allow other good happenings to bypass us while other bad happenings may continue to cause us to unnecessarily suffer physically, mentally, and financially. And that does not bode well for reaching our goal of happiness and a lot less suffering.

A little research proves that successful people have similar kinds of problems other people have. So the whole thing boils down to a matter not of problems, which are common to all of us, but our ability to solve them.

Remember, you will become and you will achieve what you think about. That is if you stay with it, you will reach your goal.

Anything that comes to us in the future will almost certainly come to us as a result of the extent to which we use our minds. And yet, it is the last place on earth, it is suggested, that many persons will turn to for help. Think of this – just one great idea can completely revolutionize your work and as a result, your life.

The only thing in the world that can take you to your goals in life is your mind, your effective use of it, and your follow-through on the good ideas it supplies you.

I refer to this part of my writing as the Human Relations section. As you have read, it pretty much suggests that to get along with other human beings and for other human beings to get along with you, you have to go "tit4tat" with each of them. What I mean here is a very simple thing to remember. If you remember it and do all your deeds in accordance with this concept, you will be the one to determine the magnitude and quality of your good life.

The "tit4tat" (like for like) concept was established, to my way of thinking, during "Moses'" days. In scripture, the proverb, Matthew 7:12, according to the KING JAMES VERSION:

"Do unto others as you would have others do unto you."

Remember this also – You cannot achieve anything of meaningful value if you are not able to do it with and through other human beings. I sincerely hope that each of the readers fully understand and accept this statement. REMEMBER!!

Do not fougedaboutit

WOW! There is a lot to consider when you are a human being trying to do well for yourself.

Give People a "Hand!"

Good HR is giving people a "Hand." Giving others a "helping hand" <u>EARNS</u> a "helping hand" in return.

There are two ways you can give another human being a "helping hand." Either way will be very helpful, but both ways much better.

<u>One Way</u> – You can "applaud" him or her whenever he/she has done something that is nice, kind, and beneficial. You can applaud by just clapping your hands together, if that situation is then appropriate. Or, you can verbally praise him/her for their accomplishment by using appropriate words of praise and encouragement. This always creates a good feeling.

<u>Second Way</u> – You can give someone a "hand" by extending your hand filled with compassion and physical and financial help as and when needed. Creating a HABIT of extending a "helping hand" is a habit worth its "weight in gold" in fostering good and meaningful HR.

Giving and receiving a "hand," when needed, is a great way to be a "survivor."

This is a Very Big World!

Our world is large and complex. And "Today" full of uncertainty. Our world is full of good people, but unfortunately there are a few "bad apples" in the "basket" too. To my way of thinking, we were not brought into this world to live a tough and unpleasant life, but quite the opposite.

The unpleasantness we may encounter is, I believe, as a direct result of us not using our resources in a more productive way. When you think about it, we <u>all</u> want the same things from life. "We all want <u>happiness</u> and have <u>no suffering</u>."

How should we describe HAPPINESS? This is the author's "take" on a definition. Happiness evolves, or develops, gradually from being a human being with some specific qualities. If you are a human being who strives to be <u>useful</u>, <u>responsible</u>, <u>honorable</u>, and <u>compassionate</u>, and you live your life by these qualities, you will find happiness. And the desire to have <u>NO SUFFERING</u> (or as little as possible) will be satisfied by setting in motion the cause and effect phenomenon.

Perhaps some of you will have a concern about this "promise" as you read it. You may wonder – "If I follow this understanding, will I be guaranteed happiness and no suffering?"

Having a guarantee usually means that things that are promised to you will be there at all times with no exceptions. Well, don't be disillusioned. There are no guarantees in life. But if you live the exemplary life as suggested above, you create the best possible chance for yourself to have happiness and the least amount of suffering.

The word "Reality" means to see things as they really are. I keep referring, on occasion, back to the beginning of time, our time, when God created "man" in His own image. Because of Adam and Eve's "debacle" reality, the way I believe God intended went up in "smoke." The reality we are all experiencing today is really – "What happens, happens." It is up to each of us to do our utmost to make everybody else's life and ours a pleasant and productive life.

The word "Evil," which, according to our dictionary, means "violating or inconsistent with moral law" has entered our lives. And we (some of us) as human beings are adding fuel to the "fire" of discontentment.

I have no clue if the "Fire-Breathing Dragon" in some of us will ever run out of "fuel," and life will be continued on the imaginary island called Utopia. But I do feel strongly that each of us will have to, for a long, long time, continue to do what we can do to build and live a good life for ourselves and, along the way, help as many less fortunate people as we can to do the same.

As long as each of us has a breath left in our body, we have opportunities to do the right thing for others and ourselves. There is no age limit for starting and trying to live the best life possible for ourselves. All we have to do is <u>really want</u> to do it.

What Do You Think Our Life Would be Like If:

-   We, as human beings, talked <u>with</u> each other more and if we shared our positive thinking with each other more?
-   We, as human beings, asked each other more questions about what we each thought about various matters of importance to all of us?
-   What we, as human beings, would do, specifically, to deal with certain matters?
-   What or how specifically we, as human beings, would actually do certain things to overcome, or change, or correct, or mend whatever was needed?

Point being?

Sometimes, perhaps more often than we realize, we decide to do "our thing" based on only our own thinking and however it would turn out it may be okay or just so-so. However, if we told ourselves, or admitted to ourselves, that others may have had to deal with, or confront, the same situation that we are now faced with (whatever it may be), and if we knew how they handled their similar situation, perhaps it would give us some "clues" as to how we could best handle ours.

<u>Asking questions</u> for the purpose of gaining advice or information that would give us a "leg up" when we are confronting matters to which a solution would permit us to continue on the road to living a good life <u>is not a sign of weakness; it is truly a sign of intelligent thinking</u>.

We already know that it is an unalterable fact that there is absolutely no one human being who knows the absolute correct answer to all matters that affect our daily lives. Why should we not be guided by that fact? And if we have learned about and if we exercise good human relations, we should have available to us all the human resources needed to allow us to proceed with our lives in a very positive manner.

Lest we forget! Our goal, our objective, is to always and firmly stay on the "road" that allows us to "live a good life." Let us always remember to, and never hesitate to, ASK well thought-out questions from our friends, acquaintances, and strangers who all make up our "human relatives." After all, we are all members of a very large human family.

"Differences"!?

When we refer to "Differences" in this writing, we are referring to the human race only. We are referring to the ethics of humanitarianism, the doctrine that "man's" obligations are concerned wholly with the welfare of the human race.

It would be good to know a little bit about some of the reasons "differences" in human beings sometimes create such negativism within us and what we may be able to "do" to mitigate "war-like" actions against each other whenever disagreements, of all kinds, develop.

Every single human being is "different" from every other human being in many, many ways. You will remember how the Dali Lama explained the "one human family." The one Supreme Being, God, Allah, created all human beings with the intent of being different so we could learn from and support each other's efforts to live an "all around" productive life.

The word "difference" is a word you will find in all languages that, I doubt, will ever be obliterated. Some of the differences in human beings in how we think about things, how we live our lives, our customs, habits, mannerisms, religious interpretation of what our "creator" intended for us, etc. will probably always be the "hang-up" preventing total agreement in all mutually beneficial things.

What did we just say? We acknowledged that differences between human beings have always existed and will continue to always exist. We may all now start to think – if differences are "here to stay," what is the big deal? "Why can't we just get along?" This is an old saying that, to my way of thinking, has turned out to be just words. However, this old saying is an "ideal" saying if it could be effectively integrated in everyone's mind. And actions toward each other are always civil.

So here we are, "ALL DIFFERENT!" How can we manage, what should we try to do to live our lives in a manner that will allow us to have happiness and the least amount of suffering?

The answer to this question - I have "no clue" as to how all of us can get together on one specific answer. But I do believe that as an individual human being, one by one, we can come up with a workable answer to deal with this matter, independently, for ourselves. The whole idea being that life for us will go on, Okay, if we can create a "NO HURTING" self-imposed policy toward all others.

How can we cope with perceived "negative differences" when a "difference" causes us to be intolerant of others? Can we put negative differences on "hold" to placate the cause? Unless a negative difference "carries" the potential to cause mental or physical harm to us personally, or to someone we care for, we should be able to be "indifferent" to difference. After all, we all still have the right to "choices" every day of our lives. Whenever a difference appears in our midst that may negatively affect us, we can always "duck" and choose to avoid, ignore the whole scenario and only do the intelligent thing, which would be to "bow out" in a respectful manner, leaving nothing behind that can be interpreted as "unkind." This is probably what we also call to "suck it up" to avoid unpleasantness and harm.

Some additional factors! When you start thinking about all the "differences" that do exist between all human beings, and there are many, you will realize that there are so many nice, complimentary differences and, of course, there are some of the very opposite. These are the perceived differences declared among all human beings.

When many of us talk about and refer to differences "today," our tone of voice and our demeanor seem to always suggest that "difference" is a "dirty word" and this, of course, usually results in much negativism.

When "human difference" enters a conversation and our thought process, as long as "EVIL" is not a factor it is not a matter of liking or disliking, it is about accepting that which is. We, as part of the human race, to my way of thinking, will never ever become "one," as one exact same kind.

For all of us to fully accept "difference" in human beings, I think we have to first fully accept that we are ONE OF THEM. We add our equal amount of difference to the whole bunch of us, which I suppose means that we should consider our own contribution to differences first and then to convince ourselves that our own "differences" do not matter because we are only different in every possible good way. Oh yes! There is nothing egotistical about this last statement.

The following is meant only as a thought, expressed "out loud" for some "food for thought." It could be controversial (not meant to be), but also very practical (meant to be).

When differences appear, there is always a "fence." You can live on either side of this "fence." When it comes to "living" with "different" human beings, the good thing is, to my way of thinking, that every human being has a very clear choice (most of the time) in this matter as far as living on either side of the "fence," as long as "both sides" always accept and abide by the "LAWS" of life.

The "laws" of life direct all human beings who live on either side of the "fence" to <u>always</u> observe, show, and give RESPECT and KINDNESS to each other. And this requirement shall not be diminished unless and until either side creates reasons not deserving of respect and kindness. This concept runs parallel with the "Tit4Tat" concept.

Know that if "I" do the nice, kind, and respectful "things" to and for you – that is exactly what I should have the "right" to expect in return from "you."

Now, the choices we can always make as a human being is this. If our mannerisms, our culture, our strong desire for living our good lives in certain specific ways so sharply contradict the strong desires for "the other side" to live their lives differently, we can always choose to live our respective lives "separate." And we should have the right to do so. This is <u>one choice</u> that can be made by anyone. The <u>second</u> choice is, if it is strongly desired by either side, to move to the other side of the "fence" for the purpose of sharing the other side's mode of living a life they should be able to do so by <u>first</u> accepting and accomplishing certain specific requirements stipulated under the concept of ASSIMILATION.

It will be to follow the understanding of an old saying – "When in Rome, do as the Romans do."

When a decision like this is made, it should be based on a solid understanding, requirement, and acceptance on the part of the "guest" side to, as completely and as quickly as possible, "ASSIMILATE" into the "host" side. This very important consideration should not, if this philosophy is adhered to, create any serious negativism. However, the question would still remain – is this a valid possibility to expect to have happen among human beings? Or should equal and separate apply when "differences" are extremely different?

By the way, the need for "ASSIMILATION" is ever present in our daily lives. It is a very strong and positive "TOOL" for every human being to effectively use when searching to gain HELP, ASSISTANCE, COOPERATION, FAVORITISM, and all around good guidance and personal positive results in the quest for living a good life.

"Assimilation"

What is this all about? Is it important? Is it necessary?

It is <u>all about</u> "getting along" in a positive manner with "new" situations for yourself that you will be depending on for living a good life. It is very <u>important</u> because you could be affecting the lives of many other human beings. It is <u>necessary</u> because you will be relying on other "new" human beings for your ultimate success, and they must have their "mind set" to want to help you and to focus on helping you.

Think of it this way! Anytime you want to and decide to "play" out your life on a different "team," with your intent being to BETTER your personal situation, the "new" "team" must first know what you can contribute to help them become more successful. And based on this knowledge will make the decision to invite you or not invite you. When you change "teams," you have to ASSIMILATE into the <u>new team</u>. You have to quickly learn to be a good "new" team player and play your part so that the entire "new" team will benefit from your efforts. You will have the responsibility to change and to become "ONE" with your new opportunity.

This scenario will apply to anything; everything you wish to do that will cause you to become "indebted" to others for helping you to succeed by offering you opportunities.

Positive human relation is not difficult to comprehend and to activate on your own. If you understand and accept that every human being is "different" in so many ways and, I dare say, have a common goal with all other human beings of living a life that produces happiness with the least amount of suffering, then this old saying will always apply – "Do unto others what you would want them to do unto you." And I will add, be not selfish, "but do it first."

Important to remember – and keep thinking of it! If you want to <u>benefit</u> from what others can help you to do for yourself, you need to develop, within yourself, "the art of assimilation." People will do positive things for you if they have strong feelings that you want to be "one" with them.

Just in Case!

To anyone who may be obstinate.

What not to think or believe.

This brief side note is just in case any of us have a tendency to forget our place on the "TEAM" and employ imaginary "regal power" to try to accomplish what we need and want.

Listen! You can be <u>you</u> 100% of the time and <u>you</u> can do whatever <u>you</u> want to do and <u>you</u> can say whatever <u>you</u> want to say and <u>you</u> can behave in whatever manner <u>you</u> wish and <u>you</u> can dress and look in the manner <u>you</u> choose – ALL in total indifference to all others.

This could work for you as long as you will not have a need to rely and count on any other human being to help accomplish your objectives.

However, when you understand and realize that there is not a "snow ball's chance in a warm oven" that you can accomplish anything meaningful without the input and help of many other human beings then you will quickly mellow and accept that you will have to do whatever you have to do to "PLEASE OTHERS." These others will, in effect, be your "guiding light" for living a good life.

The "*quid pro quo*" is simply "you give me what I need and I will give you what you need."

It is a fair game of Tit4Tat and it is <u>REALITY</u>.

When in Rome ...!

"When in Rome, do as the Romans do."

This saying, the dictionary tells me, goes back to about 390 AD.

It means, "It is polite and possibly advantageous to abide by the customs of a society where we are a <u>visitor</u>."

Also, it means, in other words, "Follow the rules of behavior that govern your environment; obey the social rules that prevail."

The meaning of this saying, when followed, will not only be useful to you when you are traveling and meeting "new" people. It will be equally, if not more, useful and helpful to you if you think in this manner when you are seeking employment or you are seeking needed help and assistance from someone who can and is willing to help you.

Remember what this book is all about. The content of this book is dedicated solely to give you a clear "heads up" as to what will be required from any human being who really wants to live a good life for themselves and their family. And never forget that it is "other" human beings who will either help make it easy and beneficial for you to accomplish your objectives, or they can make it more difficult for you, if not impossible, to reach your goals.

Always remember this "POINT." Always choose to exhibit your very best and most conducive to cooperation, behavior, and attitude, and you will be on the "Winner's Podium." However, if you receive the "gold, silver, or bronze" medal, it will be strictly up to your own efforts.

Why do I bring this up now? Well, I have some memories from when I was "working" and had several opportunities to interview and offer employment to younger people who wanted to start out in life.

There were many times when making a decision to offer someone an opportunity for work was all "pleasure" because everything of importance "fell into place." The resume fit well. The work experience, the formal education was good, and the person's demeanor, perceived attitude was acceptable. But what happens, sometimes, with some people – they stopped behaving in a satisfactory manner and their "work" and relationship with their co-worker started to go "south."

These people would be counseled with and given opportunities to make an immediate 180 degree turnaround. Sometimes this worked out well; other times it just had to be "good bye."

These are things of importance when you are dealing with other human beings in a "work" setting or "socially." If there are no harmonious feelings between "the parties," the required results from the required "work" that needs to be done usually suffers, sometimes, greatly.

When "work" suffers and if not immediately corrected, the business can suffer financially. And if a business suffers financially, the person in charge of that part of the business will usually also suffer. When this happens, it does not bode well for anybody.

The point with all this "bickering type" talk is to make something very clear to all of us. When we have the good fortune to be offered a good opportunity to earn a good "wage," commensurate with our abilities, we overcome a large hurdle toward reaching our goal of living a good life. It is up to each of us now to nurture this opportunity and to build on it. And the sure way to do this, in addition, of course, to performing the job we were employed to do with the very best of our ability is to exercise our expertise in Human Relations.

Your relationship with your co-workers should be such that you "trust" them and they "trust" you. And perhaps equally important, you should get into the habit of "champion" your "Boss" and praise your co-workers for good work where appropriate. If anything appears to be "wrong," you go to the other person involved and discuss it and settle it, if possible. Never spread bad news. Instead, fix it and move on if the circumstance permits.

Can Difference in Human Beings be Good and Bad?

The very first thing we all need to keep in mind when learning about HR is we must recognize and accept that every one of God's human creations are different in many ways, and this should, under normal circumstances, not be an injurious detriment to any of us. The reason we are all different will be a difficult task to comprehend, but it should not really matter what the reasons are. What matters is that our Father in heaven, a/k/a God, created the differences on purpose. After all, what would it be like if all of us looked alike, acted the same, created the same things whenever we decided to be creative? God's intention and purpose, I believe, was to design differences into all of us so that we could all derive positive benefits from diversity.

When it concerns human beings – what does being different really mean? The word "different" means not identical, not ordinary, unusual, dissimilar, to be at variance.

Okay! We are all different in so many ways. But different compared to what or to whom?

Let's see! "I am what I am, I do what I do," – "You are what you are, you do what you do," and we both function in our daily lives in, most likely, totally dissimilar ways and manner, but with no evil in mind, and we are still human beings whose physical looks and manner may also be totally dissimilar. The only thing we may not differ in is our mutual love for living a good, peaceful, healthy life. Assuming neither of us are of an "evil" demeanor – why is it we cannot find sufficient merit in our "being" to go beyond "differences" and live our respective lives in uneventful harmony?

Is it our respective feelings and concerns for our individual "comfort zones" and our "personal security" that is the culprit? Are we concerned that our, perhaps, deeply rooted comforts, habitual peculiarity of manner, how we "drive" our personal daily lives, cannot withstand any kind of disruptions or diminutions? Which effect, if or when it happens, would or could "spell" unhappiness and dishevelment of the lives for one or the other?

If this kind of scenario is what is potentially troubling to most, if not all, human beings, is it to be called <u>selfishness</u> or should it be identified as wanting to protect an inherent personal need for <u>self-preservation</u>?

It is very easy for anyone to stand up and shout, "Let's all get along," "Why can't we all just get along?" This thinking brings out another scenario as "food for thought." However, first, let us ask ourselves one question. Answer this one with 100% honesty. "Knowing (and this is a presumption on my part) that most, if not all, human beings are and will always be concerned with, and ready to protect in the best way they can the good portions of their lives for their future that they are now experiencing – how can we envision a successful and effective forever for all, "commingling" of so many differences in human mannerisms and cultures?"

How many "sure fire" responses will we have to contemplate?

How about one more "food for thought" scenario. I will make one more "presumption." "Every country in our world, and I have read that there are about 195 separate countries, do experience some degree of internal dissatisfaction "arising from having a constituency with varied ideals for living their lives." Think about it!

If these differences turn out to be of a magnitude that they will materially disregard and possibly destroy a peaceful mode of living for all concerned, and the cause of the dissatisfaction is not due to an arbitrary hostile attitude by the authorities towards specific "groups," <u>then</u> could it be doable to employ a concept of "equal and separate?"

When a fair and well-planned "Assimilation" approach has been tried and given sufficient time to "take hold" and has failed – what should or could be a next step to a potential human unification? A unification that will allow an "<u>EVEN</u>" opportunity to <u>ALL</u> to have the same access to all available "tools" needed for living a good life.

This section, or any other writing for that matter, dealing with human differences that are not "100%" accepted by all human beings is a very interesting and highly serious enigma. I do not have any answers for a potentially good outcome. All I can do, as I have done here, is "think out loud" and invite anyone else to <u>ADD</u> anything positive they can think of.

I do not wish for this section of writing to be confrontational. After all, I did suggest earlier that this book is a non-friction writing. Please – "Differences" are always a cause for the use of "understanding" and "compromise."

Do We Have a "Clear Picture?"

Do we have a good, clear picture of what our individual lives are meant to be like?

If we do not, as of this moment, why don't we try to put in perspective a "human being's" life in general?

I use the word "Utopia" in this writing. It was first used by Sir Thomas More in year 1516 in describing his book *Utopia*. It describes an imaginary ideal society free of poverty and suffering. A perfect society in which everyone works well with each other and is happy. It is an imaginary island described as enjoying perfection in law, politics, etc.

I wonder – Would we dare to even try to imagine a "Utopia" today?

I trust that we all remember the Adam and Eve debacle. When God created Adam and Eve, he created us human beings in His own likeness. Adam and Eve were the first two human beings, as we know human beings today. God gave Adam and Eve specific instructions not to eat the fruit from the Tree of Knowledge. And as the reward for honesty and respect, they were to live in the Garden of Eden and experience a Utopian-like life.

Well, as we all know, the "Serpent" of mischief, "Lucifer," entered history and lured Adam to be dishonest and disrespectful to God and, as a result, Adam and Eve were both forever locked out of the Garden of Eden and left to fend for themselves.

At the very moment, Adam took a bite of the apple from the "Tree of Knowledge," our lives, or shall we say our lives, as we believe God had intended for us, changed forever. We could have, according to our beliefs, been living a Utopian life surrounded by happiness, free of poverty and suffering. This was not to be.

All of Adam and Eve's offspring were left "holding the bag" as it were. God never gave us any promises or guarantees that our lives would be fair and equally rewarding to all of us. As we have seen up until now and as it will most likely be into our futures, life is not fair, life's rewards are not equally distributed to all. Life is very difficult and demanding.

However, we should always remember that even though we passed up our only invitation to live in the Garden of Eden and experience a "Utopian" life, the one Supreme Being has always assured us that although we must now live our lives for ourselves, we do not have to live our lives by ourselves. All we need to do is <u>BELIEVE</u> in God and <u>Ask</u> (in that order), and we shall receive all the help we will need to live a good life.

I do not know how Adam and Eve, personally, made out in living their lives, but I bet they "kicked" themselves every morning for not having honored God's directives and championed the concept of honesty and respect.

But we keep on moving forward and as we do it seems that we, many times, continue to "step in it" and somehow we come out of it "smelling like a rose." This positive result seems to happen if we are personally successful in rebuilding, in the eyes of all human beings who touch our lives, the true concept and reality of Honesty, Respect, and Compassion.

I said earlier, "I wonder." Well, I do not think there is anything to wonder about when it comes to the behavior of all human beings, all of whom should somewhere show up on one of the branches of Adam and Eve's "Family Tree." We all learn something good and sometimes something less good from our parents and some of these teachings carry on in perpetuity.

Each of us, in our current situation, has available to us a "tool" that if understood and used properly can assist us in working through and overcoming the toughest of obstacles in our way to providing a better life for ourselves. That "tool" is simply <u>good knowledge</u>.

And since the Human Factor is involved with all that we do, there are no exceptions. The knowledge and understanding of the subject "Human Relations" should be considered (my opinion) as one of the more important, if not the most important, pieces of knowledge every human being should attain and live by.

Please understand I am not suggesting by my compassionate feelings on the subject of Human Relations that it is a subject that is an easy subject to thoroughly learn and understand. It is not easy and the whole subject is more involved than I can totally comprehend. But like mathematics, you can learn enough of the basics that will allow you to see and understand that you are getting the correct change in return from shopping.

This book, *Tit4Tat*, is written very simply and easy to understand (I think). It is intended to give each reader a reasonably good understanding of how each of us human beings reacts to each other when we are put upon to give a reaction. As we all know from personal experience, a reaction can be a good/positive reaction or it can be a bad/negative reaction. It will depend on what the action was that initiated the reaction. What we must deal with every day of our lives between us humans is the cause and effect of all that we do.

The Past and the Future

I believe that the peace, happiness, productivity, fear, unhappiness, and man-made destruction we all, to some degree, have experienced in the past and, no doubt, will experience in the future has and will continue to depend entirely (100%) on how we humans exercise our individual positive abilities. For instance, we should exercise our ability to develop amicable approaches to every single thing of "human importance" we want to accomplish. Would that not be another "humdinger?" We should take the "yes we can" approach for a starter. I believe we do have the ability. However, "the jury is still out" on whether there would be enough of all of us who will fully understand the benefits of that move. After all, the only thing that should matter to <u>ALL</u> of us is the benevolent position of human beings' attitudes and feelings toward one another when it comes to living together in harmony. We should also accept that differences in each of us, as human beings, can be attributed to the "Supreme Being's," on purpose, reasons for creating differences in all of us. And that is so we could all learn from each other and be much better for it.

Trust – Is a rare commodity today (I think) which, when found and verified, should be treasured and nurtured.

"<u>Trust But Verify</u>" (President Reagan's observation) – When you think about it, it may be the best combination for seeking and obtaining the REAL TRUTH and understanding.

"Trust" – This word alone and its intended meaning today, I believe is on shaky ground.

Whatever do I mean?

Well, first, what does the word *Trust* mean? Our dictionary notes the following meanings:

> "Reliance on the integrity, justice, etc.; of a person, or
> some quality or attribute of a thing; confidence."

The word *Trust* and the saying "Trust Me" or "It's the Truth" today, in my opinion, has less real value and meaning than ever before in our lifetime.

Why would I say that?

Well, I suggest this not because I do not believe most people do not want to tell it like it really is, but because again, in my opinion, most people in today's societies do not themselves know what the truth about many things really is and the value the truth is intended to have for the recipients of the answers. Or if they do, they seem to have plenty of reasons to want to disguise real answers or "truthful" answers.

Why would I think that "Trust but Verify" is a good and safer thing to do? Think about it! If you have a serious need for a "100%" correct and truthful answer to a question, which answer you must rely on for your health and well-being, then you owe it to yourself to VERIFY the responses you receive to any questions of importance to you.

Of course, when we assume the VERIFICATION posture, we can very easily depress our relationships between ourselves and the person we received an answer from when they realize we are attempting to verify their answer or verify that they are working on the agreement or the promise they made to you.

Well, if we value our relationships with people, we should try to avoid, at all costs (perhaps), any opportunity to "depress" them. However, if the answer you received to an extremely important (to you) question which you intended to rely on "100%" to try to improve your own well-being and you did not VERIFY that it was a good and reliable answer, and the answer turned out to be incorrect for your needs, then a more depressed or perhaps devastated person could be you.

So what should we do? How will we know when we hear the real truth?

Well, as an example, if we (hypothetically speaking) were told by our doctor that we have a severe illness, which could require a major operation, we most likely would seek additional advice in the form of a second and perhaps third opinion from other medical experts. And if the "experts" unanimously agreed with the original diagnosis, we would most likely feel a high degree of comfort and feel it would be okay to proceed. In other words, the original answer (diagnosis), being verified, now makes sense to you and you feel good about proceeding. To you, this "verification" now represents the truth. However, do remember that there are no guarantees in life, but we pray for the best.

To any important question, the answer on which we must rely we cannot or should not proceed to implement the answer until we personally know and feel it is a totally workable answer, for us personally, and we have a way to evaluate and verify the progress to be made or being made.

How do we handle the responses we receive from many different people to a lot of different questions? How do we "trust but verify" everything we hear? Well, you do not; you cannot and you do not really have to!

Why not?

First, let us remember that we are here talking about and referring to a person of "one," an individual. When it comes to knowing and working with the real truth, you, as one person, personally need only be concerned with answers to questions, which you have a direct responsibility for handling the correct way. Yes, this "trust but verify" philosophy should apply to you personally in your personal life as well as in handling your business and/or fiduciary responsibilities.

What Do You Want to Do With Your Life?

This is a very important question for you to ask yourself, and the correct answer is even more important. The point of this question is obvious. What do you want to do to earn a living for yourself and your family and create a better life for yourself?

These are important questions which, when answered properly at the earliest possible time in your life, will benefit you the most.

This is a question, which more often than not, is not easy to answer, especially if you are young and just starting out in life.

This is a question, which too many people are not giving enough attention and it should be given much attention.

The "proper" answer to this question, if there is a proper answer, may, many times, depend on the environment you grew up in. It may depend heavily on your personal circumstance, the life experiences you have already had as an adolescent, what your parents and other family members have been or are doing now as way to earn a living. You may have seen or know of people who are doing interesting and profitable work and you may want to do the same thing.

If you happen to "fall into" an endeavor that you think you will like, that you understand, can "picture" a future for yourself, count yourself among the lucky ones who will have this kind of realization early in life. If you are someone like that – GO FOR IT and don't waste any time starting to prepare yourself for a good and challenging life.

If your circumstances are such that you do not have a "family background" covering, to your way of thinking, interesting and personally challenging work to use as your own "base," you have to start "fresh." So when planning for your future, you need to develop your own "plans." You now have to find out, by yourself, from "ground zero" what work may interest you the most and that you would want to spend a good portion of your long, beautiful life doing on a daily basis to earn a good living.

If you are already thinking and working on this challenge, you will be way ahead of most young people and some older ones. But please realize that it is <u>NEVER TOO LATE</u> to plan your future.

Do you realize why a realistic answer to this question is so very important for you? It is important for you, exclusively, not for anyone else other than, of course, your future family or your existing family. All of us, including you, now and into the future have and will continue to have NEEDS and WANTS. The reality of living a good life is that without "money" that you will receive from "working," creating things of value, you will probably not fulfill all your needs and wants and that will make for a NOT SO GOOD LIFE. Now do not be "scared" at that thought. As you must realize, your life, your future is a "do-it-yourself" challenge. You are the only person responsible for making it happen. But you will, <u>if</u> your attitude toward people, life, and responsibility is always honest and positive, receive help from others if you only ask.

Some people know early on in their lives and others take longer to decide how they should move forward with their lives. And, unfortunately, some people never make a decision on what they want to do. And instead sail through life doing whatever "work" becomes available to earn them enough money just to get by. This "never-deciding" way of earning or trying to earn "your keep" must be hard, frustrating, and very unsatisfying. I do not believe there is much self-esteem that can be had from this kind of attitude toward work and life.

Is it a self-taught attitude or is it that some people have not been given an opportunity to have had some good, solid guidance from caring people?

For anyone seeking to make a decision on how to proceed with their life's journey, finding the right "niche" for themselves is an effective way to start. Without a "vehicle" (a proper fitting job, career), you are at a standstill. You do not have anything solid to base your plans (dreams and hopes) on.

If you are someone who is really trying but cannot seem to be able to take the initial step, give some thought to this idea. Be a "copy cat!"

What do I mean? I mean, sit down, put on your "thinking cap," and run through, in your mind, all the jobs you can think of that are being done today by regular people like yourself. Pick out a few of those "jobs" that look and sound interesting to you. Learn what is required, from a point of view of knowledge and work experience, to qualify for these jobs. If one job "stands out" more than all others to you – BINGO! Move as quickly as you can toward getting yourself prepared for that opportunity.

You have to accept the fact that you will have to spend a certain amount of time obtaining the required knowledge. This may be in a "school" setting or a "work" setting. But whatever it is, <u>DO IT!</u> And remember to always use effectively every day for the rest of your life what you know and will learn about Human Relations. Do this and you will be on your way to feeling satisfied and content, and that is a good start to living a good life. Set your goals and work diligently every day to get a step closer to reaching them and "NEVER LOOK BACK."

Look around you – think deep and long! Who do you see (recognize) that can do and is willing to do for you what you need to have done to create a good life for you if you refuse to do it? Anybody? Nobody? <u>Okay, you are it!</u>

This was just another way to try to convince all of us that when it comes to "living a good life," we are all in the "Do-It-Yourself" arena with the Tiger (Life) staring at us. And we know that the only way out "safely" is to tame the Tiger and move on to a good life.

Time is the most fragile resource we have at our disposal. If we do not use it, we lose it.

THINK!!?? What does this word really mean? When we use a word like "Think," we all know the meaning of this word. The word "Think," however, has several synonyms. It is interesting to note a few here:

> "Conceive – Imagine – Visualize – Focus on – Take to heart"

When you read this book, I would like you to really THINK about what is written. In addition, I would like you to form an opinion and IMAGINE,

VISUALIZE, and FOCUS on what the message is. Moreover, if you understand and accept what a 'REMINDER" can do for you, I would like you to TAKE IT TO HEART and make it an integral part of your daily life 24/7.

Information alone does not create transformation. Information plus your added actions can cause or create transformation.

This book is written exclusively for those who read it, but intended for all (Go Figure!).

Do not make anything complicated to understand when it is intended to help human beings live and work together to "FEED" their NEEDS and WANTS.

We should all do everything reasonable to satisfy our <u>needs</u> and put us on the right track to obtain some or all of our reasonable <u>wants</u>.

I am finding that one of the more challenging parts of writing anything is to be able to clearly bring out a strong desire from the reader's part to want to read and re-read all that is written. In addition, to anticipate receiving clear, interesting, helpful, and challenging knowledge that can help fulfilling the reader's NEEDS and WANTS.

I am hoping that by writing this book, it can all be defined as "COMMON SENSE STUFF." Stuff that has already been validated since the beginning of time, as we know it, about 4,000 years ago.

By simply living with and observing other human beings as well as ourselves, do our own things each and every day, we have learned how we human beings can get along with each other. Let us face it! We can get along and at times we seem to not get along. And the reasons are that we sometimes do the right thing <u>FOR</u> each other and sometimes we do the wrong thing <u>TO</u> each other.

Time and Knowledge

Time and knowledge have something very important in common! What?

Think about it! <u>Time</u>, if you do not use it to your advantage, it is worth zero to you.

Think about it! <u>Knowledge</u>, if you do not act on it to your advantage, it is worth zero to you.

How about that – the two most valuable resources to human beings can be worth an awful lot or can be worth "bubca" (that is absolutely nothing). And guess what? <u>You</u> and only <u>you</u> can decide what the VALUE to you of each of these resources will be.

"Do Unto Others ..."

If you do to others that which pleases them and in return your actions reward you with what you like and need – how bad is that?

When you think about it, the "Tit4Tat" concept and how it is supposed to work in real life – that is the way it works.

It is probably the easiest way and the surest way you can progress your life in a very positive and most pleasant way. Believe that and do not spend any time trying to find ways to negate that thought – that would only be a negative move.

NOTE: Think about it! You are the "innovator," the "fabricator," the distributor" of the most thought-after "need and want" product in the entire world and (assume) you can do all these things, all by yourself, without any help or assistance from any other human being. You can almost be referred to as a human being who is totally self-sufficient from the viewpoint of "earning a living."

In other words, you can almost accomplish everything by yourself. Notice the word "almost" is being used here. This is to prove a very important observation. You still will need the potential consumers of this "product" to help you reduce your "inventory" of what you have created. This simply shows that you are very dependent on, in this particular scenario, other human beings, the consumers, to help you make it "BIG."

If you wake up each morning and feel that you are an invincible "powerhouse" that can do whatever you want in whatever ways you decide to develop your day, and have no apparent concern for any other human beings, then you are truly on the wrong "track." For your own sake, you need to "get off" at the next stop and find the "track" that will deliver you to the "Tit4Tat" station.

WOW! That seems to be a lot of writing just to try to convince you (if it was necessary) that there is no such thing as a noticeably successful "LONER." You need other human beings and other human beings need you. We all need each other to safely and productively live our lives in the best possible way.

Are we in agreement on this deduction? I hope we are because that will benefit all those in agreement.

"The Ability to 'Work' Effectively Through and With Others"

To my way of thinking – positive human relations is based on a very sound premise which is that each human being in our world of 7 billion plus is just another human being like everyone else. And this, to me, simply means that how we behave toward each other in a most positive way should be exactly the same.

Understanding the cause and effect phenomenon is an integral part of how human relations plays out in real life – good or bad.

I am going out on a limb here, but some of you (readers) who have been around for a while may be able to verify the following. I am suggesting that the origin of the cause and effect concept was borne at the same time God created man in His own image – about 4000 B.C. What! Not even a chuckle?

You may all remember learning that when God created Adam and Eve, God gave them specific directions and instructions of what NOT to do and they did it anyway. This, in my opinion, was the beginning of "selfishness" and "disrespect." It took God about 1,500 years to about 2500 BC to become so fed up with His human creation that He decided to drown them all except for Noah and a few others, and the animals Noah put on the Ark. This would allow God to start over again. God gave Himself another chance to get it right.

And here we are. It has now been about 4,500 years since the big flood and God's attempt at retrieval. How is God doing? Well, I know God is great and doing well. The question should really be – How are we humans doing?

Well, all I can suggest is that we humans should all be doing much better. I am wondering if God is contemplating another "Retrieval" maneuver. If He is, could we blame Him?

Perfection! Perfectionist!

The word "perfection" as most of us usually thinks of it, means, broadly speaking, *something, anything in a state of completeness and flawlessness.*

To Aristotle, the word *perfect* meant, "Complete" ("nothing to add or subtract").

Vanini and Scaliger (1500-1600), two writers and philosophers said, "If the world were perfect, it could not improve, and so would lack 'True perfection,' which depends on progress."

So maybe we can agree that "perfection" is anything that is in a state of completeness and flawlessness, and that will fully serve its now intended use.

What is a "Perfectionist?"

A *perfectionist* is a person who refuses to accept any standard short of what he/she believes is perfection. In other words, a purist, an idealist. Perfectionists are far more critical of themselves and of others than are "High Achievers." While High Achievers take pride in their accomplishments and tend to be supportive of others, Perfectionists tend to spot tiny mistakes and imperfections in their work and in themselves, as well as in others and their work. They focus in on their imperfections and have trouble seeing anything else, and they are more judgmental and hard on themselves and on others when "failure" does occur.

High Achievers tend to be "pulled" toward their goals by a desire to achieve them, and are happy with any steps made in the right direction. Perfectionists, on the other hand, tend to be pushed toward their goals by a fear of not reaching them, and see anything less than a perfectly met goal as a failure.

It seems to me that a true Perfectionist can easily overwork, to his/her own detriment, the "perfectionism" in any attempt at achieving an objective or goal. Now let us make it clear that by not being a Perfectionist, you still are not accepting sloppy, inaccurate, incomplete, poor workmanship in the completion of any objective or goal. You are simply not reacting to minutia that can be easily fixed, as if it was "the end of the world." And by not being a perfectionist, you would achieve more positive "mileage" from all the people with whom you are involved.

Okay! I have now written a few words giving my thoughts on the meaning of two words – Perfection and Perfectionist. Why?

Well, first I wanted to try to give a clearer understanding of the meaning of the word *perfect* in our world. And I have had some negative feelings about people acting as perfectionists toward others. A perfectionist's actions or relations with others can definitely upset an individual's manner toward positive accomplishments if not effectively toned down. Since practically everything referred to in this book has a very close relationship with our main subject, Human Relations, I felt it appropriate.

To Champion!

To champion <u>someone</u> or <u>something</u> is to defend, support, protect, vindicate, and advocate that someone or something.

You are a defender of what you believe.

We should visibly "champion" all human beings who help each of us, individually, to do better and be safe.

About Being REMINDED!

Does being reminded about things, a lot, get you riled?

If you are a person who needs a reminder on occasion, or maybe you are someone who constantly needs reminding of what you "need" to do, either one, if you receive reminders you should feel gratitude. You should not get riled. You should simply smile and return a "heartfelt" thank you to the person offering the reminder. I will suggest why.

To my way of thinking, people who remind other people of "things" are doing it out of concern and to be helpful and not to be spiteful.

It is probably true, to some extent that many of us may not need much reminding about what and when we should be doing something that helps us fulfill our responsibilities to ourselves and others. But think about it! Have you ever been reminded by someone of something that you needed to do which, if it had not been done then, would have been embarrassing for you or perhaps would have caused you some negative results?

What? Did you answer, "I have never needed a reminder." WOW! – NO! You are kidding me, right? Okay!

Since I believe most of us, if not all of us, reading this book is very much involved in juggling all daily intricacies of living our daily lives we need help to remember things at times.

It sounds safe to say, we all need help, at times, to remember to do many things and, therefore, we should never "burn any bridges" over which timely reminders can come to our help.

Think About It! If we do not show gratitude in a proper manner to any and all who, in their own way, are trying to help us, we could soon eradicate all avenues of assistance.

I realize that in the total scheme of living our lives a reminder is but a small part of all the help we may need. But to allow us to live our lives well, every little bit will help.

Always foster and show respect and gratitude in addition to a sincere smile. A sincere smile (try it) will always bring unexpected pleasure to both the "smiler" and the "smilee." How do you like those legal terms?

Think About It!

"**Tolerance** is giving to every other human being <u>every right</u> that you claim for yourself."

(Robert Green Ingersoll)

Personal Finance

Personal Finance

"I am indeed rich since my income is superior to my expenses, and my expense is equal to my wishes."

(Historian, Edward Gibbon)

This quote represents a human being who has managed to satisfy the greatest NEED by all "mankind" – "to feel and be satisfied with what he is achieving."

This is a "do-it-yourself life"; prepare yourself with a <u>realistic</u> vision of your NEEDS and WANTS and "Go For It."

Personal Finance
Think About It

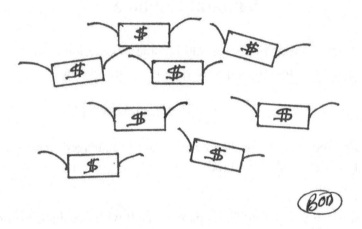

Money seems to be "flying" around everywhere. What you have to do to cause enough to land in your "pocket" is something you have to be seriously concerned about for the rest of your life.

Follow your own REALISTIC PLAN

Personal Finance

Think About It

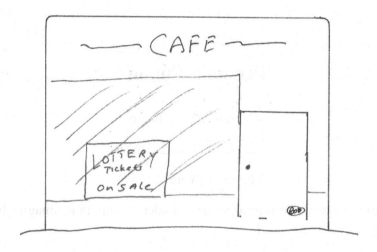

You see this sign and you think, "winning is
critical to my retirement project." Do not allow
that thought to linger in your mind.
Follow your own realistic PLAN.

Personal Finance

Maximize Your Income

Minimize Your Expenses

Maximize Your Savings

When you are performing all these "wonders," you cannot imagine how good you will begin to feel.

"Some Food For Thought"

Think of it this way – you have money – you spend money – you have no money – where did it go? Would you not want to know? We have to learn to control the controllable.

Do not tell yourself that you do not have the time to figure out what is happening to you financially. If you do not know where you are and where you are going, I can guarantee you will not like it when you get there. When you look at details, the more details the better; you will discover many things, good and bad. The more "bad" things you discover on this matter, Personal Finance, the better off you can help yourself to become. "Bad," on this matter, simply means "items" of cost you could probably live without if you are in a "pinch." These will be "things," if removed, that would improve your "bottom line," but would not necessarily, materially diminish your lifestyle. Sometimes we spend money on things we never give a second thought, and if that is the case, why spend the money in the first place?

"Remember, No 'GPS' can guide you to your destination if it does not know your starting point." And if you have not decided by virtue of a well thought out "PLAN" where you and your family want to be later in your lives, your answer to yourself, at some point, may be a simple "I wish I had."

Now, the obvious – if your current lifestyle causes you to spend more money than you actually earn and "have in hand," then you are obviously getting yourself deeper and deeper in debt. The only solution here, if you really want a solution, is to "CHANGE," tone it down – your lifestyle or find a way to earn more money.

Personal Finance "101"

Let's talk about money! After all, that is what personal finance is all about.

MONEY! Having money is very important to our physical as well as our financial health. If and when you treat money with the care and respect it should have, it will become like a very good friend to you. It will be there when you truly need it. The reverse is also true. If you treat money as if it will always be there for you and you begin to take it for granted and do not maintain your "pockets" in good repair to prevent the money from running out on you, you will be saddened and depressed.

We always say that our overall physical and financial health is the most important assets we have and that we must do all we know to do and can do to keep our good health "up to par." This is a truism.

At the risk of sounding trite, what is personal finance?

Simply put, it is the "management" of your money. Less simply put, it is the "understanding" of how to effectively handle your money to enable it to do the most good for you.

In order to properly manage your money, you first must have money. This must be the most profound statement ever made. All kidding aside, many of us who are fortunate to be able to count on expecting a paycheck every week or month can become somewhat lackadaisical and start taking for granted that this present opportunity to garner a "paycheck" every "pay day" will continue on forever. And if so, this kind of false secure feeling can lead to an attitude that creates an over-exuberance to spend your money in any particular non-planned manner. And this is counter-productive to preparing for living a good life.

Needless to say, but all of us must accept this fact that there are no steadfast guarantees in life and, therefore, our own cunning ways to financially secure our own future must prevail.

This last sentence is pretty much what personal finance should be about. How to put yourself in a position that will enable you to work and earn money, and to want to learn how to save money and, of course, to learn how to intelligently disperse your money all in the name of "living a good life" and knowing that "tomorrow's" pleasures requires "today's" preparations.

Personal finance is so closely related to Human Relations. There will always be human beings on both sides (employer and employee) who all need to be on the "same page" in order to get good things to happen. Remember when it comes to personal finance, like so many other things, you can only do so much with what you have. The cause should always be to do the best with what you have, keeping in mind the needs of all concerned. Flexibility, diplomacy, and reality are the "order of the day."

"Til debt do us part." This, unfortunately, becomes reality to some families. But it should not be your family because you will have a "heads up" after you complete reading this book.

We should always do our very best for ourselves and for others.

We should all live our lives the best way we can and in a most proper manner.

Living our lives well and allowing ourselves the luxury, at times, to do some unusual things that are fun and that we, as individuals, perceive as very much needed and important for us and our family. However, there is a word that can and probably will be very troublesome to us if we do not give due respect to its meaning and potential negative impact on our lives. The word is "EXCESSES."

There is a saying, albeit an old saying, "Too much no good but plenty okay." I am not certain how this saying originated and what it was intended to mean. However, this is how I could interpret its meaning. "It is okay to acquire what you can clearly and easily afford. But when you do not know when to slow down or stop in your acquisition mode, you are entering into the realm of excessiveness, the cost of which you cannot match with your available funds." And the financial outcome for you and your family can or will become an unnecessary economic unpleasantness.

You should always be guided by your personal financial frugality. Ask yourself, "Do I really need this?" If you cannot give yourself an honest, practical answer, do not get it.

To live our lives, to live a good life should be simple. When it becomes complicated, it is because we made it so for ourselves.

How dare I say that? I say that because I believe it is true.

Financial difficulties in your life will be the "bane" of your potentially good life. Who created the financial difficulties? Whose life is it? We created our own difficulties! It is our lives! It is a "do-it-yourself life" and that fact will never, in our lifetime or ever, change.

When you use your intelligence, accept the facts as outlined here and adapt the behavior of a highly practical and common sense individual. Do this all the time, no exceptions, no excuses, and your future will be what it will be, but you should not have any financial difficulties.

Accept that your success in life will be guided essentially by two "things." To my way of thinking, these two "things" are both valued on the scale of 1 to 10, 10 being the very best. They are your ABILITIES to get specific "work" done and done well, and having a good understanding of how positive HUMAN RELATIONS works, in real life, and practicing same every day for the rest of your life. Where are you on this scale?

Now, to live our lives, to live a good life, know that your personal finances will be a very important part of how well your life plays out. Also, keep in mind that the magnitude of your ABILITIES (the more you know) and your understanding and positive use of HUMAN RELATIONS will decide your level of success.

The foregoing was easy and fun to write because it makes so much sense. The word "value" is what our individual lives are all about. Look for the definition of value in your dictionary (mine is the *American College Dictionary*).

"VALUE = That property of a thing (your life) because of which it is esteemed, desirable, or useful, or the degree of this property possessed, worth, merit, or importance."

Put it another way – "value" in the context of this book is the quality of each of us human beings that render us desirable and useful to others. Further, the "value" of human beings in the eyes of other human beings "rides" heavily on our <u>KNOWN</u> reputation for, in addition to being useful, also responsible, honorable, compassionate, disciplined, and having a positive attitude and integrity.

The value of a human being is relative to value given and value received. To my way of thinking, you must <u>ALWAYS</u> first give, provide value, before you can expect to receive value – in that order.

In some respects, it is unfortunate that "MONEY" needs to be considered a good and appropriate "medicine" to help maintain our good overall health, but it must be. THINK ABOUT IT!

If you do not always have sufficient money available to you (money that is all yours, no loans), how can you expect to satisfactorily satisfy your most important needs?

You can outline so many good and valid reasons why and how money can help you live a good life <u>without</u> touching on or using the word Greed which, incidentally, in this conversation is considered tantamount to a "cancerous tumor," which if it exists and not successfully "treated" can cause much personal grief.

Maybe some readers are questioning why I would write this way. The answer is very simple and it is 100% selfish. When I do not have real knowledge of how someone I care for very much is doing with living their life, I worry. I feel a strong concern for their overall welfare and well-being. Therefore, I want to share my way of thinking about what I consider important ingredients that need to be present in everyone's physical and mental make-up.

What I write about here I know works well for me, and since most all human beings are basically the same with somewhat similar needs and wants, it should work well for all of us.

All one human being can do for another human being is to share all the good, positive thoughts and hope it will be helpful.

However, I believe there is, sometimes, some kind of mental resistance, to varying degrees, in many human beings in making a valiant effort to understand, believe, and create their own vision of how positive "thoughts" can contribute to so much positive good. If any positive thoughts are clearly understood and the potential results envisioned, they could help others resolve many difficulties if they culminated into the specific action required for the thought to materialize.

When you decide to be a "teacher," you are somewhat limited to how completely you can instruct the students to help them envision what "new knowledge" can do for them. The students have the responsibility, to themselves, to do what they need to do to fully understand how this "new knowledge" will further all their efforts to live a good life.

Let us all do our very best to LEARN more, to EARN more, and to react more positive in all ways that can lead us to a better life.

Just to recall what we are all saying, telling each other, as if it were, and it is the ONLY practical, most consistent, and most dependable solutions to our respective potential "money problems."

> "Live your life BELOW your means."

> "Spend less money than you earn."

> "Never borrow money (excludes home mortgage) or use credit card money to satisfy your "wants" unless you know with certainty that you will be able to comfortably pay it, totally off, when your "bill" arrives and you do so."

Guess what? THINK ABOUT IT! It is the only way you should think and act with your money in order to do "justice" to living your life well and within the power and productivity of your own ABILITIES.

If this philosophical as well as factual introductory piece of writing on MONEY has not convinced you this is the "doctrine" you need to follow to always be at your financial best, you should make a much stronger effort to convince yourself. If you do not, who could you point your finger at for not being successful?

Total success in anything does not happen "overnight." Total success is adding together all your smaller successes over time until your "Maker" calls you home.

NOTE! If you are comfortable and satisfied with what you already have and with what you do to earn a living and how much money you earn, and you do not want to do anything else, consider yourself a very fortunate human being. However, if you do at some point in time want more of anything of substance, you must find a way for you to do more. There is no other way. It is always your choice.

As I keep on writing on this subject as well as the other subjects that we deal with in this book, you will find that I get repetitious on several points. This is on purpose. I consider them of such importance to all of us that they are worth repeating.

Personal finance is a subject that should or must be, for all practical reasons, of serious concern to all human beings who are hoping for and striving for a positive and good life.

If you "play it down" to something like "I will deal with it when the need arises," you will probably be too late. The damage may be done and any possible repairs more difficult to make.

The obvious! To manage your personal finance, you must first have created for yourself a way to generate an income flow on a consistent basis. You do this by using all of your current ABILITIES and your cunningness to perform "SERVICES" that will satisfy the needs and wants of lots of other people. You, in essence, must learn to FIRST create "value" for others and only after you have first created value for others should you expect "value" to be returned to you by those for whom you first created value.

When you have reached this point, you now have to create a "visual" plan for yourself. This plan should tell you at a glance how your personal finances, at any given time, "add up" as you review your total actual income received and the total financial obligations that you have assumed.

In simple terms: your total current income received LESS all your current obligations to pay specific amounts due (=) money left over to be used for personal savings, funding retirement plans, and LAST, to a degree, some frivolous spending. NOTE: The total amount to be shown after the (=) sign above is the critical number that will help determine the overall quality of your good life.

Let us see how we can tackle this challenge. Believe me, our personal finances will, to most of us, always present an ongoing challenge; a very important challenge that we, by ourselves, must control. By controlling, I simply mean we must learn how to always stay ahead of the game, so to speak. We must create, within ourselves, very strong HABITS where we consciously and subconsciously consistently live BELOW our financial means. No compromises, NO "I will start tomorrow" kind of rationalizing. You start now and learn to live without some of your "wants" or postpone getting your "wants" if you cannot afford them without scraping the bottom of your coffer.

PRACTICAL

Keep this in mind when you consider your personal finances. A "NEED" should be something you and your family should have to allow you to sustain a "healthy" life. A WANT should be something you would like to have for yourself and your family because it will help make your life a little more meaningful (better).

What would you call something that does not quite fit into either a NEED or a WANT? "FRIVOLOUS"? Perhaps. If so, why don't we give this "frivolous" thing a few extra "think it over" before we open our wallets? It could be very beneficial to us.

MORE PRACTICAL

What do we do when we have a family with young children and we, perhaps, do not have the financial wherewithal to satisfy all the WANTS presented to us by our children based on what their peers have or what they want, etc.? Well, keep in mind that the feelings and the expressions of love and kindness and a keen sense of what is really important to you and your children's life is what resolves all questions concerning the unfortunate inability, at times, to financially satisfy all "wants."

You should proceed to discuss reality with your children as soon as their maturity reaches the points when they are prepared to understand what economics is all about. If you cannot perform certain parental desires for your children because of your family situations, physically or financially, take the mature, realistic, and highly practical approach – TALK WITH THEM!

Develop a loving, kind, sincere, honest, and realistic explanation for why certain things cannot be done "NOW." Remember, a parents' own well-being, health and comfort, is important to enable the continuance of building a good life for all family members.

If you do not have, you need to consider this criteria. You must learn and accept to be satisfied with what you do have. But do not ever lose the desire to find new ways, to do more for yourself, and thusly put yourself in a position to do more for your family.

Remember that as long as you can provide the <u>basics</u> for yourself and your family, you are doing okay. Basics = shelter, food, clothing, and perhaps the biggest part of the basics, love, patience, and understanding. Also, never say never, but work toward "more" in a very positive manner. Do not feel embarrassed or afraid to <u>ASK</u> for assistance if things get totally "out of hand."

Remember that asking questions and asking for help and assistance that are pertinent to your good and healthy life is extremely important, so you should never "hold back."

<u>PERSPECTIVE</u>

Here is an attempt by the writer to help provide a workable perspective, mental view, of each of us in relation to how we "look" to the rest of our world.

Here goes! We are who we are, we are not someone else, we know what we know, we do what we can do to accomplish what in our minds we need and want to accomplish. When we do accomplish what we need and want, we feel satisfied and content. We applaud all others who also fulfill their commitments to themselves. We look with some awe on those who have managed to accomplish much more than we have personally. We will not feel resentment toward anyone more successful than ourselves. But we may try to emulate their success if that is what we want.

We know that there will always be someone in our sphere of life who will be more accomplished, more successful than we are personally. And we also accept that we personally are more accomplished and successful in our own lives than many others. We understand and accept the tough fact that if any human being wants to accomplish more in their lives, they must acquire more ABILITIES and discover new ways to create more "value" for others.

Interesting thought! When you read this made up perspective, which is the result of my "pen" and not any scientific studies, would you agree that this could be a "perspective" of perhaps most any of the human beings who inhabit this earth?

My guess would be that it is "one for all and all for one."

Do realize that our personal life, anyone's personal life, is "a mirror of our attitude and expectations. Know that the 'world' plays no favorites. The world is impersonal. The world does not care who succeeds or who fails. Nor does it care if we change. Our ATTITUDE toward life does not affect the world and the people in it as much as it affects us."

Know this fact! In the eyes of other human beings, as long as we <u>are known</u> to be useful, responsible, honorable, compassionate, and disciplined human beings and loaded with integrity, we can do "no wrong" in each other's eyes. Do understand that by being known as a "good" person with integrity, your future efforts to earn the "values" you will need to live a good life will become more effortless on your behalf. Just do a lot of what you like and what you do best and live a good life.

Only show your caring and concern for others when you sense that by "stepping up to the plate" it will help you to sustain old friends, make new friends, help someone in need, or satisfy a client, customer with your service.

I think I covered all eventualities, but just to be on the safe side, do "step up to the plate" at all opportunities with your "Spartan attitude" and help make life better for someone, including yourself.

Remember that as a human being you have the exact same rights as every other human being – to live a life that brings you happiness and the least amount of suffering. NO human being has the right to interfere with or take away and stop another human being's positive efforts to build a healthy, happy life for themselves.

So you may wonder – if no other human beings can interfere with your positive efforts to build a "good life" for yourself, why is it that there are such large differences between how people live their lives in reality?

Think about it! Opportunities to live a good life for yourself are all over most of our world. However, our individual ABILITIES to recognize these opportunities and being able to "work" these opportunities to our personal gains DIFFER SHARPLY in most human beings.

What I am suggesting here is that we human beings are NOT EQUAL when it comes to our individual abilities to accomplish positive things for ourselves.

You noticed I used the two words – "Not Equal" – that usually sets off hostility toward such an assertion. It is not meant to be demeaning of any human being. But to my way of thinking, in this situation, I believe that it is an accurate and understandable statement.

So? Well, so we need to accept the fact that we must always be working toward increasing our own ABILITIES to make positive things continue to happen for us.

Then, given this "hurdle" to overcome, meaning we have to make a decision for ourselves to accept that our learning process will never stop. If it does, we STOP where we are at that moment. I think this is how we arrived at our saying and belief that our life, all our lives, is definitely a "do-it-yourself life."

If we "buy" into this concept, and we should, we need to do certain things for our own benefit to cause this concept to work wonders for us:

FIRST – We must make certain that each and every day we do ONLY things for our physical and mental health that will assist us in maintaining a good to excellent status. This should only cost you a good dose of self-discipline and your own positive "plan" for proceeding.

SECOND – You must give yourself some "thinking time" to view, in your mind, what personal accomplishments would give you the most pleasure and pride. You should write these down and keep as a reminder to yourself of what pleases you.

THIRD – This one is important for you to fully understand. Your current ABILITIES? What are your abilities as they will relate to you accomplishing some of the things that give you the most pleasure and pride? Do you have the qualifications, presently, that will give you the ability to do the work satisfactorily to accomplish the required results?

If you come up "short" on your current ABILITIES, are you willing to tackle the challenge to increase your abilities so that you will qualify to do the "things" you want to do? If you are, do proceed to do that and always keep in your mind what you want to do and why you want to do it. Then very simply, "Go for it!" Show yourself how well you can do the positive things for yourself – and keep going.

FOURTH - This one is also very important to your success in life. As a matter of fact, it may be much more important to your overall success than ONLY your abilities, even if your abilities would be rated "A+++." It will be your knowledge of and how you express yourself from the viewpoint of good Human Relations. What is important to overall success in life is how we interact with all other human beings that "touch our lives" daily. It will be the combination of your abilities and good Human Relations.

FIFTH – This final suggestion should probably be referred to as the "icing on the cake." It is what you should do to make certain that your objectives are completed as planned.

What you should do DAILY is observe, monitor, and verify with your own eyes as soon as any project/ objective starts a forward movement that your path toward a successful completion remains clear of potential obstacles, i.e., inaccuracies, mistakes, wasted time, etc. This being done, with care, should make you proud of your accomplishment.

Why Them? Why Not Me?

You may have had thoughts on occasion as you were out and about or driving or parking your car in some "wealthy" neighborhood – "Look at all these expensive cars!" Some people are driving cars worth several hundred thousand dollars. You may think to yourself, "How did these owners manage to purchase these cars; what do they do to earn a living?" You wonder what "causes" did these people generate to give them opportunities to have this kind of effective "spendable" income. Why them? Why not me? I am hoping you will find a clear answer as you keep on reading.

Well, I think we all realize and understand that every human being in our world is different and have different ways that they apply to meet their daily needs. They provide "value" of some kind to others who, in return, provide "value" to them in ways that meet their needs. The magnitude of each individual's perceived needs differ greatly. Some human being's needs are very basic – if they can feed themselves each day, keep a roof over their head and manage to stay healthy – if they can do this for themselves in a healthy but not extravagant way, they seem to be happy and content. And, on the "other hand," some human being's perceived needs are bordering on the "extreme" scale.

I personally have always wanted to have more, but I have also always respected the feeling of being satisfied and content with what I already have. However, I have tried to maintain a strong feeling and good attitude toward wanting and needing to accomplish higher goals. Since my needs now are met on a daily basis, these higher goals would represent gaining some of the "wants" I would like.

The writing in this section has now brought us to the meaning of the word "wealth." "'Wealth'" is having things of value to you in greater quantity."

You must understand and accept that life's wealth is up for grabs. It is there. But we as mere mortals must first devise a <u>PLAN</u> which, when adhered to, will allow us to grab a fair share of the available wealth.

We cannot achieve wealth simply by expecting it to come to us. We shall acknowledge and accept that we must be prepared and willing to do the right things in order to receive a fair share.

All of us, at one time or another, take so much for granted. We expect only good things, only the best to happen to us. And when it does not, we immediately feel stepped on; we feel we have been treated unfairly, and we show off our sadness, anger, and frustration by treating others around us with malice and disrespect.

It is very appropriate for all of us to expect the best. As a matter of fact, we should not expect anything other than the very best.

However, to "expect" it and to "deserve" it is not the same thing. We should expect it and, at the same time, we must be willing to personally always do whatever it takes to deserve it.

How will we know when we are deserving of a fair share of life's wealth?

We will know that we deserve it when the "value" we have created equals or exceeds the "value" we expect to receive. In that order.

When we receive what we expect, then we have achieved a degree of success. Accept that there is no continuous or steadfast success without great commitment on our part to First create value before we can receive value.

We also need to understand that there is no such thing as failure, only results or outcomes. If we did not achieve the results we expected, we keep changing our approach until we achieve the results we expect. I think we know, when it comes to creating more for ourselves, there will always be a gap between the less affluent and the more affluent. And I think we also understand that one of the reasons this gap exists is that the more affluent want what they want so much more than the less affluent want what they want. Having a very strong feeling about wanting something acts as a great impetus for getting it. And also, if you want to be with the more affluent, you have to prepare yourself in whatever way necessary to put yourself in a position to take advantage of the opportunities for more gain as they appear. To clarify what I mean when stating, in my opinion, that the less affluent people do not seem to want what they want as much as the more affluent people want what they want. I mean you have to be willing and prepared to go the "extra mile" to achieve more.

Here are some "one-liners" that I believe leave important messages so please read them carefully and make certain you understand their full meaning.

"Patience is a sound investment principle as well as a virtue."

"A consistent approach may raise the level of our rewards."

"If we want to widen our profit potential, we need to widen our horizon."

This last one, to me, is a super important message:

"Tomorrow's comforts require today's preparations."

Do not be the individual who will say, "Gee, I wish I had done that."

If you ever wonder why sometimes nothing ever gets done, why your progress is stalled, keep the following in mind:

Remember that a person's <u>thoughts</u> are the basis for his/her goals and objectives. A person's <u>accomplishments</u> represents reaching those goals and objectives. The span between the <u>thoughts</u> and the <u>accomplishments</u> is <u>DISCIPLINE</u>.

I know that you know what this means, but let me give you my version anyway. Once your mind has given "birth" to a potentially good, practical, and beneficial to you – <u>THOUGHT</u> (something when completed that will be very beneficial to you and your family), you picture in your mind what the goal, your objective, will be like for you and your family. Then you establish the "steps" (your PLAN) you need to take in order to reach your goal. Now you have to start taking and completing each "STEP" so you can reach your goal. But for some reason, you do not start or may start and complete some of the required "steps," and then stop and go no further. Hence, no goal reached.

Why did you stop?

Here is where the meaning of DISCIPLINE takes over. The word "DISCIPLINE" means, at this point in the game, "to act in accordance with rules." The rules being referred to here are the "steps" you had decided would be necessary for you to take and complete in order to reach your goal.

If you want to do what you have decided that you should do for yourself and your family's benefit – YOU have to do it – No one else will.

Also, so you can reap all the benefits that may be made available to you from or by others, do this. Reach out to people from all walks of life. You never know what insights or solutions may come to you in unforeseen contacts with people. Keep up with "old" acquaintances and continue to make new ones.

The fastest way to become financially better off is to take a long-term approach. It may take a few years. Remember that small things add up. "Wealth" is an accumulation of little things over time.

Please accept my thoughts on this – money is not everything, but it helps. However, the real quality of the life we live often has more to do with our outlook on life, our relationships with others, our health, and our family than it has to do with the amount of money or other material things we own.

"Rich" or "Wealthy" can mean a lot of things. But here I use it to describe a person who knows what is really meaningful to him/her and in that regard does not have to worry about his/her material resources; one who has the means to do what he/she wants with his/her life, who is free from stress and strain of having to keep up with bills; one who is confident, at ease, and SATISFIED WITH WHAT HE/SHE HAS.

If there are any secrets to building "wealth," it is probably "HABIT." More than 2,000 years ago (I read about this), the philosopher Aristotle explained that the secrets of success in anything was "HABIT." To him, it was the crucial ingredient of all geniuses. And it was nothing more than a recognition of the concept of "compound interest" applied to life itself. Aristotle recognized that people do not simply wake up one day with the idea for a great invention or get rich. All progress is made by small increments compounding over time.

If you think of it this way. "A great builder lays one brick at a time and, over time, builds great monuments. Also, a great artist works day after day and, over time, produces great works of art. So, too, we build our wealth a little each day and, over time, we become wealthy."

So, you see, I think we can accept that it is all in <u>POSITIONING</u> ourselves properly so the small habits of our everyday life build wealth for us.

The quality of our work and our ways of interaction with other human beings must, at all times, be of the highest grade. We must understand the "principle of incremental degradation" and never take advantage of it. Remember that small cutbacks in any quality are often impossible to detect. But put together a lot of small undetectable cutbacks and soon you will have a noticeable inferior "product" or human being. This principle applies to more than quality control. It applies to the way we run our lives, including the way we run our financial life – it is another way of saying little things add up.

Sometimes you will read something and it "catches your eye," but you do not quite understand its full meaning or suggestion to you. Do not just skip over it. Do yourself a great favor, figure out what it is really suggesting to you. You can do this by simply thinking about it and/or have a brief conversation with someone who may be able to help you gain more clarity. My point is simple. If you are really striving to do more and better things for yourself and your family, make certain you fully understand the whole process.

I am hoping that there will be many individuals of all walks of life who will read and accept what I am REMINDING them of. And whose way of life, as a result, will change for the better. There are individuals now whose lives differ greatly from one another. Some individuals will be well on their way to enjoying an extremely good life in all respects. Others will be making certain adjustments to their own way of pursuing life for the better. And still, unfortunately, there will be individuals whose life, at the present, may seem to be so unbearable that they do not yet know which "end is up" and that they may feel they carry such a heavy burden that they see no light at the end of the "tunnel." I pray they will come to understand the many ways they can improve their own lives by making certain adjustments in their daily behaviors and attitudes toward themselves and others.

We should ALL also understand that the one "Supreme Being" helps those in need who, first, tries to help themselves. And, also, that ordinary human beings, like you and me, will gladly step forward and help others in need who show a sincere desire to help themselves. But what all of us should remember is that our journey through life is just that – a journey that will not end until the one "Supreme Being" "blows the whistle." And between now and then there will be the ongoing need for continuous nurturing on our respective behalf to keep the good life on track. And the more human beings we can help, train, and coach to help themselves, the better off we will all be.

When we say that "integrity" is a principle that never fails, everyone knows that having integrity means that you are and also known as an honest person and a truthful person, and that trait will be extremely valuable to your efforts to live a good life. Without these valuable traits, you will not stand a chance of having the good life as the majority of human beings think of a good life.

I will suggest that it is very important to all of us to understand who we are as it relates to our knowledge, our abilities, our goals. The richness of a life depends not only on the amount of happiness it achieves, but perhaps more important on finding out who one is. Such as about one's unique combinations of "Powers" – the word "power" here means the combination of our knowledge and abilities. And then through "experimenting" and careful considerations of which directions your life should move forward in order to allow you to most productively utilize your "power" to build the most advantageous life for yourself.

So what this book is all about is you. How should you live in this world for your stay here to be the most productive and pleasant?

As you will realize, every day for the rest of your long and good life you will be directly involved in the daily challenges of "People vs. People." You can never escape these challenges nor would you want to. Keep this in mind every time you are dealing with people.

Everything in this entire world we want to do or get done, we must do with and through people. EVERYTHING.

So, again, to summarize what we are aiming for with this writing is, in essence, simple to understand. Meaning, that once we identify ourselves to ourselves with who we are as it relates to our present knowledge and abilities, then we will know what we are capable of doing. Now, the second part of this analogy, which has to do with "getting done" what our knowledge and abilities indicate we can do, is going to be the most difficult task for you. This task will involve several important "steps" for you. These "steps" will begin at the earliest time that you, yourself, start to view the world you live in and you begin to realize that your "security blanket" will soon be removed by your parents.

Hey! What is happening?

If you have the kind of parents who have been trying to "instill" in you common sense and the understanding that before you can do something, you must be something, you should be well ahead in this wonderful "game" of life. And if you are starting out "cold," it may be a little tougher on you – but not to worry.

Not to belabor these important "steps" which, when we think about them, will be quite obvious. I will briefly mention them here and this writing will repeat them several times.

Step #1   Understand what a good ATTITUDE means to you and all others with whom you will have contact.

Step #2   <u>Understand</u> what we mean when we talk about People vs. People.

Step #3   <u>Understand</u> what we mean when we say "Before you can do something, you must be something."
                    (Referring here to your knowledge and abilities.)

Step #4   <u>Understand</u> why you cannot be successful without a "well thought out" PLAN of approach to your future success and living a good life.

When we are truthful with ourselves and taking responsibility for making the best use of what we have, we are on our way to living a good life.

So we ask ourselves, "What do we have?" Good question! Well, this is what I have learned from several authors who have commented on "our brains." We have our underutilized brains which, to me, would be interpreted as meaning we have substantially more brain capacity than we ever seem to use. What if we "doubled" what we are currently using? We will probably still have plenty left over. Why not enter your "BRAIN" in many more daily positive challenges for your own good and gain and see where it takes you? Generate more interest in productive things for yourself and <u>THINK</u> about whatever you feel will be positive to you, and pursue it with vigor.

Then we have our current knowledge and abilities. Also, we have perhaps the most valuable commodity on earth, which is <u>TIME</u>. As you know, <u>TIME</u> never stands still – you either use it or lose it. These are our possessions. This is really an immense amount of "wealth" that belongs to each of us. And it is investment of our "wealth" that will determine our rate of return and the quality of living the good life.

We should all be keenly aware of what causes financial problems. What is the cause? The only cause? Perhaps not the only cause, but I will venture a guess that it may be the number one cause (#1). It is creating more financial obligations for yourself than you have a moral right to do. It is you and nobody else. So look to your personal behavior for your solutions.

What Does it Mean to be "Well Off" Financially?

I think you would have to say that the answer here is very personal to each individual. However, here are my feelings on this subject.

Listen! Strictly from a financial point of view until you have reached your personal financial goal of being debt-free at the end of "each month" (except for your home mortgage) and you have accumulated your "secure money cushion", you should not consider yourself a person who is financially well off. Think about it! Does it not make sense?

I realize what I just wrote may be considered a somewhat arrogant statement. However, I do not want you to stop remembering and considering the importance to you personally of actually reaching the point where you can tell yourself that you and your family are financially well off.

It is not easy, but it is a goal well worth going after. But perhaps you will not comprehend its importance until you need to rely on it. Why not be the person who will thoroughly understand and feel its importance "up front" and thereby truly benefit 100% from its accomplishment.

Don't Be Afraid!

Do not be afraid to start saving your money. Each time you get yourself ready to spend some of your money on things other than what you truly need – THINK ABOUT IT. Tell yourself that you are going to need some of it later in your future. And at the same time, also think about how you will cope with living your life if you do not have it. Your personal finances are just like your personal health. You have to show them both great respect and treat them always in a manner that will represent good, solid preventive maintenance. Because having one without the other as you progress in age will not bode well for your continuing good life. And if you do not have either one, you are "you guessed it."

I Believe in Many Things

Here are a few examples. If you like, help yourself.

- ➤ I am all in favor of earning as much money as I will need to live a good life in accordance with the style of living I am comfortable with.
- ➤ To each his own. "Differences" are good. Figure out the good part and use it, and neutralize the bad parts.
- ➤ Know what truly pleases you and makes you feel comfortable. Then arrange your plans so you will attain it.
- ➤ I believe we all have to learn how to create "VALUE" before we can expect to receive "VALUE."
- ➤ I believe we should know the "road" we need to travel on to live a good life.
- ➤ I believe in proper proportions of everything that has to do with living a good life.
- ➤ I believe "too much" no good, but "plenty" alright.
- ➤ I believe we should be fully aware of our ABILITIES and work daily on increasing our abilities to enable us to create more "value."
- ➤ I believe in fair "capitalism," meaning earn as much money as you can but never at the personal "expense" of another human being.
- ➤ If you feel you have to perform "underhanded" in order to achieve personal gains, "fougedaboutit" – you will end up on the losing end with, usually, extremely unpleasant personal results.

"Value" Comes and "Value" Goes

How do we attain "value?" We, as individual human beings, create value through our cunningness and strong desires to satisfy desirable and realistic needs and wants for ourselves and others.

Why, sometimes, does part or all of our "values" go away from us? Because we as stewards of these "values" do not do enough on our respective parts to maintain the values we have acquired.

What are "values?" In the context of this writing, we identify "values" to us as any and all things that play a significant positive role in providing us with the opportunity to live a good and healthy life.

Sometimes, perhaps for many of us, we do not recognize and appreciate the "values" we have in something until we start to have feelings that we may lose it.

What is that all about? It could be called "taking things for granted." As we know, when we think about it, it occurs when we expect something of value to us to ALWAYS be there for us and, therefore, we pay little attention to it.

It could be referring to our personal health, our family's "adhesiveness" to each other, and/or our friendships with others.

It could include our "work" and our "personal finances." When we are doing well, meaning we always seem to have enough money coming our way to do with whatever we want to do to live well, entertain ourselves well, we do not think far enough ahead. And as a result, we do not do enough to adequately cover ourselves by providing a "safety net" for our future when we may no longer continue to receive a consistent "fresh" input of money from having provided needed and valuable efforts to others.

What this really means, at the risk of sounding trite, is simply that the time will come when your body and mind will no longer be able to be as productive for you as it has been. This could stem from personal feelings of not wanting to work more, or it could be if misfortune should appear in your life and your mind and/or your body simply cannot handle any more value-driven activities as in your past.

Remember that "tomorrow's" comforts require "today's" preparations. Being prepared is something you need to do for yourself and your family. Preparedness is not something that is in your future just waiting for you.

There is no greater comfortable feeling than to know and realize that what you have provided or will provide for your own and your family's future will allow you to continue to live a reasonably good life as you "ride into the sunset."

Will you be prepared to comfortably "ride into the sunset" based on your current goals and objectives? Only you can give the best answer to that question. THINK ABOUT IT! And do something about it. Start now if you have not already started. The only true beneficiaries of your positive actions are you and your family.

"Nothing For Nothing"

This old saying still means if you do nothing, you will have nothing.

"Food for Thought"

Some more "food for thought" concerning your personal financial situation.

We should all accept the fact that MONEY is very much a LIMITED necessary resource to most of us.

What do we all need to consider doing when faced with having to deal with all types of important limited resources? We have to find ways of conserving them. MONEY is a conservable limited resource. We must protect its consistent availability to each of us. We must see to it that it will be available to us as we really need it. We must plan the use of our money in the most effective ways. We must focus on the "VALUE" of our money as it will relate to our ability to consistently live a good but frugal life. Frugality must become an integral part of our daily life in order for our lives to make financial sense. Of course, if you win the BIG ONE on the lottery, you can modify the last sentence a little bit.

Try to understand and picture in your mind what, basically, is happening "TODAY" economically speaking all over the entire world. And that the effect of these happenings could and most likely will, to some degree, affect each and every one of us in many uncertain, negative, uncomfortable ways.

It would not be "stretching" it to suggest that the majority of the U.S. citizens are confused about the true state of the U.S. and the rest of the world's economy. Everywhere we look and listen, there seems to be opinions moving in all different directions, each telling a different story of the condition of and the prognosis of our world economy. Even more troublesome is that nobody seems to know if anyone is on the "right track."

A further troublesome thing is that most of us "working stiffs" may not really become aware of any financial economic calamity until it may be too late to take any prudent pro-active steps to mitigate potential serious personal financial problems.

If you are following this thinking and you share the sense of the potentially sad financial state we could find ourselves in, how could you not immediately focus your efforts on "building" a "PLAN" for yourself and your family to hopefully allow yourself to have sufficient financial security on hand to permit you time to "hunker down" and let the "storm" pass.

Remember, if you have planned your financial life so you can reasonably handle a "temporary" bad economic downturn, and if it does not happen as badly as may have been anticipated, then you could find yourself in a better financial position when times get better.

In "today's" perceived uncertain world economy is this not a positive thought that should be acted upon?

How to Stop "Fighting" About Money

(Does anyone really do this?)

Money can be and usually is the number one (#1) cause of marital strife and tougher times to live a good life.

Listen! THINK ABOUT IT! It is very easy to start a fight over money – Don't Start!

Well that sounded like a "know-it-all" sounding off.

However, when you think about what is at the "bottom" of all such fights, if and when they do take place, and if you exercise your God-given intelligence you know that it is due to one or more family members spending more money than they have available to spend. Now, if you agree with this statement you simply have to stop spending more money than you have. You need to find a way to pay off whatever debts you have incurred. After you have done that – change your thinking about money.

"Money does not grow on trees." If it did, we would all be involved with arboriculture. Money is a very valuable and necessary commodity that deserves great respect and "T.L.C."

When you get together with your family to discuss your personal finances (do accept that calmly talking about the subject is of utmost importance), make sure that at the end of the discussion the "heads" of the family are on the "same page." Remember that during this entire discussion, patience and flexibility will be a driving force to a successful resolve of a problem. And this should include a well thought out and realistic "PLAN" for how you agree to spend your available money in the future. Remember, you are the co-owners of the problem (if married) and you will be the co-beneficiaries of a good resolution (if you stay married). This, I believe I can say without fear of contradiction, will give all involved much peace of mind.

How you perform this "miracle" by yourselves should not be all that difficult. Your agreed upon "outline" of what you need to do is the easy part. Following your "outline" that you have agreed to will be the difficult part.

Start out by clearly identifying where your total income is coming from. What is the "TOTAL" spendable income (gross income less any deductions, i.e., taxes, health insurance premiums, etc.) you can "count on" every pay day (assuming a "monthly" pay day)?

Now, if you have absolutely "NO EXPENSES" or other obligations to pay for – you would be in a great financial shape. All the money you would have at that point you could use for frivolous spending. WOW! – if only our financial lives were that simple. However, if it were so, "THINK ABOUT IT." What would our surroundings be like? Just spend a few moments imagining. I think you would find yourself in a very strange place. (My attempt at a little humor.)

Look – the last part of the above paragraph was kind of silly. But the important lessons we <u>must</u> learn (as if we do not already know) is that we <u>must</u> have available to us money to allow us to purchase each day a piece of the "good life." We must also <u>PLAN</u> for each day into our future to have the financial wherewithal to, in a timely fashion, be able to pay for our NEEDS and WANTS.

I will <u>REMIND</u> you now of how your "PLAN" needs to look to you when it is agreed to and ready to put into action.

You will need your <u>TOTAL</u> spendable income that you can count on, that you can expect each "pay day" (assuming a "monthly" pay day).

Here comes the part that will be the deciding factor in how well your finances will serve you. It will be a list of <u>ALL</u> the expenses (show in detail with clarity) that you have obligated yourself to pay because you are receiving something in return. This will be expenses like:

- ✓ rent/mortgage
- ✓ various insurance premiums
- ✓ utilities

194

- ✓ food
- ✓ clothing
- ✓ car payments
- ✓ car service/maintenance
- ✓ gasoline
- ✓ savings account
- ✓ retirement account
- ✓ miscellaneous things necessary or unnecessary

Add additional expenses that I may not have included. It is very important to you that _every_ expense that you have an obligation to yourself and others to pay is included. Double check; you do not need to fool yourself. Develop and show all of the expenses on a "monthly" basis. As an example – if you pay something quarterly, every six months or every twelve months – calculate what you will need each month to have the total needed when the "expense" is due. Then total all the expenses (for each month) to see what you are obligated to pay out each month.

Now you simply deduct from your spendable income all of your obligated expenses that come due in each "pay day" (assuming each month). Again, a very simple mathematical move that you, I am sure, already know.

NOW – WATCH OUT!

Do you have a positive balance or do you have a negative balance?

Do you have any money left? Are you in the "black" or in the "red?"

If you are in the "black," then you can consider yourself to be in reasonably good shape, financially speaking. However, you may not be satisfied with the total amount that you have left. You want more money left over.

If you are in the "red," you are not doing too well so now your tenacity and willpower will be your "saving grace." You must now figure a way to either earn more money, or spend less money, or do both (the best way) until you put yourself in the "black" and remain there.

You will have to scrutinize very closely each and every "expense" item that you now have to pay for. You have to decide on those expenses that may not be able to be easily cut or reduced, i.e., rent/mortgage and car payments, and leave those expenses in place. However, all other types of expenses that may present you with an opportunity to either reduce or totally cancel out must be taken into consideration by you. Your expenses MUST be severely dealt with by you in order to allow them to be totally covered by your available income. Cut, cut, cut – Ask yourself, "Do I really need it?"

When you are looking at your expenses, I suspect there may be a tendency on the part of some readers to immediately go for more "broke." And to cover the expenses by starting to "max out" credit cards, getting bank loans, or worse yet, borrow from family and friends. Do not fall for this "solution." That is not the "solution."

So what should you do?

Well, first you have to agree with yourself and your family that everyone should "tighten their belts" and begin to focus on reality. However you do the rest that needs to be done; only you can decide.

Remember, when things get "tough," the "tough" find a way to overcome.

A suggestion! If you ever find yourself in dire need of help to get out of a bad financial situation, do this. Develop a PLAN for handling your existing "shortfall." Show on the PLAN what you will agree to do to put yourself in the "black." Now, if you are known to be an honest, sincere, useful person, and you have a credible plan to "get out of the hole," I would be very surprised if there would not be "help" waiting for you "around the corner." Usually relatives, friends, credit unions, local banks, etc. would be willing to "have your back" within reason.

Bottom Line – you have to learn to live below your means. You must plan for and consistently "feed" your savings account and your retirement account. And so, so, so important – if you want, really want more of anything, you have to figure out a way to do more. How? By increasing your ABILITIES to do more "valuable" work and becoming a knowledgeable and sincere practitioner of effective and positive Human Relations.

Remember the saying, "trust but verify." (President Reagan's contribution to our well-being.) This, to me, is a most profound saying. And it can be used by each of us to make certain that once we are on the "right track" with our financial life, we stay on the "right track" for our future and our good life. TRUST yourself that you will stay on the "right track." But, at the same time, also keep a "sharp eye" on what you do and VERIFY to yourself that what you are doing is doing what it will take to keep you on the "right track."

A good, thoughtful "PLAN" made by you will be your GUIDE.

Consider Our World "Today"

Our world "today" is more interdependent than it has ever been. And much economic uncertainty is looming on the horizon. It used to be that when something happened with the economy on the other side of our world, geographically speaking, good or bad, it would not necessarily affect us in our country. Now, "if the Chinese sneeze, we can catch a cold." That is how interdependent we are becoming "today." And I believe that interdependence is a "non-stop" growing phenomenon.

It would be a very comfortable feeling if anyone could accurately advise us that all of these changes toward more interdependence would culminate in a "Utopian" world setting. But that "ain't gonna happen."

Living well in a highly interdependent world will depend a lot on good, generous, positive human relations. However, at the present time as we are becoming more and more interdependent we are subjecting ourselves to the more potentially negative parts of being interdependent. THINK ABOUT IT!

The economies of all the countries involved are, in a manner of speaking, being "commingled" as a result of "world financing" – everybody borrowing from each other, lending money to each other, investing money, creating demand for goods and services, etc. It is capitalism in its highest form, but without, it seems, adequate controls to help cause "countries" to have the financial success needed and necessary to, in a timely manner, pay for their "FUN."

When you think of it, our "world family," when it comes to "Global Finance" and living within their means are really no different (except for being super-size) than our own independent families (husband, wife, children).

As "one" human being, "one" human family we can only hope and pray that our world leaders can take care of the "unstable" economy that appears to exist in many countries and convince its citizens to learn to cope with "less" until "more" can be realistically justified. If this cannot be done, we may all be "more" or "less" without.

As I have mentioned earlier in this writing, we are not "out" to try to "change the world" albeit a nice thought. But I believe that we can prepare ourselves, individually, for living a reasonably good life under most circumstances.

We are dealing here with a very important part of our daily life. It is about our positive personal finances without which living our daily lives now, in the present, and then in our future would not be a pleasant thing to look forward to.

Money, it has been said many times, is the "root of all evil." Money, in real life, is of extreme importance to all of us. It is the "thing" that allows us to have the material "stuff" that help us with living a good life. Money is a necessity. However, the "LOVE" of money can be evil. The meaning here is do not become obsessed with money; do not allow money to become a dominant influence on your "being"; it can, without proper control, become a bad omen.

In order to deal with our personal finances, we need to have an inflow of money to our "Hands." This means we have to have certain "ABILITIES" that we can offer to "others" that they are willing to reward us for. In other words, we need a "job." Okay! We have a job; we have had a job for a while and we have provided ourselves with some niceties and necessary things to help us live our daily lives.

We know what our "present" is all about. How do you feel about your present situation? You are either doing very well or you are doing less well.

If we are in good health, we can usually deal with any situation we get into, in our present, which causes us to be doing financially "less well." But our future is filled with unknowns. Unknowns can turn out to be good or to be bad as they materialize. As we may remember from our past experiences, when good things happen to us we can handle it without any difficulties. So we really feel – "bring it on," the good "stuff" and we will enjoy them.

But, and this is a BIG BUT! What will happen to us when some of the unknowns turn out to be "bad stuff" and we will not know what it is until it is staring us in the face? Are these not potential happenings we should try to prepare ourselves for? You may ask – how can we prepare ourselves to adequately face "unknowns" in our future?

For each of us, individually, we have to learn to control the controllable. Our health - yes, our health – to my way of thinking, is for the most part controllable. I say this because I feel strongly that you will agree with me when I suggest that if we treat our "body" on a daily basis the way we all know how a human body should be treated to give us the strength and longevity we all desire, we will attain such goals. With our health "up to par" we will have the clarity of mind and physical strength to deal with many things that may appear as "road blocks" in our future.

Our personal finances should be 100% controllable by us. After all, we can always find a "Black Hole" and throw our money into it without showing respect and regard for its "value" to our future. If we can do that, we certainly could come up with some "fresh thinking" on the very valid point that "tomorrow's comfort requires today's preparation." And as a result avoid, in totality, the "black hole" until our financial security is secure in our "hands." Then and only then should we allow for some frivolous spending activities.

Our financial well-being is represented by the positive effect of our health, our abilities, our respect for and understanding of the real importance of money as it regards our individual lives in the days, months, and years to come. "Money does not grow on trees." If it did, we would all be involved in arboriculture (I said that already).

This is a lot easier said than to actually do it. But I can only write it this way to try to get a point across. You and only you can foster your own good and comfortable future. You are directly involved in a "do-it-yourself life."

If you do not prepare yourself for your future, how do you think you will feel when you arrive there? Preparation is a must to reach a successful conclusion of all endeavors.

Let's dwell some more on "preparation." This is to be very practical in our thinking. Instead of trying to note "bad stuff" that could happen, let's look at it this way.

If, as we move into our future, what if we thought about what we now, in our present on a daily basis, <u>need</u> to function and live a good life. We need "<u>WORK</u>" that we enjoy and can be very good at that will provide us with an "income" to meet all our reasonable "cost" obligations. We need reasonably good "shelter" for ourselves and our family. We need to provide healthy foods for our family. We need our health to enable us to do for ourselves what we need to do. We need personal HABITS of doing pleasant, healthy fun things that will give us that always thought-after feelings of "HAPPINESS." We need to develop within ourselves a healthy but frugal and realistic attitude toward "material" things in general. We need to establish for ourselves – "Do we need it" in order to live a good life?

Now, these are the things we will need in our "present" to live a good life. Feel free to add to this list.

How should we prepare ourselves so we can have a "degree" of assurance that our future will contain most, if not all, of these things?

A very simple answer, but not necessarily easy to attain, is having a secure "money cushion" of sufficient size to help you maintain what you now have into your future while the tough conditions, if and/or when they occur, hopefully work themselves out.

What about a "secure money cushion?" Where and how do we start? How about right now! "TIME" can equal money, in a manner of speaking. So if you do not use it, you lose it.

Listen! Each of us, individually, have "limits" that have been put on us because of our personal life situations. These are "limits" pertaining to what each of us is capable of accomplishing for ourselves. Sometimes, many of us find proper ways of "lifting" or increasing those limits by doing whatever it takes to increase our own "ABILITIES" to create "higher values" of our accomplishments. You learn to do more things of value to others. This is one very certain way of creating more for yourself. Increasing our ABILITIES to create "value" is a measurement we should all try to properly "stretch" on a daily basis.

Now, back to the "secure money cushion." We each know what we have to work with. Our "paycheck." Our personal situations will dictate how we handle the building of this "secure money cushion."

The HABIT we must develop, regardless of our individual situation (exempt are those lucky people who have more money than they know what to do with), is always to play the "frugality card." In other words, you "earn" $X each "pay day" – your lifestyle should dictate that you will have a balance in your "account" of at least "$1.00 plus" when you receive your next "pay day." This is important! The "$1.00 plus" you have left at the time you receive your next "pay day" is AFTER you have paid ALL your financial obligations due each "month!" This should mean that each month you will have settled 100% of all outstanding debt due to be paid that month. The "$1.00 plus" you have left should be used, without fail, to build your "secure money cushion."

You, I, all of us need to learn and accept to live our good life BELOW our means.

Now, of course, you all realize that the "$1.00 plus" balance used in "dramatizing" this part of the writing is simply a "mathematical illusion." Not to insult any readers' intelligence, but you obviously cannot effectively build a "secure money cushion" with only $1.00 at a time. However, the "$1.00 plus" is symbolic and intended to indicate the total amount you have left at the time you receive your next "pay day" and that total should be devoted to building your "secure money cushion" account.

If you start and continue this mode of saving, you will be developing a very important and valuable, to you, HABIT. And, of course, the more money you can earn the larger and faster your "money cushion" account will grow.

How large should a "money cushion" be? It has been suggested by many "money-savvy" individuals that a family's "money cushion" (savings account) should contain a sufficient amount of readily available cash to cover and pay off, each month, for 10-12 months, all your financial obligations coming due during this period. The thought behind the "money cushion" is obvious – it should give you time, during "bad times," to maintain your way of life until you can get back on "good times."

Once you have "mastered" or "accomplished" your adequate "secure money cushion," you "lock it in" to make certain you only use it for its intended purpose. Then you start, immediately, to work on your "retirement investment" account.

I want you to learn and understand that the basic difference between a "savings account" and a "retirement investment account" is its intended purpose.

The "savings account" is a simple operation – you give your bank your "leftover" money and "today" the bank will give you a "pittance" in interest for holding your money in "safe keeping." Your money will be reasonably safe, FDIC insured up to a certain amount for each account holder. And the bank will provide you with readily available cash from your account when you absolutely need it.

Your "retirement investment account" is importantly different. In this type of "account" your intent will be to "save" your money in such manner that it will "grow" reasonably safe and as much as possible in a good, vibrant, progressive economy, and that if and when the economy is "less good," less vibrant, and less progressive, your money will suffer the least amount of loss. And that the "bottom line," at the time you need to or should consider retiring from your daily efforts of satisfying the needs of others, there will be a "TOTAL AMOUNT" of funds available to you in your account that will allow you to continue to live a reasonably good life until the "BIG GUY" summons you to the "Board Room" in the sky.

The only thing that I wish to share with you concerning how you should be investing your money in a "Retirement Account" is this.

Investing in stocks, bonds, and many other "vehicles" is not an easy task. However, some readers may be, in their own right, well equipped with proper knowledge and experience to make their own decisions on where to place their money and they proceed accordingly.

But if you are a "NOVICE" in the world of "high finance," and I sincerely believe that most of us are, do not rely on your own emotions, "gut feelings," friendly advice, or "talk with my cousin," or "I have a friend who is doing very well," etc. If you are not in the "business" on a daily basis of investing money in the "market," do not fancy yourself as any kind of an expert and try to go it alone. You could, and probably will, become very disappointed with your overall results and perhaps BROKE!

Investing for your "Retirement" should be a "long-term" effort. The "MARKET," if you follow it, acts like a "yo yo" sometimes and can scare the heck out of you. But "historically" the "stock market" over longer periods tend to favor the positive side if the companies your money has been invested in are smart, strong, and progressive companies.

Who should advise you on where to invest your money that you need to have growing for you to help provide for your comfort when you have done your "work?"

For most of us, it is my opinion that we should consider utilizing (professional) investment companies that are large, well-known, have an excellent and successful track record over several decades, and with an unsurpassed record for honesty, integrity, and discipline. These types of companies have the ability and resources and do develop good, needed analysis of the better businesses to invest in. And they stay current on all happenings in our economy and the economies of the rest of the world.

It has been my experience that large progressive investment companies "welcome" smaller investors and help them set up a most effective program for their future financial needs. Do consider any and all "moves" with your "hard earned" money with great concern when it is being invested.

As an example of a concern you should have is this. If someone approaches you with investment advice and they tell you that they can offer you a "DEAL" that will pay you a "return" that will be much larger than any of the legitimate large financial institutions suggest is a possibility at the time – play it safe with your money – just say "no thank you" and walk away.

Think of all the "SCAMS" that are being portrayed all over by "NICE" people every day. Do not fall for it. Do not do it.

Some "Retirement" "Food for Thought"

At some point in our lives, we will probably say "Thank You" for the day we finally retire from our "Bread and Butter" work. But when should this day be?

It is not an easy question to put a good answer to. We are all so different when it comes to the subject of "retirement." Some of us would probably opt to retire "yesterday," if we had the option. Some of us, because of how positive we feel about the work we do and how much we like it, may dread any date set for retiring.

However you handle your thinking about this subject, you must make certain that you have a clearly defined "Plan" for how you intend to realistically fund your retirement. The obvious thing you must get straight in your mind is that when you retire from remunerative work (your paycheck), what will you replace it with?

You do not want to be a "pedant" on this subject. You do not want to be someone who has acquired all the book learning on the subject of "how to retire successfully" and, at the same time, forgotten about the practical wisdom of smartly applying all this knowledge for your exclusive benefit.

At the risk of again sounding trite, when you retire you will always have some very important <u>NEEDS</u> to continue to be filled and here are some of the important <u>BASICS</u>.

- ✓ Good health
- ✓ A home that has been properly cared for and fully paid off
- ✓ Newer model car(s) that are fully paid for
- ✓ Money (cash available) monthly to pay in a timely manner for the comfort and peace of mind you receive from:
  - o Food
  - o Utilities
  - o Taxes
  - o Medical and long-term care insurance
  - o Property and liability insurance

o Fundamental other operating costs (i.e., car maintenance, clothing, and your more frivolous pursuits like entertainment and vacation travel)

Let me insert a little "drama" at this point. You have had a long life, full of positive happenings and perhaps some negative happenings, but all in all a pretty good life. You are nearing your "day" when you will retire and continue to live the balance of your life with "peace of mind." You are starting to notice the "light" at "the end of the tunnel" as the saying goes. The question that, hopefully, you provided yourself an answer to earlier in your life is when "the light at the end of the tunnel" becomes so bright that you realize you have arrived "at the moment of truth," your retirement date, is all your "financial luggage" following you and arriving at the same time?

Arriving at your "peace of mind" destination without a financial life "support system" that you should have "prepared and packed" earlier in your life for this moment would be – guess what – devastating to you and your entire family.

So many of us, in our youth, never give this subject much serious thought. However, it is probably on our minds, taking up some space. But the thoughts attached to the subject seem to be – "Yea, I know" or "I will deal with it someday."

Well, well – Listen! "Friends, Romans, and Countrymen, lend me your EARS" – the time to DO, if not before is NOW.

Enough with the drama. But let us stay with reality.

The obvious thing with all this planning and the absolute "NEED TO DO" exercise is to seriously focus in a sufficient degree on the timing for "the light at the end of the tunnel."

Working and enjoying your life at the same time is what life is meant to be all about. When you have "worked" long enough to your way of thinking, you will see "the light at the end of the tunnel" and ideally that should mean a continuation of the good feelings you, hopefully, will have had during the "working part" of your life.

There are many things concerning your life that it is not too late to start doing. However, planning and saving for retirement when your customary "paycheck" stops coming in every pay day, is not really a safe matter to postpone too long.

Only you can plan for your own retirement needs. But one thing you must always consider when putting your plan together is "START OUT" and STAY within the realm of reality as it will apply to you personally. The nice thing to have happen when you retire is to be able to afford the continuance of your lifestyle up to that point.

I believe there are a good number of people who, when they reach the "established" retirement age, will say "Thank God," for now being able to do what I really want to do. When I hear this or some similar comment, I feel sadness for that person. Is this person giving us an indication that he/she has worked all his/her life doing something he/she "detested?" If he/she has, how intelligent is that?

Life is too short to be working at something you do not like. But, as always, it is your choice. You choose the kind of work you want to do. And if it is not your choice, it must be because you were not prepared; your abilities were not there to do anything else. Now that certainly sounds like a very nasty remark from the writer. But is it really nasty or is it the way it really is? You tell me!

If these people in question are really prepared to do many different types of work, why did they not pick something else to do that would be much more pleasing to them?

We are, of course, speaking in general terms when we talk like this, and there are probably a number of instances where a person, because of their personal circumstances, are limited to what they can do.

We have, again, digressed a little – back to what we were talking about – RETIREMENT.

From my own experience from having been retired for almost two decades, I would ask anyone who told me they are retiring, "Why do you want to retire?" If their answer had to do with personal medical reasons or other reasons relating to their immediate family, I would understand. But if I knew that they had "loved" their job for many years, I would question, why retire?

If you "love" what you do and there is still a strong need for your "talent," your abilities, why not continue on a part-time basis or full-time if the opportunity is there?

The readers now ask – What's with the question, "Why retire?" Well, there are times when a question like this is totally meaningless because, for whatever personal reasons, a person has <u>decided</u> to retire and it is "carved in stone." There are other times, however, with many people, that the "day after" they actually retired they have strong regrets about that decision.

"Today," I believe there are many opportunities for the older generation to continue in their work beyond retirement age, if they want to. And I believe that many want to, but may not feel that it is possible.

Like so many things written in this book, it is just another thing to give some serious thought to.

Here is Some More "Food for Thought" Concerning Retirement

An important question for all you younger "working stiffs" to keep in mind. At the time of your retirement, in the "distant" future, or if you must end your "working days" earlier than expected, for any reason, when there is <u>NO MORE PAYCHECK</u> coming your way on a steady, consistent basis, are you going to be adequately prepared? Will you be able to continue to live a reasonably good and satisfying life as it will concern "self-financing" your needs and wants?

This is the type of question that is extremely important for each of us to have a realistic answer to. We need a reliable answer and <u>PLAN</u> to be adequately prepared. The earlier in your "working life" you start paying attention to the solution required, to be adequately prepared, the better off you will be.

When you are one of the younger "workers," you may pay less attention to this type of question and personal challenge, thinking, "I have plenty of time to accomplish this" and "I will think about it." The problem may become that you keep on carrying this thinking "beyond a point of no return."

If this happens and you do not "deal" with developing an answer to this potential problem until, say, you are past the "middle" of your working career; will you still have time to do it?

Well, I have always believed, generally speaking, that if you are trying to do good for yourself as well as others, it is never too late to start. However, when you are faced with the need to accumulate a commodity such as "money," most of us "working stiffs" need more time than others.

When you are younger, say you are starting on a "working career," chances are, depending on your "start-out" abilities, that you will earn a "wage" that you feel is just barely enough to take care of your then current responsibilities to maintain yourself. And because of those feelings, you just do not have any extra money to put into your "savings plans" for your future.

Well, let me suggest from my vantage point of "AGE," the feelings of not "having enough" can be an ever-present feeling. However, I do not necessarily believe there is all that much valid meaning or reality attached to the "feelings" of not having enough when it comes to "funding your future needs."

Why do I say this? Well, consider the dictionary meaning of the word *"feeling."* "Feeling is a general term for a subjective point of view as well as for a specific sensation: to be guided by feelings rather than by facts." Okay! But what does that really mean? I intend it to mean and remind us of the unavoidable fact that our existence on the earth is "totally" a "do-it-yourself" objective for each of us. And it means that we have to "assign" priorities for all the meaningful things that we want to have happen to us.

To my way of thinking, there is one exception to the following suggestion. And that is if for some unusual situation where you consider your total weekly or monthly "take home" pay and you live a reasonably frugal lifestyle and you pay for rent, your health insurance, food, and other necessary living expenses, you end up with literally only $1.00 left in your pocket, you probably are a little ways off to start saving anything for your future needs.

However, if the above scenario is not what you are all about and you have, to some degree, excess funds to "entertain" yourself, "then" there is adequate room for starting to prepare yourself for your future financial well-being.

Start with "feeding" a savings account, something, on a regular basis (every pay day). And if together with doing what will be necessary to increase your overall abilities which will put you in line for more opportunities for additional responsibilities that will translate into more rewards (income), you will succeed. Just do not lose sight of your personal financial objectives.

Just to Give You a Little Bit of Summary

There is a lot you can write about the subject "Personal Finance." The net result of all that you can write on this subject, to my way of thinking, is "how much MONEY will be involved in your individual lifetime?"

We have heard it enough to probably believe it, "The love of money is the root of all evil." We have to be conscious of this saying. When we love something, we tend to go "overboard" with our actions to have it, sometimes to the point where we end up losing it.

Is money important for living a good life? Can you imagine what it would be to try to live a good life without money? First of all, could it be done? Well, as most all human beings consider what living a good life is all about, it seems quite obvious that it cannot be done. We could say that "money" is vitally important. Anything that is referred to as "vitally" important deserves respect and intelligent handling. Money is important to any person living in a civilized society. Nothing will take the place of money in the area in which money works. That is all there is to it.

What is money? "Money" is the reward from our personal productivity. From the "products" and "services" we provide to others. We, in turn, can then use the "money" rewarded to us to obtain goods and services from others to satisfy our needs and wants.

If you think that money will not help you to attain happiness – THINK ABOUT IT! Money has brought a lot more happiness than poverty has.

We are not saying that just piling up a lot of wealth is important. What we are saying is that money is important because it is the only reward that is completely negotiable and can be used by everyone.

We should try to remember this formula: The amount of money we receive will always be in direct proportion to the demand for our ABILITIES and to the difficulty of replacing us. This is as it should be.

This is why preparations for life are so important. As has been said, "Luck has been defined as what happens when preparedness meets opportunity." For every one of us, opportunities are all around us. Our ABILITY to see them will depend mostly on how well we have prepared ourselves.

While this may sound elementary, you would be amazed at the number of people who want more money, but do not want to take the time and effort to qualify for it. And until they qualify for it, there is no way for them to earn it. It is like the person who wants a good-looking figure but who does not want to change his/her eating and exercising habits.

What we are telling ourselves, and it is true, is that the WORLD will pay us exactly what we earn and not a penny more. Our earnings will always be in exact proportion to the service we provide. If you do not like the income you are receiving, you must create ways and means of increasing your service. Your service must come out of you – your mind, your abilities, and your energy.

People who refuse to do more than they are being paid for will seldom be paid for more than they are doing. You may have heard some people say, "Why should I knock myself out for the money I am getting?" It is the attitude that, more than anything else, keeps people at the bottom rung of the economic ladder. They do not understand that only as we grow in value as a person will we receive the increased income we seek.

The problem we all, at times, experience in life is not that we cannot achieve our goals. We can do that. The problem is that we do not create, set goals. We leave our future to chance and find out, sooner or later and to our chagrin that chance does not work. We just missed the boat.

So we understand – all you need is a "PLAN," the goals, the "road map." And the conviction to start the ball rolling and keeps it rolling until you reach your destination, your goal(s). You should also know and accept, in advance, that there will be problems and setbacks along the way. But knowing also that nothing in our world can stand in the way of a well-constructed "PLAN," backed by persistence and determination.

Now "Go for it" – and never forget that money cannot be sought directly. Money, like happiness, peace of mind is an <u>EFFECT</u>. It is the result of a <u>CAUSE</u>, and <u>the cause is VALUABLE SERVICE</u>.

Someone once said, "It is good to have money and the things money can buy, but it is good too to check up once in a while to make sure that you have not lost the things that money cannot buy."

It all gets back to the "laws of life" that controls everything in the universe – CAUSE AND EFFECT. The <u>CAUSE</u> must always precede the <u>EFFECT</u> or the EFFECT cannot occur.

A Final "Food for Thought"

Have you ever thought this way?

This is very personal and this is how I try to think first thing every morning when I awake. This is how I want every day of my life to be like. I do not ever want to take important matters for granted.

What <u>do you</u> want from every day of <u>your life</u>?

When I awake every morning, I want to remind myself to recognize and fully embrace the privileges that I was given at birth.

I want to feel my gratitude for my <u>eyesight</u>, my ability to <u>hear voices</u> and <u>sounds</u>, my ability to <u>employ sound thinking</u> and, most important, for <u>my beating heart</u> that will help me move smoothly through my day.

I want to enjoy a clear mind that can very easily help me remember my goals, my objectives that I need to achieve "today."

I want to acknowledge to myself, remind myself that I will need to depend on every human being who becomes a part of my life "today" to help me with my anticipated accomplishments. And, therefore, behave toward them in a manner that will make them feel they want to help.

I want to do what my "heart" tells me to do as it concerns the positive relationships that I know I will need with every human being who touches my life "today."

I want to remind myself that I have in place a positive "PLAN" for my life and that my PLAN will be "updated" and/or changed at the moment a valid reason to do so shows up. The only thing that will <u>never change</u> in my "PLAN" is my "<u>STRATEGY</u>" for living my life, which is to be a human being who is <u>USEFUL</u>, <u>RESPONSIBLE</u>, <u>HONORABLE</u>, <u>COMPASSIONATE</u>, <u>DISCIPLINED</u>, and having a <u>POSITIVE ATTITUDE</u> and be "loaded" with <u>INTEGRITY</u>.

Now, this is quite a "mouthful" of desirable traits, and why not? What we should all realize and accept is that when we <u>become known</u> as a human being, as an individual who possesses these attributes, these traits, these abilities, <u>we will</u>, in a manner of speaking, "<u>have it made</u>." Why? Because we will be a human being, to put it simply, who "everybody" wants to be with, wants to rely on, wants to be served by. And as a result, our opportunities to be given opportunities to "serve" others will grow by "leaps and bounds."

And as you must realize, every opportunity to serve others will directly reflect positively on your ability to maintain a good and financially satisfactory life for yourself and your family. <u>NO SHORTCUTS ALLOWED</u>.

This little thought-provoking section should become an integral part of how a positive good life is created and maintained. Our personal finances can very much benefit by its employment.

Think About This One!

The family who has no "secrets" among themselves and who have good, meaningful conversations with each other will "nip in the bud" all potential problems "lurking," and as a result will have a good, comfortable life together and individually.

Planning

Planning

"If you fail to PLAN,
you are planning to fail."
(Benjamin Franklin)

"Goals are only wishes
unless you have a PLAN."
(Melinda Gates)

"The best way to LEARN about 'anything'
is to start a conversation and listen."
(Grandfather)

Always stay on the level.

Always keep a level head.

Always do your level best.

(Picasso Jr.)

Planning

Ahoy! "Self-Ruler"

Do you want to change course in life and sail into a beautiful sunset? Remember, "if it ain't broke," don't fix it. However, if your sense tells you that a change in your "modus operandi" for living a good life may be in order for you, do not hesitate.

PLANNING, by you, holds the KEY to fulfilling your desires for what you want to gain by living your life. A PLAN gives you DIRECTION and PURPOSE (a reason for moving forward). A detailed PLAN that truly reflects your personal desires is the impetus, the moving force, the stimulus to accomplish more for yourself.

A PLAN, your plan, implies a formulated method of doing something for yourself that will become meaningful and beneficial for you.

"Planning" means "Change!"

When you want to move yourself from an unsatisfactory position in your life to a more satisfactory position, you must decide what that move should entail for you. You must decide, for yourself, "What do I want to accomplish in living my life?" You need to give your mind the clearest "picture" of the desired results. By doing this, you are creating a NEW BEGINNING for yourself. And you need to accept that a New Beginning, to better results for you, will include CHANGE.

Know that <u>Change Represents Progress</u>. And "progress is impossible without change; and those who cannot change their minds cannot change anything."

Planning

A good way to begin each day of your future life.

Your future starts tomorrow!

Each morning as you awake, why not put your "Mind Set" in the most receptive position to make absolutely certain that you will <u>HEAR</u>, <u>UNDERSTAND</u>, and <u>EMBRACE</u> sage advice that has a habit of appearing, to you, even if you have never asked for it.

What I mean with this is that many times, without feeling the full gist, you will read and hear "sayings," sometimes short writings that are all intended to share a "<u>Truth</u>" that can be referred to as "<u>Common Sense</u>," and truly have a positive effect on your daily life.

Know that it is <u>WORDS</u> and their intended meaning that matters, not necessarily the person who wrote them. When you truly understand the intended meaning of any writing purporting to be both positive and helpful – if it makes sense to you, <u>EMBRACING</u> such writing for your own benefit should be a "NO BRAINER."

<u>REMEMBER</u>, it is <u>ALWAYS</u> other human beings that we need to deal with for mutual advantages. Learning how to deal with human beings in a positive and fair manner will prevail to your benefit <u>EVERY TIME</u>.

Opinion!

"I can never prove your opinion wrong!"

Asking for and receiving another human being's "opinion" on any matter important to you can be very helpful. However, you must be careful as to who you ask an opinion of. The reason being that everyone you could ask will most likely give you their opinion, even if they are not sufficiently familiar with or knowledgeable of the subject at hand. When you ask someone for their opinion on something, it is usually because you want to try to help give yourself the best direction to reach a solution to whatever you are contemplating.

An opinion is being described as follows by several dictionaries:

> "It is a view or judgment formed about something or someone not necessarily based on facts or knowledge. It is the ideas a person has about something or someone, which is based mainly on their feelings and beliefs."

So you see, an opinion by someone who is known to have deep knowledge and good personal experience about the specific matter at hand can be very helpful and valuable to you. And will probably be an opinion you could lean on. Anyone else's opinion would probably be a "crap shoot."

Exercise caution anytime you plan to rely heavily on an opinion.

What About Your Own Opinion?

"The greatest deception "men" suffer
is from their own opinion."
(Leonardo da Vinci)

Your own opinion can turn out to be the BEST. But you will never know that answer "up front" unless you first compare and evaluate your opinion with others' opinions on the same subject. Do not act like a "know-it-all."

Respect the knowledge and experience of others who are or have dealt with the subject at hand. If you do, you will put yourself in a better position to be a winner.

Do You Sometimes, Unintentionally, Fool Yourself?

How can you fool yourself? Well, this is how you do it.

> "You learn what to do and how to do "things" that will truly benefit <u>you</u> and help <u>you</u> to provide a good life for yourself, <u>AND THEN DO NOT DO IT</u>."

How silly is that?

Our Future is Important!

How do you see your future developing?

How do you build a future for yourself?

Answer: "With lots of other human beings."

How do you begin?

Answer: With, in the most positive way, "do unto others as you would have them do unto you" – ONLY <u>you do it first</u>.

Planning/Goal Setting

Is This Important?

<u>Plan</u> = A scheme of action or procedure. (a plan of operation)

A project or definite purpose. (plans for the future)

To arrange a plan or scheme (for any work, enterprise, or proceeding)

Plan refers to any method of thinking out acts and purposes <u>beforehand</u>.

<u>A plan, your plan, and nothing else, will represent your vision</u> of what you need and want from living your life.

If you do not subscribe to the idea of letting yourself know, in no uncertain terms, what you want to gain or to accomplish in your lifetime, for yourself and your family, I could, perhaps accurately, assume that you will be "running" your life only on the "fumes" from your potentially abundantly productive brain.

This last paragraph is probably not the kindest thing I could have said, but so much of your future success in life is "riding on your own shoulders"; and if your potentials are not discovered at the earliest possible time, you will be "short-changed."

Every one of us has some good "news" inside of us just waiting to be let out to benefit us individually. The good news is the "unknown" about each of us. We do not know how great we can be, how much we can accomplish! How much we can love! We will not ever know what our potential is for accomplishing valuable, useful, meaningful, and helpful objectives until <u>we decide and commit to try</u>!

If you now have reasonable to good health and you feel that you have not much of anything else – what could you possibly still have?

You have opportunities "of plenty" to create and move forward with a productive and pleasurable life for yourself and your family.

In order to start moving forward, you have to recognize your own "confidence" level in what you decide to pursue. And, if necessary, find a way to build up your confidence level to meet a specific challenge. Confidence in you "is to feel full trust, belief in the trustworthiness, and reliability of yourself."

"Confidence – Thrives (grows) on honesty, on honor, on having a strong respect for the fulfillment of all obligations, on faithful protection, and on unselfish performance" (Franklin D. Roosevelt).

With confidence, you can accomplish much! Having confidence causes you to feel like you can do all the reasonable things you can think of.

So how can I recognize my own confidence level? Your feelings on specific matters, your current knowledge, and work experience on specific things will allow you to question your own level of confidence.

The questions you should pose to yourself should be directed to the requirements needed to properly deal with the specific challenges that you are deciding to face. You ask yourself, what knowledge do I need to have, what specific work experience do I need, and perhaps the most important thing to recognize within yourself is your level of anxiousness or your earnest desire to move forward with any specific project you have decided on.

Remember! WANTING very much to accomplish a specific goal is paramount to you being successful.

If you truly understand what you want to accomplish, but you do not quite possess all the attributes necessary to become a success with a specific goal, do not fret. Figure out how you can learn what you may be lacking in certain knowledge, requirements, and work experience, and then go out and get it. This move will usually prove to be very valuable to you and should add a lot to your abilities for reaching your goals and living a good life.

When you begin to develop <u>your vision</u> of your future, there are, to my way of thinking, two (2) things you need to know and seriously consider about yourself. You have to ask yourself two (2) questions and your answer cannot be "Willi nilli" or just "good enough." Your answer must be, for you, as clear and convincing to yourself as it will be humanly possible to project anything into your future.

<u>Question #1</u> – This first question has to do with – What do you want to do (What "work" do you want to pursue) to create a steady, financially satisfactory environment for yourself and your family that will help you sustain living a good life? And to support, in later years, your continuing to live a good life in your retirement. For a young person, perhaps still in school, as they read this particular paragraph and read the word "retirement" will say, Wow! And then question, do I really have to give any thought to my retirement this early in my life? All I can say in response to such question is "<u>Believe Me, You Do</u>." Things are changing fast. The "old days" with job security, employee retirement programs, and who knows the future of social security are, it seems, steadily disappearing.

<u>Question #2</u> – This second question you can only answer to yourself after you have provided a fairly complete answer to the first question. You need to tie your "vision" together with your current and future ABILITIES so you can accomplish the obvious – causing your "vision" to materialize, become reality. So your second question, to yourself, is "What do I need in my "TOOLBOX" to assure myself that I can effectively pursue my established "vision" for my future?"

The first question concerning your creation of your "vision" for your future will, by nature, perhaps be more fun, more easily completed by you. This is when your imagination can run freely without too many restrictions. However, whatever your thought patterns will follow, you must restrict yourself to reality. Whatever your decision on how you want to proceed to build your good life, you must understand and accept that every endeavor undertaken by a human being will always require specific abilities to allow "visions" to become reality.

As you keep on reading and figuring out what all this can mean to you, do realize that to put yourself in the best position to live a good life you have to be prepared and possess the appropriate knowledge and ability to perform the tasks necessary to accomplish the goals you have set for yourself.

I have this feeling that some readers may ask a couple of "fairness" questions on this subject.

"Do we all, as human beings, have the same rights to living a good life?" And to my way of thinking, the answer is an obvious and absolute – yes!

Another question might be, "Do we all have the same opportunities to live a 'realistic' good life?" Good question! But first, how should we define "living a good life?" Depending on how each of us, as individuals, define for ourselves what living a realistic good life means to us, we should be able to answer yes to this question.

It is true, however, that after we are born we all, it seems, are put into various and different positions where we, as we grow and mature, develop abilities to understand and to do a myriad of different things. Each of us will develop abilities. And the extent and quality of our respective abilities will be "all over the map."

Let us get on the "same page" as it relates to understanding and agreeing on what the word ability means.

"ABILITY = Is the inherent power or capacity of any human being to do or act in any relation. The word *"Relation"* here is essentially your being able to 'hold your own' in any and all matters involving you. It also means your level of competence in any occupation or field of action from the possession of capacity, skill, means, or other qualifications. *Ability* is a general word for mental power, native or acquired, enabling one to do things well. The word *"native"* here should be defined as being the environment in which one was born, the aggregate of surrounding things, conditions, or influences" (*The American College Dictionary*).

Having a uniform understanding of what the word "Ability" means to all of us, I wonder how we should answer the question, "Will we all have the same opportunities to live a good life?"

I think our answer to this question will have to be this – "It will depend totally on the quality and extent of our individual abilities as to the level of "quality" of our good lives." But, yes, we will all have opportunities.

Let us never forget and always understand and accept that it will be our individual abilities to get things done that will, for sure, determine the quality of our respective lives.

The quality, of the quality of a good life, will vary from one human being to another when a comparison is attempted. But remember also that each human being, as to their likes and dislikes, as it would refer to their independent lives are never exactly the same. Therefore, the only thing that will matter, I believe, is that the way each human being ends up living their good life is to them THE BEST.

Our parents or guardians, when we are born, are largely responsible for helping us develop our positive feelings for life, a certain quality of life. And also to help us create good, positive habits that will help guide us to develop and acquire specific NEEDS and some realistic WANTS. And so important a basic understanding of what we, as individuals, need and must do to allow us the opportunities to acquire or satisfy all our needs and wants.

If we do not acquire this understanding soon after we are born and of sufficient age to learn and understand "things," we will be delayed in acquiring what we all want, which is the talent, the knowledge of how to live a good life.

We will all be faced with "delays" in our lives. But if we WANT something strongly enough and if we know that we can still acquire a basic understanding of how "things work" in real life, we can catch up and overcome any and all delays.

Know this! Living a good life is not all that difficult, but it is not without some good efforts on your part. The amount of money you think you may need to start living a good life does not have to enter the "picture" as a critical ingredient to learning how it works.

The real quality of the life we lead often has more to do with our outlook on life, our relationships with other human beings, our health and our family than it has to do with the amount of money we have or other material things we own.

Please do not misunderstand my comment on money and material things. Money is not everything, but it helps. We need money to satisfy our basic needs for food, shelter, and clothing. And since living a good life, in reality, is more than just existing, we need money to satisfy our reasonable WANTS, which would be anything we should reasonably desire after first having provided ourselves with our basic needs.

Learning how to use a most effective "tool" called planning or goal setting, we can probably say, without fear of contradictions, is the "thing" that will help us "get over the top."

"Getting over the top" is again very simple to comprehend. You will be "over the top" when your completed goals bring more satisfaction to you than just being able to meet your basic needs.

Planning/goal setting is what is an absolute necessity to give you a meaningful, workable "picture" of what you want the future to be like for you and your family. It is a fact that you cannot imagine what your future can be like unless and until you have first created the "picture" in your mind and, second, you have started on the road to fulfilling your goals.

Planning! What is a practical way of describing the meaning of this word?

Let us try! When you want to accomplish something, anything, you are attempting to design an action or procedure (a plan of operation) to complete a project or a definite purpose (plans for your future). You are formulating a method of doing something. A plan refers to any method of thinking out acts and purposes beforehand.

Many times we already know what we like, what we want to have happen to us in our lives. We know that a self-development attitude is "key" to adding to our abilities. We also realize that our "next positive moves" forward to a good life can be best accomplished by us through careful and complete planning for our future.

<u>Always</u>, it will be in your personal best interest to remember this sentence:

"<u>Tomorrow's comforts require TODAY'S preparations.</u>"

As you will have read in this book, positive Human Relations becomes an integral part of anything and everything you want to accomplish in life. Everything you do affects Human Relations. Depending on what you do and how you do anything it will have a positive effect on human relations or it will have a negative effect.

When something we do has a negative effect on human relations, any benefits we were hoping to gain may be very few or none at all. So why not focus all our energy on doing only things that will promote positive human relations and be of distinct benefit to ourselves? This is what the "Tit4Tat" concept is all about.

Never forget, always be keenly aware of the fact that "THE HUMAN FACTOR" is involved with <u>all</u> that we do.

You should never, in your mind, limit yourself to what you realistically need and want from living your life. You should "tackle" every opportunity that you "come across" in such a positive manner that you increase your chances to accomplish them. Always do your personal very best, ask for help from others if you run into some difficulties. But work diligently until you get what you need and want. And chances are good that your needs and wants will be realized.

However, like so many of us human beings, you may not always reach your objective for whatever reasons. However, do not let your reason be for not trying your best. Okay!

So in those situations when you really tried but did not succeed, you can always try again at a later date. But the important thing that you should <u>add</u> to the knowledge you gained from this specific objective that did not materialize is a clear understanding of the reason or reasons it did not work out in your favor. Again, give yourself an honest, clear answer as to <u>why</u> did it not work.

You may question, "What good would this do me?" Well, it could do you much good. Think of it this way! Everything happens to us for a reason, and it will serve us. What I mean is this! Anything that would be important to you that you have tried your best to accomplish and for some reasons you were not able to do – Stop and think. Ask yourself what were the reasons that entered your project and stopped you from completing it? Look at these reasons very closely and ask yourself, "What can I do to overcome these obstacles (reasons) so that I can accomplish what I need to do?" If you personally cannot figure it out, do not fret – Ask someone you can rely on to help you think it through. Now, if you resolve your dilemma by removing the "reasons" that created the obstacles for you – Great – you win.

Looking at "the other side of the coin." You cannot remove a specific obstacle and therefore you "walk away." Instead of "kicking yourself around the block" because you are disappointed and perhaps angry with yourself that you could not accomplish something you wanted, "walking away" and forgetting about it is, to my way of thinking, an intelligent thing to do.

When we plan for something to happen – we usually plan for something we will like. What does the word *"like"* mean?

Like = To take pleasure.

Ask the following questions of yourself and let us see if your answers will "trigger" some favorable, to you, thoughts in your mind?

Question – What is like, like?

How does it feel to create and receive feelings of pleasure?

Question – What will my future be like?

What do you want your future to be like?

Question – How will I know what my future will be like?

What have you decided that your future should be like?

Question – How do I start to see my future develop?

Once you have decided for yourself what you want to accomplish in your future, you must carefully plan and execute all the "steps" you must take to accomplish your objectives, your goals.

Question – What is the likelihood or probability that I will have a likeable future?

If what you put into your plan to accomplish for yourself is <u>WHAT YOU WANT</u>, your life's journey from start to completion should have created a good life for you.

If you have lots of "ability" (acquired or native), you may end up (depending on the state of the country's overall economy) with many choices for "work" that will suit your abilities and desires. It is true that the more you learn, the more you can earn. If you are a little short on "ability" for the kind of work you would like to do, you should not be disillusioned.

If you are young, time is on your side and you should spend some of it, or whatever amount of time is required, to gain the additional abilities you will need to do the desired work. If you spend, say, three (3) to four (4) years studying a certain profession or working as a "Trainee" to learn a "trade" (in demand), it will be time well spent and it will provide you the potential for a "brighter" future for yourself. And if you are of a "slightly" older generation, there is still hope for us, if we want it, to be "re-trained" for new and different work. All we need to show ourselves is that <u>we want to do it</u> and then get going on it. It may be easier said than done. But then again, anything worthwhile pursuing is usually not easy.

Your objective with your employment (as an employee or as an entrepreneur [self-employed]) is to generate sufficient remunerations and true feelings of satisfaction and contentment, all of which turns into happiness. Consider the following on your way toward success.

What is it about successful human beings that make them "tick" in such positive ways?

What is the "vehicle" people drive to become successful? It is called "A.W.D. – GOAL."

They all have "goals." They all have "objectives" which they know, that when they are reached they are successful.

They know exactly what they want and they think about it every day of their lives.

They have a clear vision of exactly what they want to do, and that vision carries them over every obstacle.

Quite often, when we have a clear vision of what we are working toward, we become truly alive for the first time in our lives.

Goal setting is the very basis of any success. It is, in fact, the very definition of success.

Having a goal, a firm objective, means that anyone who is on course toward the fulfillment of a goal is experiencing a degree of success at that moment.

Pleasure and satisfaction come to us from serving others. For those whose goals and objectives involve the serving of large numbers of people, chances are they will be richly rewarded indeed.

Finally, a goal, an objective, must be such that it creates an impetus, a stimulus within us that fills us with positive emotions when we think about it. It must be something we want very much to accomplish. The more strongly we feel about an idea or goal, our subconscious will direct us along the path to its fulfillment.

Whatever our goal happens to be, if we stay with it, if we are fully committed to it, we will reach it. That is the way it works.

What? And Why?

These are two very important questions. The answer to which can or will be a strong factor in deciding your personal future.

Without a carefully structured (honest and realistic) answer to each question, living a good life for you may be subjected to "hurricane force headwinds" and that will not fare well for you.

Question #1 – WHAT?

What do you want to do to create a good life for yourself and your family? Your answer to this question will create/build the foundation for your destiny.

Once you have clearly established, in your mind, what you want to do with your life here on earth, that answer will be your stimulus, your moving force, your focal point of all that you will PLAN to do. This answer will give you clarity of mind, give you directions and your purpose, your reasons for being here.

Question #2 – WHY?

In Question #1, you provided yourself with an "outline" of what you want to do. In Question #2, you need to clearly understand the importance, to you, of WHY you have chosen to do what you outlined in Question #1. Why do you want to achieve what you outlined for yourself? What are the personal benefits you expect to gain? Who are the other people who will benefit from your successes in life? The answers to this question, "WHY," should be your motivation, your incentive to move forward and completing your choices.

Planning

"A plan or planning refers to any method of thinking out acts and purposes beforehand."

Planning is what can help you stay healthy, build "wealth," and become very likeable to other human beings.

If we agree with the suggestions noted earlier in this book, our purpose for living our lives, our reasons for existing on this earth is to have "happiness and the least amount of suffering."

We know, from the outset, that all of us human beings are solely responsible for our own destinies. We know that we are part of a very large human family, all of whom have been slated to live a "do-it-yourself life." Meaning, "what is to be is up to me."

Having created our "mindset" for our responsibilities to ourselves, we now must create a vision for how we want our future to "play out." We must do our very best, whatever it takes, to "paint" a very clear picture on our minds of what it is that we really want to accomplish with our lives that will fulfill our ultimate purpose for living on this earth.

To make a decision on what you <u>want</u> to do to "earn a living" or any other positive endeavor, for other reasons, and then "stick with it" and become the best that <u>you can be</u> will probably not be an easy task. The reason it may not be all that easy is because there are usually so many "avenues" available to choose from.

Many of us, when we are trying to choose, say, a "profession for life," tend to perhaps think in only one direction – "where can I make the most money."

Of course, this is very much a valid conclusion or reason. However, the deciding factor in which direction your thoughts should be heading should be totally based on your known current ABILITIES and any solid plans you have to increase your ABILITIES through additional formal education and/or actual work experience.

There are numerous "things" we want to do with our TIME here on earth. And in each case, if we want to make certain that we progress in a highly beneficial manner with new endeavors, we must decide beforehand what "steps" we need to take to accomplish the objectives. This is what is referred to as <u>PLANNING</u>.

When developing a clear, precise "picture" for yourself as to which direction you want to take your life, meaning how do you want to spend one-third (1/3) of your 24-hour day (at least five (5) days a week) to earn money that will help you satisfy living a good life? This is a very important question to which you will need a very doable answer.

Once you know the direction you want to take your life, you have to construct the "road" you will need to travel on. You, in essence, will need to provide yourself with a detailed "map" covering each "step" that you must take to reach the favorable termination of your endeavor.

Perhaps the most important thing that you need to do once you have decided on an objective to help you "feed" your good life is that you establish, in your mind, a very clear reason for "<u>WHY</u>" you are setting out to do what you have decided to do. Always keep a sharp focus on this reason. It should keep you moving forward. Consider and "picture," in your mind, the benefits you expect. Consider who else will benefit from what you are proposing to do.

Ask yourself, "Is this endeavor a #1 priority for me?" And "Do I understand and accept that in most situations I cannot go it alone?" "I will need help and assistance from others." "Am I a person known to others to be a person others want to help?"

Know yourself, know your limits, be flexible in your decisions, and perhaps the most important consideration for you is to be and remain REALISTIC in all that you wish to pursue. Do not begin a journey unless you can clearly identify your destination.

One of the more difficult things to understand and that I have personally grappled with many years is the question – "What is the reason we do not do many of the things we say we will do?" Especially if we know that the things we were contemplating doing would be good for us.

I really believe now that I have a very logical answer to this question, and I feel certain I am not alone thinking this way. It is one or both of these reasons. "We are either too lazy to do it, or we do not really want to do it." Does this not make sense? What else could it be? After all, if we really want to do something, assuming this something is within the realm of reality and our abilities, would we not find the time and resources to get it done?

Planning = Productivity

Planning <u>MUST</u> be present <u>before</u> any production can be efficiently started and completed.

Just like the "Cause" and "Effect" phenomenon, the "cause" must come <u>first</u> before the "effect" can become known.

All of this is so obvious. You have to know exactly <u>what you</u> want to do before you can actually do it.

Convince yourself that <u>you</u> need a "PLAN" for yourself and your family. And that PLAN, when completed, should, as accurately as possible (now), represent you and your family's VISION of how your future could be. You can change or modify or adjust (all same meaning) your PLANS at any time you detect a need in order to <u>stay on PURPOSE</u>.

Ever wonder why some people accomplish so much all of the time and others never accomplish much at all?

Is it because we misunderstand the reasons that do apply? We may tell ourselves that what is needed to accomplish a lot is intelligence, wealth, family, friends, luck, or education. All of these attributes do not "take away" from the real driving force behind productivity, but they are not the major contributors. As an aside, you can have all of the above nice attributes, but if you do not possess the "KEY" to the "productive engine," you will go nowhere.

The "KEY" to productivity is all about having goals and objectives, making plans and having diligence (the stick-with-it attitude).

Remember to never put yourself in a position where you are "totally" "alone." Remember that you will never have all the answers to all the important, to you, questions that will arise during your lifetime, but you will have some of the answers. Also, remember that you will never meet another human being who has all the answers, but they will have some of the answers. Having a sharing attitude with other human beings can be the "saving grace" for you when you need answers.

The following observation is worth remembering.

"You are one person, you meet another person, you each have one (1) idea, you decide to exchange ideas, and now each of you have two (2) ideas."

Multiply this kind of thinking and action by any multiplier. The more human beings you develop a meaningful relationship with, the more "avenues" marked "Help Available" you can travel on to get new ideas and help to remove "road blocks" that may prevent you from reaching your goals.

"TIME" – managing time is extremely critical since it is the biggest productivity obstacle. Time does not have a "shelf life"; you simply have to use it or you lose it.

Think About This One!

When do you feel really good about yourself and your situation? Is it when you know that you are moving toward where you want to be? Toward the things you like; toward the things that will help you to live a good life?

You may ask yourself – "How will I know that I am heading in the right direction?"

This is a very good and important question for you to have a good answer to. However, there is a very simple answer and it is this. Realize that you are the only person who can provide yourself with the correct answer. Then, really think about what you want to accomplish for yourself and your family. What do you want to create for yourself and your family during your lifetime?

Once you have given yourself some reasonably complete answers that are realistic for your personal situation, put them down on "paper." What I mean by the above sentence is, are you adequately prepared based on your current ABILITIES to pursue the goals you will be setting? If you believe you are, then LEARN which "steps" you need to take, what you need to do to accomplish each segment or task of your goals. Then put them all in the order you will need to complete them. NOTE: This is your plan.

And here comes the "hard" part. Start the "ball rolling" and complete the first step and then immediately follow up by completing "Step" 2, then "Step" 3, etc. until your goal(s) have been met. What I mean by it being the "hard part" is simply this. If you start a project and then feel any hesitation to continue, you will be "toast."

PLANNING, your planning, to accomplish what you want from living your life will ONLY have a chance to become reality if you "start" yourself in a forward motion to make it happen.

Is PLANNING a necessary, unavoidable function for living a good life?

If you need to convince yourself that the PLANNING functions need or must be an integral part of your entire life, "THINK ABOUT IT" this way: you go to sleep in the evening – while you are sleeping nothing of any consequence, good or bad, usually happens to your life. Now, when you awake in the morning, how do you think you will feel if when you open your eyes all you have is a blank stare into your surrounding space? Your "blank" stare into space is an indication that, temporarily, your brain is not feeding you any DIRECTIONS. However, all of a sudden you start doing some physical things like getting out of bed, perhaps visiting the bathroom, getting dressed, going into the kitchen for some morning sustenance, getting ready to leave for school or for work, etc. – now you are "cooking" – your brain is in motion giving you directions.

In the example noted, these directions represent the process of "turning on" your "habit" light. A habit, as you know, is an ability acquired by frequent repetitions of an act. It is, in this case, your customary practice or use of your time as you awake in the morning. This is all good. All of these habits are born from earlier PLANNING efforts on your part or on the part of your parents for you.

Try to imagine how your "day" might work out for you if you had not acquired these particular habits. And if you have not developed habits that will help you to move forward with your life in a manner that will give you pleasant and positive results – how would that be for you?

The essence of your PLANNING is for you to know how you should be using every "minute" of your time, every day, in the most "productive" way that will lead your efforts to positive results that will add to what you will need to live a good life.

Are you still wondering – "What's the big deal about "PLANNING?"

Consider this! As you move on in your life, you may find yourself quietly asking yourself – "Where in the world did all the time go?" This could be an obvious sign, or indication, that you "ran out" of time while trying to accomplish your desired goals. Planning is an answer to effectively dealing with potential time constraints. When you plan to get something done, you should be focusing only on your project! Your time should be used primarily for completing your projects and obtaining positive results for yourself.

Planning <u>ALL</u> your moves forward in your life will help you become successful in the most effective way. And your chances of "running out" of time to accomplish the important, to you, "things" are greatly reduced. What I mean here is quite simple to understand. You "polish" your "vision" of how you want your life to evolve. You confirm, in your mind, each and every "step" you must take to make your vision become a reality for you. You assign the sequence to each "step" needed and now you have a "PLAN." If you did your PLANNING well and if you diligently work your plan and complete each "step" your plan requires – you will reach a successful conclusion.

> "If you fail to PLAN, you are planning to fail."
> (Benjamin Franklin)

This saying tells it just like it is.

Not Yet Convinced?

This is for anyone who is not yet convinced that a good "plan" or "goal" for living a good life is of utmost importance to you if you want to be happy and have the least amount of suffering.

<u>One More Time</u> – Some more constructive thinking! I am hoping that you will think about this and will remember times when you have actually, yourself, experienced a feeling like this.

"You wake up in the morning, you are feeling well, you are feeling good about being awake, you are feeling like life is really pleasing you this morning. You cannot wait to get going; you are feeling motivated and full of vigor. It is going to be a good, fun, and productive day for you. What is this all about?"

Well, I will suggest this. Really, the only reason you feel this way is because, in your mind, your day is planned and <u>you</u> or <u>someone else</u> planned it to include you. And, in your mind, your day is going to be filled with many things that you will like, enjoy, and want to do, and perhaps even profit (financially) by. It is therefore that you are feeling the way you do.

To this scenario you will probably say to yourself, "This is a great feeling." And "I would like to feel this way each day, for as many days as I can, for the rest of my life."

Well then, if most of your days could feel this way for you, why would you not want to repeat having feelings like this for the rest of your life? Well, let's be realistic. If most of your days would create this feeling for you, it would be great, yes?

Okay – I will suggest the following again and again.

I believe a person can plan for their life's journey in such a way as to generate this kind of "day" for him/her almost every day.

How? Well I have been hinting and suggesting the "How" throughout this writing, and this is just another way to try to convince you how your life can feel if you just do one thing for yourself. And by the way, again, only you can do this for yourself.

If you understand and get the drift of where I am going with this and you are truly a "do-it-yourself" person, all you have to do to give yourself the most positive chance ever to living a good life is to develop your own plan, your goal, and objectives. Put everything in this "plan" that you would like, realistically, to have happen to you as you are living your life. And then start a somewhat more difficult part of your journey, which is to follow your plans and never stop until the "Big Guy" blows the whistle.

You say, Wow! And as you look at all the things you have noted in your "plans" you may say – "That is a lot of stuff on one plate." How will I know that I can do this? Well, you will not know until you actually try. But first know if you do not identify to yourself what you want to have happen, in detail, then nothing will really happen, except for what usually happens each day in your life when you are awake. Then you will have to wait until the end of each day to see what you actually did accomplish during that day. And the reason for that is that you had no idea what would happen since you did not really plan for anything specific to happen.

THINK About It!

Your "plan" will be a reminder to you of what you would like to see happen to you "each day." You will be doing what pleases you, what will make you feel productive and useful, and these are truly feelings that will cause you to have a good life. Okay?

Again – Planning/Goal Setting

Is It Important? Yes!

Throughout this writing we have been discussing the importance to each human being of the positive effects good human relations and personal planning can have on our respective futures.

Accomplishing something, anything, involves work to be done by someone. And that someone should be the individual who is seeking to benefit from the accomplishment.

I would like to ask each reader to have the following kind of conversation with himself/herself. It may sound a little weird to ask someone to carry on a conversation with himself/herself, but it is not. This type of conversation is meant to be very suggestive.

"Here I stand!

I am one!

I know that I need and want:

- Roof over my head
- Food to eat
- Clothes to wear
- And I probably will need and want many other things as well because I see what others have

How will I get these things?

I do not know anyone who is willing, able, and ready to just give me all the things I need and will want.

I have to figure out a way to obtain the things I need and want.

I wonder if this is how most people think before they develop a plan? (Yes they do). I must develop a <u>PLAN</u> that I can "work" to get what I need and want.

When I reach this last understanding and I do create a realistic plan for myself and make a solid commitment to "work it," I will be on my way to living a better life.

Wow! Thanks for listening to myself making a lot of sense."

Needless to say, most of our "PLANS" for living our daily lives are very doable to put together and exercise (get the job done). But the "PLAN" that will be needed to allow us to live a good life well into our future will take a little more thinking and be much more "long range."

But, also, it is about focusing our minds and our daily efforts on completing for ourselves meaningful tasks that in return will give us genuine feelings of satisfaction and security. We want to do "ALL" the things that will benefit us, personally, in a positive way without "hurting" anyone else.

The intent of a "PLAN," like the plan we keep referring to "the good life" plan is for each of us to clearly identify to ourselves what we want our lives to be like, from morning until night, every day, for as long as the good Lord allows us to stay on this earth. And decide/learn what we must do to make this happen for us. REMEMBER, we have to do what we have to do because we are part of the "do-it-yourself" world.

The toughest maneuver you will face after you have carefully documented your goals and determined the steps you must start taking "each day" to reach your goals is overcoming the "Get Bored Syndrome."

This is something which many people seem to be smitten by and which usually, sometimes, derails a lot of good work up to that point. Note this – when you start feeling "bored" with working toward your goals, you better ask yourself "immediately" "What is happening to me"; "Why am I getting bored?" "Do I no longer want to achieve my goals?" Why? Remember, if you can give yourself an accurate, honest answer to the "Why are you getting bored," you will most likely have your answer and perhaps you can fix the problem.

Also, remember, loudly to yourself, the reasons you personally have for putting these goals into your life in the first place. Are these reasons no longer relevant to your "good life" plans? If they are still relevant, you should get back "on your horse" and keep heading into the sunset.

However, if your goals are no longer relevant to your living a good life and it is for good sound reasons – start over again with a "new take" on your future.

"TIME"

If time is infinite – why is there never enough of it? The universe has all the time there will always be. Human beings have an expiration date on their usage of time. Human beings have to plan for the use of their time here on earth so that they can accomplish their desires.

Use Of Your Time

If you are competing in a "sporting" event, your best use of your time can make you a winner.

If you are "competing" in the "world of business," your best use of your time can make you a success.

If you are a person who believes that there is always a way to improve on the results of what you do and that better is better, then be concerned about how you utilize your allotted time each and every day.

Slow down – do not let your "hands" move faster than your "mindful eye." When you are executing any kind of work, give yourself the time needed to always think clearly on what you are doing and how you are doing it during every moment of your activity.

Think! Can this be done differently, easier, faster, or better and still give me the end result that I need?

Always keep in mind that "Haste makes waste." Sometimes "waste" forces you to cause yourself problems. "Take your time!" This does not mean wasting time. It is allowing time to be on your side to help you get things done with the right positive feelings. Also, while taking your time, if you recall in your memory the many reasons for "WHY" you are doing what you are doing, your timing, your work will bring out in you pleasant and more meaningful feelings.

We all do things for various reasons. The better, the more clear, the more meaningful our reasons are for doing anything makes the outcomes, the end results, much better for us.

Our "Time" and Other "Human Beings" – The Best Resources

You say you cannot "find" time to do all the things you need and want to do.

Why? Time does not hide! I do not know why you cannot find it. It is always right in front of you. The problem we are all having, at times, is to know how to apportion our time in a way that will allow us to get done what we need and must get done for ourselves. If we tell ourselves that we do not have time to do certain things that would be very important to us, then we are too busy.

This next "jewel" of information is something you already know, but I want to throw it in here anyway.

The interesting phenomenon about "TIME" is that each and every one of us human beings, on our earth, are given the exact same amount of time, which is 24 hours each day, every year (365 days), which total 8,760 hours. WOW! What we do with this time is nobody's business but ours, individually.

I am not sure who first suggested the following, but it is probably still a really good and practical "base" to start from. "Of the 24 hours we all have in a day, 8 hours should be devoted to sleep and restoring our bodies, another 8 hours (for 5 days each week) should be devoted to "working" to earn the "money" we need to help us live a good life, and the last 8 hours (plus the added hours for weekends and holidays) should be our personal time that we should use to prepare ourselves for each "day" which needs to include travel back and forth to work, taking care of our personal shopping, hygiene, our health, our family, and recreation.

Living a good life is not easy, but it is a very doable goal if we approach it from a positive "I need to and I want to attitude."

Remember an old saying – "If we can't find time to do what is important to us as individuals each and every day, we are just too busy." This may be very true. For most of us, it is probably the "truest truth."

So, what is the answer? Well, we cannot do anything about stretching our 24-hour day into something more, so we have to resolve this in a different manner. We can, perhaps many times, depending on what type of work or responsibility is involved, use part of the next day to complete what needs to be done or perhaps part of other future days. If we do that, it is referred to as careful and complete planning of the use of our TIME – also known as goal setting. This is by no means an easy task to accomplish, but again, I believe it is totally doable IF that is what we, as individuals, truly want to do to help ourselves to do the most in each day, week, month, year, etc.

Please allow me to digress.

THINK ABOUT IT!

There are two things in our lives, our entire life, which can help us immensely if we give it the RESPECT and IMPORTANCE it deserves.

What is it! What is it!

I will suggest that these two things should be judged by each and every one of us to be, among many things, the two most important personal resources we have available to us which, if used properly, will always, to my way of thinking, get us to where we need and want to be.

Our TIME and OTHER HUMAN BEINGS are the two resources.

TIME

We all understand and have to accept that each morning when we wake up we are all granted a "one-shot" deal for 24 hours. No more! No less! What we do with this time and how wisely we use it will show up in the results we bring to our "table."

OTHER HUMAN BEINGS

This is a powerful resource! Think About It! Take all the other human brothers and sisters that you are always surrounded by and add your

TIME resource. This, I am suggesting, is one powerful combination of resources which, when you learn how to use them together, you will have a "kick ass" powerhouse to get the things done that you will depend on for your good life. I was going to use the expression, "Kick Donkey," but that could be a little confusing and it would no doubt anger the animal lovers.

Now you may wonder – well okay – I can understand the "TIME" resource benefits that can accrue to me if I can learn to use my time effectively, but how so with the "other human beings?"

Think About It!

All the knowledge that exists all over the entire world, and all the "thinking about" and "the interpretations" of this knowledge in so many different human minds and in so many different languages is all the results of active human beings just like you and me. NOTE: ONLY human beings own all of the knowledge available.

Now, since we as a "single" human being is so limited, by comparison, to what we can learn, understand, and retain in our minds, we need and must rely on each other to help us ADD to the knowledge we need to do better for ourselves.

Now, think about the significant importance of the subject "Human Relations." As you should realize, our individual lives would come to a complete standstill if we do not have the opportunities to, in a positive way, relate to and receive valuable "input" of knowledge and deeds from other human beings.

One more thing about "TIME."

If everyone has the exact same amount of time to utilize in a day, why is it that some people can create and do generate so much more results from using their time than some of us do with the exact same amount of time?

It is a very valid question. Think About It!

We are not trying to compare the total value of results gained because that will not only involve the Time but also different Talents using the Time. We are comparing the <u>number</u> of things accomplished.

It just seems that many times when you make comparisons that some people can stuff a lot more things into a 24-hour time period and you wonder how they do it.

Could it be that they do <u>detailed planning</u> on how they could best use their time to accomplish the most? They probably have a <u>detailed plan</u> of everything that they NEED and WANT to do every day, and this is why they get good and timely results and probably (sometimes) have some time left over to add to their "personal use" column. What do you think?

Why Are We Here?

We are all put on this earth to accomplish something. And that something by each of us should be an effort that will <u>add value</u> to your life and to the lives of other human beings.

For many of us, we may judge ourselves by our <u>intentions</u> rather than by our <u>actions</u>. Others judge us by our actions. No one has ever been successful with good intentions alone. There has to be "action" to cultivate anything.

When is a "GOAL" Like a Strong Magnet?

One thing a goal <u>must</u> do for the "goal" setter, <u>you</u>, is fill you with very positive emotions when you think about it. It must be something you want <u>very much</u> to bring about.

If you do not feel a tremendous strong urge to get started and to complete your goal/objective, you should re-visit your reasons for having created this goal.

"ASK!"

This is a very helpful word to always carry with you. "Don't leave home without it!"

We all know what the word "*Ask*" means.

It is a word we should never hesitate to use when we are hoping and striving to learn more about anything.

It may surprise you to know that if you ask a question <u>in the correct way</u> from a knowledgeable human being, he or she would be most pleased to provide you with a proper answer.

If you believe that better is better, and you believe that you can always improve on something that is already good, and you are willing to do something about it – keep on asking questions. And do not forget to say THANK YOU for the responses.

Listen! Heads Up!

This is something we will all experience in our lives until the very end.

Problems, Problems, and Problems

Can you imagine what our lives would be like if we never encountered any problems?

As we all know, a "problem" is any question or matter involving doubt, uncertainty, or difficulty.

Problems are an ongoing challenge to living our lives in our preferred way. But problems of varying degrees will always be present in our lives and the <u>only positive</u> thing we can do about that is for each of us to become an exemplary problem solver.

Sometimes you are "blindsided" by a new problem; sometimes you have had a "bad" feeling about something, and when the problem does occur it convinced you that your feelings were correct. It does not matter what problem you find yourself confronted with. What matters is that you do not want any difficulties holding you back from living a good life and, therefore, all problems affecting "you" must be resolved quickly and in the most efficient manner.

Nothing should get in our way of living a good life and of reaching our planned objectives. So the <u>first</u> thing each of us must do for ourselves is to clearly identify and describe, in detail, what we believe caused the "problem."

How do you start the search for a problem-solving solution? The one and only most practical and useful way – you start by stating the problem – then you start "ASKING" pertinent questions of every human involved.

We may have to do some "digging" and also provide ourselves with a very honest and accurate assessment of our own individual actions leading up to the problem making itself known. We should not feel afraid of what the "digging" results may show as long as they represent an honest and accurate "picture" of what caused the problem. If you cannot accurately identify the cause of the problem, and if the problem, as it exists, "BLOCKS" you from moving forward, you cannot really resolve it. All you can do is start over again to try to reach whatever your objectives are.

Now, all concerned, take a realistic look at all of the information you have "unearthed" to find out Why? the problem occurred – put a "light" on it so you can clearly see. What do you see? – Unless "I miss my guess" and if you all believe that you are looking at an honest, complete description of the causes for the problem, you are also looking at, probably, the clearest, most concise answer to how to fix your problem.

Are you all with me? You have an answer to resolving your problem. How you believe, individually, when taking actions to render a resolution should be, I think, totally in line with your unquestionable good character.

See how easy it is to resolve differences or problems? Just make an accurate identification of what they are and deal appropriately with them.

Always know what the Why? represents. The Why? in Why did this happen? will offer you the answer, the solution, to most problems.

NO VISION?

NO PLAN?

NO GOAL?

Are You Floundering?

No Good For You!

Regarding all of us – We all have to deal every day with the facts of life. What are the facts of life? It is any aspect of human existence that must be acknowledged or regarded as unalterable.

You take the positives and you take the negatives and you do your utmost best to turn them both into your personal benefit.

Each of our lives is totally involved with the <u>Cause and Effect</u> doctrine. When what you do in your life never seems to close in on your "dreams." "<u>THINK ABOUT IT!</u>" And you all of a sudden realize that the "facts of life" are all about you.

Here are a few things which, to my way of thinking, are part of the unalterable facts of life.

<u>One is</u> – Life is a "do-it-yourself project." This cannot be changed, so we should all accept it and do the best we can for ourselves with it.

<u>Another is</u> – Your own thought process, the way you <u>think</u>, about all that is important to you matters must always be in the ALERT MODE. You must make yourself aware of the things that are surrounding your daily life, good or bad. And take appropriate actions to be your own protector, your own guardian. After all, who should care the most for you if not yourself?

<u>Another is</u> – Consider all other human beings surrounding you at all times. You may know them or you may not know them; they may be total strangers to you, <u>BUT</u> they all can and some definitely will affect

the quality of your life. Be an intelligent person for yourself. Afford everyone around you proper respect, kindness, and honesty, and you will be "playing the cards you are dealt" in your favor.

Another is – If you do not have the following "working in your corner," you will most likely be an individual whose quality of life is determined, on a daily basis, when you awake each morning. And you will have no idea what could be your "life" "tomorrow" and the "next" day, etc.

If you have NO VISION, you have NO PLAN, and with NO PLAN you will have NO GOALS, and the net result is a "floundering you," which is NO GOOD FOR YOU.

To be happy and have as few sufferings as possible in living your life, DO PUT A PLAN TOGETHER FOR YOURSELF that will allow you to FOCUS on and attain the "things" you want the most from living your good life.

Settle on your own VISION for your future life. Meaning, tell yourself, "This is what I want to do and accomplish." And then put your plan together, work it to completion, and you will reach your goal and that will = good for you!

Benefit From "Others!"

(Be selfish in a positive way)

Benefit from the "work" that others have already done. Read what others have already written about the subjects you are interested in, about the subjects that you can benefit from knowing.

One thing is probably very true. You may not agree with everything you read. But what you read can "trigger" your own "thinking mechanism" from which you can develop your own credible ideas of "things" that can help you and others.

It will be mentally and physically impossible for one person to generate and contain within himself all that is important and worthwhile to know. "Hitch your wagon" to all those "work horses" who, in total, know so much and who are willing to share what they know – also known as writers, authors, and teachers. That is using your "head" in a manner that will benefit you exclusively and put you on a faster track to accomplishing what you have decided are your goals in life.

You will benefit from the total of all your "Abilities." The more "Ability" you can offer to the "world," the more success you will gain. The word *"Ability"* means "to have power or capacity to do or act in any relation. It means to have competence in any occupation or field of action, from the possession of capacity, skill, means, or other qualifications."

Continue to be very much aware of the following statement. The word *Ability* and what it translates into as regards our successes in our lives is kind of scary from an emotional viewpoint. And this is why.

If you have NO WORTHWHILE ABILITIES to offer, you will have very little or no success in living a good, meaningful life for yourself.

When I refer to "no worthwhile abilities," I am simply stating that if you have nothing of consequence to offer the "world," meaning that the "world" cannot use what you have to offer to satisfy or better/improve itself, the "world" is not prepared to reward you. Without ample rewards flowing your way, you cannot acquire what your NEEDS dictate, and the desired WANTS you would like.

Conversely – the direct opposite of what I just suggested will move your life in the right direction.

The "Bottom line" is simple to understand, but will require work on your part. You must develop good, useful abilities.

Once you have developed abilities that will be useful to you and be equally and more useful to others, and you are able to exercise a good basic understanding of human relations, you will have no place to go with your life except up and forward to your personal success.

Always remember and accept that "If it is to be, it is up to me." After all, it will always be a "Do-it-yourself world."

When you think about the subject Human Relations, to my way of thinking, you should be thinking in the selfish mode. I will suggest why right now.

Human Relations, in a "nutshell" is all about getting along with people in the most respectful and honest manner. Therefore, you, personally, will gain so much more of what you will need and want to allow you to live a good and productive life if you end up, at the end of each day, with more people feeling positive toward you and your abilities and trusting you.

Be Mindful!

In All That You Do

By being mindful on a continuing basis, you can avoid many accidents and know, most of the time, where exactly you are with your personal health and your personal and business finances. This does not add to your existing workload. It is not doing anything other than being aware of your actions all the time.

Say nothing, know nothing, have nothing.

"Nothing" is a lousy word to have to put up with. So why do we? Beats me!

What is MINDFULNESS?

Mindfulness is a state of active, open attention on the present (the moment).

Being mindful is, for the moment, thinking only of and doing only those "things" that are of real importance to you. Keeping all things separate and in a workable sequential order. You do one thing at a time – no "multitasking." However, FIRST you need to have decided and know what is and will be important to you. This is no different than having carefully decided on what your goals will be for living a good life and what daily "steps" you need to take to get there. It is important to your success in accomplishing your goals that you do not allow anything else to interfere or interrupt your forward motion. ONLY "new" situations that are imminent and are of an "Emergency" caliber should be allowed to temporarily interrupt your forward motion.

The "things" we are referring to here are intended to include in your daily life your sleeping, your waking up, your eating of breakfast, lunch, and dinner, your attention to your personal health and well-being, your attention to your work (as an employee or as an entrepreneur), your attention to your finances (personal and/or business). When your mind considers <u>one</u> of these events, allow your mind to <u>only</u> dwell on it until your thoughts are completed, then consider another event, etc.

You should have your own prescribed, written goals to cover your personal life. Also, you should have your own prescribed, written goals to cover all your activities to "earn a living."

The whole idea of living a good life is to always be mindful of what you need to do, the steps you need to take to accomplish your set objectives/ goals.

The <u>ONLY</u> obvious reason and the <u>ONLY</u> factual reason for doing this should be <u>so clear to you</u>. <u>IF</u> you do not already know where you are "Heading," the direction you must follow to obtain what <u>you have decided</u> is important to you, how will you ever get there?

Chances are that you will NEVER ACCOMPLISH what you would like without carefully designed directions. That is a terrible thought. But a thought you do not need to contend with if you go about preparing yourself for only good, positive things and then faithfully follow the DIRECTIONS that are needed and that you have proposed to yourself.

One very important thing that can, and most likely will, be a direct positive benefit to you personally is whenever you do, whatever you do, or about to do, in the moment, REVIEW in your mind the REASONS, to you, why you are doing it. This kind of acknowledgement to yourself usually causes you to do "the thing" in a way that can bring you greater satisfaction. And at the same time it may "trigger" thoughts of future betterment when you do the same thing the next time, etc.

Family Concerns – Consider All Matters
As Important to a Family's Well-Being

When you are having a family conversation which, I believe, would be appropriate to have on a consistent weekly basis. All family members who are of an age to be able to "understand" should be present during the conversations and be allowed to have their voices heard.

All family conversations should be productive and pleasant and always in a positive vein, whether on the humorous level or a serious level. But ALL parties should allow the time needed to do it without haste. Haste makes waste, and probably less productive results.

The "two heads" of the family should always and frequently bring to a current point the status of personal health, questionable feelings on any subject that could affect the family's well-being and thoroughly reconcile personal finances to make certain to avoid financial "pitfalls." And to review where, as a family, they are on the "road" to reaching their preset goals.

Of course, if you are a single person, you should always think of your overall well-being and keep a sharp eye on the "road" that you mapped out for reaching your goals.

Why Don't We Do For Ourselves What We Know We Should Be Doing?

WOW! This must be one of the more important questions we need a good answer to.

Watch out, your "worst enemy" may be hanging around! – Procrastination!

Well, when your life seems to be turned upside down and not bringing you the pleasures you feel you deserve as a member of this large human family, something is happening to affect this feeling. Listen! Things do not just happen to you personally to effect feelings of dissatisfaction with how your life and well-being is changing.

Remember Cause and Effect?

Well, "Cause" is the reason for any change to your life, good or bad.

When it comes to your own total well-being, including your personal health and finances, there is one very important question you need to find the answer to. What or who is it that totally put you on the road to the total destruction of your life instead of putting you on the road to freedom and happiness?

How would you feel about learning it is <u>YOU</u>?

NO! NO! NO! – This is not a scare tactic to again try to convince you to move forward and do <u>ALL</u> that you know is good for you. It is simply to try, again, to bring <u>real reality</u> into your thinking.

From having read and hopefully understood all the intents to be helpful, you should have a very good idea of what we human beings (all 7 billion plus of us) need to do to significantly improve our own lives. Again, we <u>are not</u> focusing on changing the entire world (even though that thought is probably on every writer's wish list). We are only concentrating on changing ourselves, where needed, one individual, <u>you</u>.

The writer, when writing on subjects like this, will automatically make an assumption that each reader has or may have or will have at some point in his/her life the need to want and try to improve it.

If you are a reader who has been so "Royally" blessed and who may not have the need to generate any change to his/her life, then perhaps you would consider coaching others who are less fortunate. And in such situations, this writer will consider it a win for his efforts.

The question noted at the beginning of this "section" was "Why don't we do for ourselves what we know we should be doing?"

We have available to us good and undisputable knowledge of what each and every one of us <u>need</u> to do to substantially improve on our personal health, our personal financial situation, and our human relations.

    a. Some of us will be very successful in accomplishing these needs.
    b. Some of us will be only partially successful in accomplishing these needs (because somewhere along the line we stopped our activities that would have led to being very successful).
    c. Some of us will not be successful at all because we never got around to start any of the activities needed.

So the "$64,000" question is (now that is dating myself) "Why?," when they know they needed to do it, were the people included in B and C above not doing what could generate tremendously positive results for each of them?

Well, after trying to come up with an answer to this question that could not be refuted – I drew a "blank."

The only person who can come up with a real and honest answer to why they are not proceeding to help themselves is the person to whom this question applies. In this case, <u>you</u> – if you "fall into" this category.

Why? Why? Why? not do it for yourself?

I can only offer some reasons and/or remarks that could easily be interpreted by others as perhaps insensitive and unkind. If that is how they would be interpreted, I ask what else could the answer be? After all, many people immediately buy into and act on any concept that can be substantiated as a workable move to a better you, a better life.

Here are some thoughts on why I think you do not do certain things for yourself that you know could be good for you.

1. Because you really do not want to help yourself do better! (You want someone else to do it for you! It can't be done!)
2. You are so selfish that you only want to satisfy your immediate desires.
3. You are simply lazy and do not care about yourself.
4. You only want to feed your "emotions" to your own detriment.
5. You have not been able to clearly visualize a better future for yourself because you have not planned for it. (Why not prove this statement totally wrong and create a clear plan for yourself that would cover and materialize all your pleasant thoughts about living a good life. It may be the answer that cannot be refuted.)

If you understand this whole scenario but refuse to do it, and there are no "pills" that can work your mind in a positive direction, and there is no spiritual awakening within you of the importance to you of this – what is a person to do? Should we "let it slide," "let the chips fall where they may?" Sounds inhuman, but what else?

Being Organized!

When you know what you need or must do every hour of every "working" day, and you have the "materials" and the "tools" and the "manpower" at the ready, you will be able to accomplish the most, at the least possible cost, to you. The majority of the cost to you that you will reduce has to do with "labor." If "labor" is not <u>working</u> on a consistent basis for you, <u>it becomes "paid for" wasted time</u> and your "wallet" will be a lot lighter. This is a very simple observation that is much ignored and not considered in everyday planning. Those who practice being organized will agree with me 100% on this one.

Convenience

A Convenience is Definitely an Advantage

Make your "work" as convenient for you to do as is humanly possible. You will be pleasantly surprised how much pleasure and progress you will derive from being less stressed and able to get things done faster. When you do things, "work," that you have to do many times over for a long time, such as building a profitable "Career," THINK ABOUT IT as you progress.

THINK – "How can I do what I do better and faster? "What do I need to help me accomplish this?" Well, here is my "two cents." Planning and organizing comes to mind as a first step. This is not to insinuate that you have not been "planning" or that you are not organized, but simply to suggest that you review your present situation and make any necessary and essential modifications that may be called for. New and better "Tools" comes to mind as a second step. The right "Tools" at the right time makes work a lot easier and faster.

Planning and being organized is a great way to create convenience for yourself. It is like eating good food when you are very hungry – it makes you feel much better.

Maintenance

Who are we kidding? Maintenance is important to our overall well-being, but grossly overlooked by many.

If we used our intelligence, just the bare minimum, we must understand that maintaining the values we possess and will acquire as we live on is a direct result of preventive work on our respective parts.

It is caring for, strengthening, and continuous recognition of those values that help us to live a good life. This rationale pertains to everything that we value. First, our health and our family and friends. Second, all those material things ("Tools") that help us accomplish what we need to provide ourselves the best life possible.

Let us all stop living our lives through the eyes of a "throw-away society." If it is valuable and it "breaks," fix it!

So Whaas up? Is it time for some self-assessment and change?

Personal Health

Personal Health

Remember

"Every Body Matters"

Our dictionaries tell us that HEALTH is "soundness of body; freedom from disease or ailment; the general condition of the body or mind with reference to soundness and vigor."

Now, from reading this book up to this section, you know that I have suggested that the soundness of our personal finances and our knowledge and personal actions of positive human relations play a very important role for us in living a good life. How should we rate the value, the importance of HEALTH, to a human being for living a good life?

We could easily tell ourselves that each one of these categories, human relations, personal finance, and personal health is equally important to us for living a good life. However, we have to employ some prudent thinking here and decide which one should be THE MOST important category, understand why, and accept a reason, and live our lives with that reason foremost on our mind.

In expressing the following thoughts, I am not telling you about a new discovery; I am simply REMINDING you of what I am convinced you already know when you allow yourself time to think about it.

Think about this one! We are still dealing on a personal basis so this is again very much of self-interest to us.

Let us say this! "We are in a fortunate position in that we are okay with our personal finances and we are doing very well in our positive handling of human relations." What if our personal health is not "up to par"? What if we have to contend with physical and/or mental agony to a point where our personal finances and our good relations with other human beings do not seem to offer any helpful relief?

The above is kind of a sad way of trying to make a very important point, which again happens to be that we, individually to my way of thinking, are mostly responsible for how we will fare with our health throughout our lives.

WOW! We are still coming back to what seems to be another unalterable fact – the onus is still on us, individually, to do the right things for our own health. By now we must realize and accept that the reason for this "situation" is that we are the only ones who can, without a doubt, adequately effect proper CONTROL over what we need and must do for ourselves to provide for ourselves the best of all important things "Healthwise."

However, LET US THINK ABOUT IT!

What if we ALL, who understand what having "common sense" and applying it to all our efforts can do for us in a positive way, think about it this way.

Now, dear reader, this is meant to be nourishing "food for thought," not a directive for an "all end" conclusion.

Your good health, both physical and mental, is, in a manner of speaking, what will be the biggest factor to your ability to live a good and productive life. Your physical health will provide you with the strength your body will need to cope with all physical matters that you need to perform each and every day. Your good mental health will help you to stabilize and prioritize your thinking about what is and will continue to be important to you and a positive productive life. "Progress" with complete peace of mind is a goal, for each of us, well worth our time and effort.

Once you experience "progress" for yourself, however slow or fast you attain it, peace of mind will follow. And that is what makes all the positive healthy "things" we do for ourselves worth every "minute" we have to spend to accomplish it.

Take care of your body; it is the only place you have to live.

We do not have any guarantees in life as to the longevity of our mental and physical health. But we can personally be the best "conduit" for greatly reducing risks for unhealthy happenings to us.

Being in control of your life and having realistic expectations about your day-to-day challenges is the key to stress management, which is one of the more important ingredients to living a happy, healthy, and productive life, and something else very helpful and most necessary that is so simple to do for yourself and so easy to understand.

The knowledge of exactly what we need to do to "MAINTAIN" and keep our "human vehicle" running smoothly is disseminated, daily, through the media just about everywhere in our civilized world. And for some reason, which only we know personally, we seem to be the biggest procrastinators when it comes to giving this knowledge the "action" it needs.

We tend to delay some things until the opportunity to benefit by it is LOST or greatly diminished.

Listen! When it comes to your body, your "internal human vehicle's" proper functioning, ingest only the NUTRIMENTS your body NEEDS, NOT what your "eyes" tell you. And give your "body," each day, sufficient physical movement (exercise) to make it feel it is alive and well.

THINK ABOUT THIS! Creating and maintaining good health is not about doing good and proper things for yourself "sometimes," or "once in a while," or when "I have some free time," or when "I feel better." This is about starting now and doing it every day as part of our daily life. It will work for us without failure as soon as we create a HABIT of the important healthy things that need to be done. When you do "good" things over and over again, you soon create a habit which will prompt you to continue to do that "good" automatically.

Do not take the following statement lightly! Really put these thoughts in the "reality" light and give yourself a clear understanding of WHY this is one of the more important "common sense" moves you can make for yourself. It will take a degree of selfishness and stamina. But the "pay off" for you will be "Golden."

"Remember, you do not "MAINTAIN" your health by eating properly and exercising to get younger; you maintain your health to get "older."

Always "listen" to your "body." Maintain a sense of what is "going on" inside you. Are you feeling "good" in your normal ways? Are you feeling different away from the norm? Do these "not feeling good" signs persist for several days? If they do, obtain a medical opinion of what is happening without any delay.

Prepare yourself; do preventive maintenance on yourself to help retain your strength and vitality. This is something you can do for yourself at all times. This is something you will always be able to afford for yourself now. But if you wait or decide not to bother with doing anything and then if a true physical or mental difficulty arises, you may have to "pay" dearly for any possible health corrections. You may have to "pay" in a manner of missing much time from living a good and happy life.

What I am doing here is comparing us, our human body's potential conditions with the conditions of our country's existing "infrastructure." Our country's "infrastructure," it seems by all accounts, is not doing well at all from a safety and functional point of view. Our country's infrastructure appears to have been badly neglected for a very long time and is now in need of necessary "BIG TIME" maintenance and replacement work. And the big question is, "How do we 'pay' for it all?" And who will pay for it?

It is too late now to "PREPARE" ourselves for this infrastructure correction. It is already here and the total "Cost" will be huge. And the "inconvenience" to all involved – very great.

Getting ourselves into as good a physical and mental health condition as we can and maintaining it with NO DELAYS, and even "building" on it is tantamount, to my way of thinking, of giving ourselves a better than even chance to live a good and pleasant life within our financial means.

You notice the word PREPARATION! It is everywhere you "go." Preparation is a most essential part of our lives that will help us to live under a "sunny, clear blue sky" even if we have rain and snow sometimes.

Remember the saying, "Tomorrow's comforts require today's preparations."

What about our immune system? According to a Harvard Health publication (from the Internet), "For now there are no scientifically proven direct links between lifestyle and enhanced immune functions." "Researchers are still trying to understand how the immune system works and how to interpret measurements of immune functions." "In *the meantime, general healthy living strategies are a good way to start giving your immune system the 'upper hand'."*

This will not be about any "specific" thing that you should be doing for yourself to maintain good health. Instead, it will be about how I believe we should all think about personal health. There will perhaps be more questions than answers. However, as it concerns most of the answers, the correct answer for you, as an individual, will be your responsibility to develop in your mind.

The quality of your personal health can change in a "New York minute." Not from bad to good, but from good to bad. This usually happens as a direct result of not preparing your "internal system" on a daily consistent basis to stay healthy.

There is a tendency by all of us, if our bodies feel good, we forget about it.

The health choices you make right now will affect the quality of your life as you age. Most of us humans were born and blessed with a "body" that was assembled with 100% perfectly operating parts. Let us not take anything for granted.

However, once we are born, our work (initially our parents' work) begins. This body we were blessed with MUST be properly maintained and properly nourished "100%" at all times in order for it to grow and remain "perfect." This is each individual's direct responsibility to himself/herself. Do not confuse yourself by thinking and believing that you can effectively assign this responsibility to someone else because you will never, in the long run, receive the full benefits you need.

Draw a comparison in order that you may perhaps more clearly understand the impact on your body if you do not perform your own daily maintenance.

Example: Take something obvious, but not necessarily common to all – the "Rolls Royce" car engine (and everything else). The proper maintenance of the Rolls Royce car will cost an "arm and a leg" every time it goes in for service. And if you neglect doing this for a long time, you may end up with a very expensive car that does not perform well for you and may even "die" prematurely.

The good thing about your own body is that by "value" comparisons, in my opinion, your properly functioning body, over time, is "worth" to you many times more than the most expensive "toy" you can imagine. The other good thing about your body, the cost ($) to you for your proper and timely maintenance of it is but a very small fraction of the expensive car maintenance. And your properly functioning body will provide you with more happiness and productivity than you can ever imagine, and more often for a much longer time.

The only thing you must first overcome is, for most of us, the seeming ongoing procrastination to <u>START</u> and <u>continue</u>, without interruption, your daily "maintenance work."

Remember, "Nothing lasts forever." However, if while it is lasting it is functioning as nearly perfect as is humanly possible to make it, you will be farther ahead with living your good life than those who may have compromised their own situation.

It will be impossible for anyone besides yourself to be totally on the "lookout" for things that your personal health needs to be protected from.

So because of this impossibility, the responsibility, the job necessary to do this falls completely on your own shoulders. Are you prepared for this? If not, how can you prepare yourself? It is basically very simple, but you have to do it; you cannot just wish that it will happen.

Listen to your body; "Look, see, and feel your body." If you notice something on your body, in your system, that you have not seen or felt before, or hear something that makes you wonder what it is – say something, ask someone (family doctor) and do something. Actions like these, on your part, will help protect your physical and mental well-being. If your body sends you a signal that it feels different (not good) from your norm – pay attention to it.

"Let food be your medicine and medicine your food." When it comes to our health, truer words have not been spoken. (Reportedly, a famous saying from Hippocrates, Greek physician known as the Father of Medicine, about 400 B.C.)

Medical research has proven (you can read it everywhere) that the proper food cannot only cure physical illness, but also improve and potentially cure mental health issues.

It will bode well for all of us to be regularly updating our knowledge of the many personal health benefits we can gain from eating the "correct" kind of food daily. The correct kind of food for each of us is all kinds of food that competent nutritional/medical experts recommend. Also, we should not forget the physical movements our bodies need, in moderation, daily – it is called exercise.

God, I am sure, will bless all with better health who regularly adhere to this universal advice and who will not retreat from this self-fulfilling obligation.

Whenever you do things with good intentions for yourself and you wonder "how much is enough or too much," remember this – "Moderation in all things, including moderation."

If we think about our personal health in the way I am suggesting, and if we do it with sincerity and consistency, we will be giving ourselves a really great present.

There are no "magic pills" that will replace our own personal efforts to improve and maintain our health. We have to cultivate our habits so that we do the things we must do for ourselves – "automatically." We have to eliminate all excess body weight and we have to keep up with the conditioning of our bodies.

Nourishment (Yah, Food!) – Food can be the "Devil" in disguise and most of the time it seems we have no problem welcoming this "Devil." But it is a problem for us which usually becomes a BIG PROBLEM.

To remind us of body nourishment and excess weight, the *"Harvard Heart Letter,"* which I receive on a regular basis and would recommend to all readers who show a great concern for a healthy life, is extremely informative on how we should treat our life-producing engine, OUR HEART. (Letter Volume 25, #5, January 2015 issue). You obviously need to focus on all parts of your body when it comes to relying on it to help you live a good life. However, ask yourself and think about the answer, "What could you do if your heart stops functioning?" The answer is, again, quite obvious. There is absolutely nothing you can do. R.I.P.!

"Excess weight can boost blood pressure, blood sugar, and cholesterol values, <u>ALL</u> of which burden the heart."

THINK ABOUT IT – it is *"Tit4Tat"* all over again. You <u>FIRST</u> do something good for your body. Then your body will do something good for you. Remember, consistency of doing good things for your body is "KEY" here to develop consistent good return from your body.

When it comes to our personal health, the first line of defense is <u>PREVENTION</u>. Dr. Oz very aptly said this – "If you don't have a reason for your heart to keep beating – it won't."

Be aware! If you do not have this, you have absolutely nothing. Our heart, the "engine" that drives our good life.

Medical experts state unequivocally that "a heart attack can strike anyone, anytime – healthy or not." This following information is from an article written by Melissa Jacobs for a magazine called *"Main Line Today,"* the January 2016 issue. It is a "happy ending story" about a young lady, then 45 years of age (now 56 years of age) who unknowingly created a "nightmare" predicament for her heart health by overextending her weight lifting exercises to a point where her "blood pressure skyrocketed, pumping so much blood through her heart that it tore the inner lining of her artery."

To make an "eye opening" story short, Dr. Francis Sutter, the Chief of Cardiothoracic Surgery at Lankenau Medical Center, Wynnewood, Pennsylvania, "performed emergency quadruple bypass surgery" and the young lady "left the hospital with virtually a normal heart."

I try to always have a good reason for most everything I do and write. My point for sharing this story with you is simply this. We do not know what it is like to be physically vulnerable and not trust our body. Perhaps if we did, everyone would do anything and everything possible to try to avoid a heart attack.

Remember, our lives, how we live, how we maintain our health is very much a "do-it-yourself job." This should mean, to all of us, that we are to ourselves the line of first defense to our health and happiness. We need to know what to do and never procrastinate one "nanosecond" when it comes to seeking immediate help in all instances when our body is "talking to us" and telling us that things may be starting to go asunder.

Read the following carefully and never put yourself in a position where your only answer to what you should have done is "I forgot" or "that will never happen to me."

First on the list when it comes to education is recognizing the symptoms of a heart attack. They include:

- ✓ "Rapid heartbeat
- ✓ Dizziness
- ✓ Shortness of breath
- ✓ Extreme fatigue
- ✓ Nausea
- ✓ A cold sweat or clamminess
- ✓ Pressure or pain in the center of the chest, the arms, the stomach, or other areas of the upper body, including the jaw and neck."

You know when something is wrong in your body. Listen to the "voice" that tells you to get to a hospital.

THINK ABOUT IT – There are so many wonderful, happy, and productive accomplishments each of us wants to fulfill in our lives, so why not focus on the "health" of the one and only "body part" that will have the only full ability to take us to where we want to be.

Always tell yourself each morning as you awake, "Today is a good day" and "Life is good." Believe what you say and you will not have a bad day.

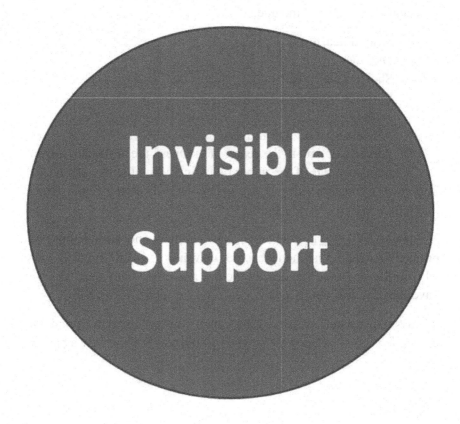

Spiritual Nourishment

Beget

Invisible Support

Prayer is the world's most reliable wireless connection to spiritual nourishment.

Religion

The quest for the values of the ideal life involving three phases: the ideal, the practices for attaining the values of the ideal, and the theology or world view relating the quest to the environing universe.

When you are a <u>BELIEVER</u> in a religion that professes true love and equality for ALL mankind, you are, by all accounts, on the right "track."

If you have questions, if you feel doubtful or uncertain about any of life's trials and tribulations, and you are seeking to improve your personal situations, apply your mind to the available "invisible" support system and **<u>FOLLOW THE DIRECTIONS</u>**.

Religion and Spiritual Nourishment!

For me, a most private subject matter.

Spiritual nourishment for the mind and soul, to me, is just as important as the proper nutriment for the body.

If you think nourishment is just food and drink, in the appropriate sense, you may be misleading yourself. Spiritual nourishment is what many of us think of as "invisible support" for our soul and for living our lives.

As we know, the "soul" is the spiritual part of "man," as distinct from the physical. Both aspects of a human being will always need the most effective kind of support to bring living a life to its fullest potential.

When we think about, talk about, write about, and using the words "spiritual," spiritualism, and spirituality, we are, of course, referring to the subject of religion. Religion is a subject that is an integral part of every human being's life, albeit part of their lives in varying degrees.

The subject of religion is probably the most "<u>private</u>" domain of every human being seeking the "invisible support" that it will always provide. Since I am not "all knowledgeable" on this subject, I will not attempt to "preach" to you, but I do want to share with you my personal "TAKE" on that "invisible support" awareness phenomenon. I am writing this as a Christian follower.

FAITH!

Again, let us all get on the same page by having a mutual understanding of what having "faith" can mean to us.

"Faith is having confidence, trust, and belief in yourself and a person or thing. Belief, which is not based on proof, belief in the doctrines or teachings of religion, the doctrines which are or should be believed."

From having faith in God and in yourself, you will find the strength, wisdom, and clarity of mind to live your life in the best possible way.

Without faith in all that is good, you will be standing alone at "the crossroads of emptiness."

Religion causes "recognition on the part of "Man" of a controlling superhuman power entitled to obedience, reverence, and worship." It is "the feeling or the spiritual attitude of those recognizing such a controlling power" "The manifestation of such feelings in conduct or life."

Prayer is our declaration to God that we are dependent on Him. God knows our problems. But God wants us to know what our problems really are. We need to be very specific with God when we pray for His help! Not loosy goosy. It will be like sharing our "PLANS" with God – then He will know how to help us. To my way of reasoning, PRAYER is the world's most reliable wireless communication system for attaining spiritual nourishment.

When you pray for a "good day," do not only have in mind the weather. Foremost in your mind should be that you will have a good, constructive, and productive day and that all positive things you need to have done will get done with the help of God, which will strengthen you.

Trying to write about a subject such as religion and spiritual nourishment can be quite intimidating because the available knowledge is so vast and most of us know so little. But every piece of knowledge and guidance we can garner for ourselves will be worth a better life for us.

Based on the many religions, in order to put yourself in line to receive a fair share of "invisible support," which is "spiritual support," you must be a BELIEVER in the creator of heaven and earth. This I learned by listening.

As I indicated above, the subject of religion is so vast and even at my age I can only claim knowledge of a highly diminutive portion. However, I believe it is very important for each of us to have, at least, a basic understanding, albeit perhaps very basic, of what we believe in and why we do believe. And how helpful spiritual nourishment can be to help foster a good life for ourselves.

Remember that "God" will help those believers who FIRST make a valiant effort to help themselves. There is "no free lunch," so do not bother to look for it. As you know from reading this far in the book, we are all members of the "do-it-yourself" world. This simply means that each one of us is responsible for carefully and thoughtfully planning our future and effectively executing our plans to promote the good life we all want.

Know this! When it comes to "needing," "wanting," and "receiving" some of the invaluable "invisible support," it is not a matter for you to just ask for it and you shall be given it. To my way of thinking, it has always been that you have to "EARN" this support first.

This simply means, to me, that you must know exactly what it is that you truly need and want and then you must take the "first step" by doing all that you can do, on your own, to achieve what you desire. This will be a clear sign to God that you are sincere about what you need and want. Now, if while you are pursuing your goal (plan) you run into some difficulties which put a temporary hold on your progress, THIS IS THE TIME where you ask God, through prayer, to help you figure out a solution. And all the time you continue, on your own, to work toward a solution by thinking about the outcome you need.

You have made it known to God, through prayer, with specificity, what you believe your problem is and you have asked for help. However, you continue to work on your own on a solution and then you will find that all of a sudden you have "clarity of mind," which will point you in the direction of the solution that will allow you to reach your goal (plan).

My writing of this part is intended to be reflective on my personal experience with problem solving in my life.

The one thing you should never forget to do in your spiritual relationship with God is this. Never not Thank God for His help, and confirm to God with your "thank you" that "I believe and that is the truth – Amen, Amen."

Do all you can do for yourself to learn more and more about the religion that applies to you, whose primary and only "goal" is to help "man" exist in our world with the best possible life with happiness and the least amount of suffering.

As a world society of human beings, notwithstanding our sometimes very strong but not intended by God to be negative, contrasting differences.

IF we can all learn and understand "Why?" we do the negative things we sometimes do in our daily lives to each other and, at the same time, acknowledge, in agreement, a common sense positive <u>PURPOSE</u> for existing in our world, we could perhaps be able to more successfully and more positively deal with each other. We may even figure out, in common, how we "can get along."

How about if we try to greatly reduce "negative greed" and start exercising with gusto the meaning of compromise? What do you think?

BELIEF!

You want your beliefs to change. That is proof that you are keeping your eyes open, living fully, and welcoming everything positive that the world and people around you can teach you. This means that people's beliefs should evolve as they gain new experiences.

The following are some very worthwhile quotes to keep in mind.

"People of all ages have ascribed to the idea that if you believe that something will happen, it will take place. It is the power of belief that causes things to happen in our lives."

"Most people define beliefs as inward convictions, a feeling of certainty about what something means. A belief is both mental and emotional. It is imbedded in the mind and in the heart."

What will we need to allow us to refer to ourselves as a <u>BELIEVER</u>?

Here are some thoughts!

- When we feel something is true.
- When you have confidence in something.
- When you rely through faith on something.
- When you accept and have confidence in an alleged fact or body of facts as true or right without "first-hand" knowledge or proof.
- When you, in your own mind, have learned of the cause (the reason) to believe in the truth of what is alleged, the end or purpose for which something is done.

When we have attained these feelings, I believe we can refer to ourselves as Believers.

I believe you have to live by faith in a very uncertain world. If your life is not going well, you should choose a new path – a different path from the one you have been on. Follow a new path – meaning set a new goal. Belief in a "divine power," I believe is universal.

A book to read for a very good insight and understanding of what the *Bible* teaches us is *The Journey* by Billy Graham (2006).

God speaks to us in words we can understand, and those words are found in the *Bible*.

"God created us to be His friends."

"God is everywhere at the same time."

"God is real – but so are evil and suffering."

Once we understand this, accept this, and do for the "Glory of God," what friends do for each other our lives will be the best ever.

Another question that may be in our minds as we think about this subject is this one. What exactly does it mean when "God made us in His own image?"

What exactly this means is apparently not an easy question to answer. Based on what I have heard and read, my imagination suggests this plausible answer. However, I will, of course, readily "bow" to any theological authority who has other thoughts.

Considering that God is invisible, intangible, weightless, soundless, and devoid of any heat signature, any claims to a physical resemblance appear pretty doubtful.

Then there is the fact that since we are utterly incapable of even approaching God's sinless nature, any attempt at arguing for a moral or spiritual resemblance seems destined to fall as well.

The image of God, in my mind, is "an absolute inspiring spirit with limitless superior dignity." And this image, I believe God decided to "stamp" and endow every human being He created with. Thus, He created all His children in His own image.

Now we should all realize that when God created "man" in His image, He turned over the "job" and the responsibility to all human beings to MAINTAIN and SUSTAIN the positive "VALUES" of the entire earth, into eternity.

With all the love and respect, God is, to me, the "spiritual answer man with limitless dignity."

Question: "How should we measure or grade ourselves as to how we have lived or are living up to God's expectations from humanity?"

How about a few more "THINK ABOUT IT."

Think About It! – Sad events in your life can be a "wake-up call." We do not fully appreciate someone or something until it is lost. Let us make certain that if we are true BELIEVERS in God, we do not lose "touch." There are times when we take certain things, important to our lives, for granted, even when we know we should never take any meaningful thing for granted. There are people who spend many of their waking hours feeling sorry for themselves. How useful it could be to put a daily limit on self-pity. Just a few tearful minutes, then on with the day. A better tomorrow depends on many things. But perhaps the most important thing is our relationship with God, our Father in heaven, and all human beings who touch our lives each and every day.

Think About It! – Have you ever found yourself in a personal situation when you were very concerned about what was happening to you and around you but you did not know exactly what it was and what you should do? And all of a sudden the "clouds" lifted, your mind became clear, and you knew then what your concern was and you "fixed it" and moved on with your life. Whenever I have such feelings and I experience an "uplifting" outcome, I know from where the "fix" came. I also always try to do the best I can first to try to "fix" any short-comings I experience and then if I need help, and I usually do need help, I ask in the spirit of our God for some "daylight." And when I receive it, I "fix" the negative situation and move on with my life.

Think About It! – The more you know about yourself, -- what makes you "tick," – what makes you happy, -- what makes you sad, -- what makes you angry, -- what makes you feel smart or stupid, etc., the more you will know and understand about all other human beings. How so? Because the feelings most all human beings have "run" pretty much in the same vein.

Take inventory of yourself, "ID" yourself to yourself, and then do to and for others that which will help give them the same positive, helpful feelings you like to have.

Create a life for yourself that feels good on the inside, not one that just looks good on the outside.

As a Matter of "Fact"!

"Coincidence is God's way of remaining anonymous" (Albert Einstein).

"Science and religion are not at odds. Science is simply too young to understand" (Dan Brown).

"My concern is not whether God is on our side; my greatest concern is to be on God's side, for God is always right" (Abraham Lincoln).

"My religion is very simple. My religion is kindness" (Dalai Lama).

"Above all else, guard your heart, for it affects everything else you do" (Anonymous).

"Life is not about finding yourself. Life is about creating yourself" (George Bernard Shaw).

Remember!

FAMILY

Is
Our refuge from the storm.

Is
Our link to the past.

Is
Our bridge to the future.

PRAYER

Releases the power of God
To those who have FAITH, no explanation is necessary.
To those who have NO FAITH, no explanation is possible.

KNOW

An atheist is a human being who has
NO invisible means of support.

Spiritual Nourishment!

Spiritual nourishment helps to build invisible support to each and every human being who is a true BELIEVER.

<u>Spirit</u> – "The divine influence as an agency working in the heart of man, a divine inspiring influence."

The human spirit "is considered to be the mental function of awareness, insight, understanding, judgment, and other reasoning power. The human spirit is the principle of conscious life. The accepted or professed rule of action or conduct awaking to one's own existence."

Divine spirit "is the godlike, acknowledged, rules of action or conduct for living our conscious lives. These are rules of action and conduct that need to be renewed, in our minds daily, through the discipline of prayer and learning the "WISDOM" from the *Bible*."

Invisible Support!

Receiving "invisible support," at times, during our life should not be totally "foreign" to any of us. When we think about it, we have all, at one time or another, been the unexpecting recipient of these blessings.

Some examples of such times may be: "catching yourself when falling and not being hurt," "starting to drive your car, a little late after the traffic light changed to "green" and thus avoiding another car who was "running" the red light," "your eye catching the site of a young child running out into the street, allowing you time to stop and not hitting the child," and also, perhaps, finally "seeing the light" to resolving, favorably, some really tough predicaments you may find yourself with," etc.

NOTE: God works in mysterious ways, but always in positive ways (practical ways). Coincidence is God's way of remaining anonymous.

Remember!

The mutually successful conclusion of any dialogue that may have been negative, in part, between human beings should <u>END</u> in a genuinely sincere manner with one of the following statements as relevance dictates.

"I am grateful for your understanding" (or
your help, or your "attitude")

OR

"I am sorry"

Neither of these parting words would ever hurt you. But they will show your elegance as a human being. And they can have the effect as a "neutralizer" on any possible leftover negative feelings.

Words, as among many other things, matter.

Remove a Fog of Doubt

To many of us, the reading of this book – knowing God's work and practicing our spiritual beliefs (you have them, right?) gives us the opportunity to see all things more clearly and up close.

It is like looking for and finding answers through a very powerful telescopic lens. Things like answers to solving our problems become so much closer and so much clearer and so much more understandable, making our lives more enjoyable in all respects. It is all about the "invisible" support that is afforded us. There is no visible evidence other than the personal results, the experiences we will gain. It seems that without this invisible support we do not have as much personal gains as we might otherwise have.

Do you understand what it means to you when you underestimate something? Well, in life if you are not, in your mind, completely clear about what positive effects your current thinking may have on the results you are opting for, you tend to not give it the appropriate support it will need. And by not providing the appropriate support (be it attitude, knowledge, manpower, or money) to gain the results desired, you fall short of your goal. In other words, you lose something which you could have gained if your estimate had been more "spot on."

When we are attempting to accomplish "big things" and achieve highly satisfactory results, we need all the assistance and support we can muster. Do not sell this type of thinking short. That could be very shortsighted.

Each New Day Can Provide a New Beginning

When we awake every morning, I am certain most of us have, figuratively speaking, millions of thoughts running through our minds. Where do we start choosing which thoughts we need to deal with "today?"

Well, to my way of thinking, there is one thought, in my mind, that surfaces pretty much immediately. And that is that this new day will be filled with countless opportunities to build on what I believe is already a good and constructive life for me and my family. So my thinking leans toward those opportunities which I can identify will help me to continue progress of furthering my good life.

This is the manner in which I will plan to pursue this new day and every new day. You could too.

A new day, a new beginning. Let us start here every time. Make each day better than the day before. Remember always that better is better.

"Good Morning World"

I think it would be a **POSITIVE** for all human beings if this saying became representative of our feelings when we first open our eyes every morning.

I think the word "suggest" is a more quickly acceptable word to use than the word "tell." Why? Because when you suggest something to someone, you are bringing an idea, a proposition before a person's mind for consideration and possible action. Nothing is final, that someone makes the decision on what to do for himself/herself.

So here is a suggestion. When you first open your eyes every morning, the first thing you say is, "Good morning world." Then if you follow a religion that glorifies God, the creator of our world and the universe, you acknowledge your appreciation to God for being alive.

One way you can acknowledge your appreciation to God is through a morning prayer before you get out of bed.

Then you open your thinking section of your mind and put in place the best <u>ATTITUDE</u> that you sense will be needed, by you, to accomplish all challenges that usually come your way plus any unusual or surprise challenges.

Then you remind yourself that the "world is your oyster" and that there are many "pearls" out there readily available to those who are "good fishermen."

If you are wondering what I mean by being a "good fisherman," this is it.

The "world is your oyster," to my way of thinking, simply means that in our world there are countless beautiful, practical, useful, meaningful, healthy opportunities for living a good life (the pearl) if we have prepared ourselves properly with the correct tools needed to "opening the oyster."

However, in any given "oyster," there is a chance – but no guarantee – that a pearl lays within. So it is with life. But nothing ventured, nothing gained. We need to take <u>"educated" chances</u>.

To be a good "fisherman" in the "sea" of all worthwhile endeavors, you have to know, understand, and remember that perception is reality in the minds of human beings. How others see us, what they hear about us, what they understand about us will form their perception of us. And their perception of us will play an important role in forming their attitude toward us.

A good "fisherman" may be well known for the complete "tackle box" and "fishing rods" he always has with him. In this attempt to clarify each of us as a "good fisherman," we need to wake up each morning with the absolute correct ATTITUDE waiting in our minds to "explosively" express itself. All of us human beings have so many different attitudes stored in our minds and ready to be used, and the one attitude usually chosen by many human beings is solely based on the first encounter from other human beings.

I want to circumvent a long discussion here on the subject of variable attitudes and get straight to the only one that has science somewhat perplexed because it works every time it is exhibited.

Your attitude cannot help but to be reflective of your accepted purpose for living your life. If your accepted or acknowledged purpose to yourself for living your life does not include all of the following descriptive words of a person's known qualities, you could ask yourself why they are not included and then perhaps make them become an integral part of the future description of your own person. This would then be a true win-win combination for you.

If you are a person who is known to others as someone who is living his life with the purpose of being useful, responsible, honorable, and compassionate, then you should not have to be concerned what ATTITUDE you will be exhibiting to others once you get out of bed and get going.

Will to Perform

Devote yourself to understanding and properly responding, in a faithful manner, to what your "brothers' and sisters'" needs are.

Realize that God made us co-creators and stewards of this, <u>OUR</u> entire world. Let us all make certain that we honor and comply with the responsibility bestowed on us.

Why not think of this section of writing, albeit the last section, but, for certain, the most potentially powerful stimulator for peace of mind, as the "super glue" that can effectively hold it all together for us?

MAKE THE MOVE!

What could be the ultimate positive "move" you, I, and everyone else could make on each other?

"To give to others, and always support every
RIGHT that we claim for ourselves."

Truths

of

Infinite

Importance

INVENTORY!

What do you have?

If you have your good health – you have a lot.

If you have a meaningful job that you like – you have a lot.

If you have "no debt" (excluding a reasonable mortgage) – you have a lot.

If you have many very good, sincere friends and acquaintances - you have a lot.

If you are an individual who is known to others to be a person who is <u>useful</u>, <u>responsible</u>, <u>honorable</u>, <u>compassionate</u>, <u>disciplined</u>, and loaded with <u>integrity</u> – you have much more than a lot.

You do realize that all of the above "paints a picture" in our minds of a human being who does have a lot and that <u>you</u> and everyone else would probably feel privileged to know and to be involved with, every day, for the rest of our lives. It is the kind of human being who will help foster great mutual benefits.

All you need to do to become a good partner with "living your life" is to make certain that you fully understand the meaning of the words used here. Moreover, making certain that when living your daily life you will always "live up to" their meaning without fail.

Guarantees?

There are no real guarantees in living your life. But what is usually the case is that the "smarter" and more intelligently you "work" and the more consistency you put into your efforts to reach your realistically planned GOALS, the better your chances for success become.

The only sure thing, "Guaranteed," that we know will eventually happen to each of us is that we will "Pass On," returning to our "Maker."

Well, what about everything else that can and usually does happen between the time of birth and when we pass on?

There will be things that we can do to help ourselves to fulfill our purpose for living on this earth. The things that will happen to us will depend very much on our "own doings" as well as the "doings" of others, both human and nature. The things that can and will happen will be both happy/positive and sad/negative things.

When we decide to give the meaning of the word RESPONSIBILITY the kind of attention, understanding, acceptance, and action it is deserving of, we may all come to realize and accept why the quality of our lives here on earth is truly a "do-it-yourself project."

Home Depot and Lowes are two major retailers catering to "DIY" customers, who want to do their own (as much as possible) home repairs and renovations. The customers' reasons for doing this are usually "two-fold." They like to hone their skills at this type of work and they, most of the time, save good money.

Well planning and executing the work essential to living a good life is also very much a "do-it-yourself project."

If anyone questions this statement with a "Why?", the only answer I can offer here is "Why not?" This answer is what you may refer to as a nebulous answer; it is indistinct, it is not immediately a useful answer, it gives you no specific direction. But wait! Maybe it does give us some kind of direction. The fact that I answer you, "Why not?" should prolong your thinking time on this subject. It should get you started on

THINKING, why is creating a good life for yourself a "do-it-yourself project?"

Well, the first question you should ask yourself is, "If I don't, as the task force leader in my mind, develop and set in motion a plan, which when adhered to will allow me the luxury of living a good life, who would do that for me?"

If I asked you to list the names of at least ten (10) other human beings whom you believe would do this plan for you so that you could just sit back and enjoy life, how long would it take you to write down the first name?

Here, again, I am trying my best to convince each reader that there is no one else who can take your place in creating a plan for the kind of good life that will appeal to you individually. Therefore, it must be a "do-it-yourself" job.

Do We Need to Make Adjustments in Our Lives?

Here is something else to think about! Now, as you continue reading this book, do not misplace in your "memory bank" what I have said, that the full intent of what I am writing here is to offer a "thought process" that may require you to think about you and your future a little different and to be more focused.

I do not believe that we can, any of us, go through life trying to be the exact same person we have been up to now. "Things Change," and we have to "roll with punches" (in a positive way). Therefore, we too need to consider changing certain things about ourselves. But also keep in mind that if what you are and do today works well for you, remember "if it ain't broke, don't fix it."

Now here is that something else to think about! Accept that certain ADJUSTMENTS at times can be very helpful to your overall well-being.

To ADJUST is to "move into proper positions for use, to make something useful in a new way." This can apply to a human being.

Live your life as a true "Diplomat!" Focus on being pleasing, likeable, and tactful. Learn how to say or do things to avoid giving offense. For some of us, being a "Diplomat" in all our actions is "second nature." However, for some of us it will take some individual effort. But, believe me, the "Earnings" you can put into your own coffer will definitely grow when you perform your life as a "Diplomat."

We all need to ADJUST our ways of living our lives, from time to time.

We will always be heavily dependent on our personal health and our personal finances to live a good life. Some of us may not have too much of what helps to provide a pleasant life. And some of us may, by comparison, have an overabundance of the stuff that helps to provide a pleasant life. In this case, it is what it is. However, the one thing we must never do to ourselves is to pretend to ourselves and others that we have a lot (money and material things) and then borrow money to try to prove it. The results will be NO GOOD.

It is true that your personal health and your personal finances will help to dictate the kind of life you will be living.

Think about this too! There are two old sayings with a very strong mental appeal if you let their meaning sink into your consciousness.

"If you can be happy with a 'little,' you have a lot to be happy for."

"We seldom think about what we have, but constantly on what we don't have."

If you have a lot, FINE!

If you don't have much, well, that can also be okay as long as you are enjoying reasonably good health.

NOTE THIS: Having a little now does not mean that you cannot have much more in your future. It is up to you.

Think this through! First and foremost, get your mind set on an even playing field. As you go through each day, you should never forget that being a human being, from our Creator's point of view, on one hand, no one else in the entire world is better than you and, on the other hand, you are not better than anyone else in the entire world. The only thing that changes in our world is based solely on what each of us provide for ourselves and how we use it to live our lives.

And the other thing to keep in mind always is that the world plays NO FAVORITES, it is impersonal. The world does not care who succeeds or who fails. The world does not care if we change. Our ATTITUDE, mind you, toward life does not affect the world and the people in it nearly as much as it affects us.

How can this be? Well the world is neutral and everyone in this world is just an independent human being DEPENDING SOLELY on what he/she can accomplish for themselves.

What is my point with all this writing? Again, making a meaningful point can be extremely tough sometimes. The point of making a point, in the context of the contents of this entire book is to try to assist those of us who may have questions about how best to create and live a good life.

We will probably always have words to categorize groups of human beings, such as the "HAVES AND THE HAVE NOTS." I am not exactly sure how this description came about. I think, though, that the "HAVES" are human beings who have gained the feelings of contentment and comfortableness with what they have accomplished and been able to accumulate in their lives until now. I think the "HAVE NOTS" are human beings who are still trying to figure out what they need to do to become "HAVES." They are either on their way to completing those feelings for themselves or some may have run into some "road blocks" that they need help to remove.

I do not believe that there are any human beings in this entire world who do not long for having feelings of contentment in their lives. Unfortunately, there will always be some who, finally, totally give up on doing anything to help themselves. And all I can suggest here is that if you do come across a human being in such a situation, at the least try to help them see a glimmer of "light at the end of the tunnel." Do what you can! And if you think you cannot, please think again. BUT if you absolutely feel that you cannot help, at the very least do not hurt them.

Who is the "Master Chef"?

Remember, understand, and accept that <u>you</u> are the "Master Chef" for creating your own "lifestyle" menu to be used exclusively by <u>you</u> for <u>your</u> living a good life.

You will read this several times throughout this book. I may refer to you in different ways, i.e. Producer, Director, or Master Chef. The bottom line is you will always be the Boss, the CEO of living your life. The reason for this is the importance to <u>you</u> of accepting this fact and working it "to the bare bones" for your personal benefit.

Now, with everything that needs to be done, we have to start somewhere, which is usually at the beginning. So in this case, Master Chef, assemble the essential ingredients needed for your "Masterpiece" (your good life).

If we are going to create something very good for ourselves that we want our MIND and soul to ingest, we have to create a credible recipe. We have to adopt a philosophy or strategy for living our lives based on knowledge and past experience that has been proven to work. We can call it our "Recipe for Living a Good Life."

The essential ingredients that <u>MUST</u> be included in this recipe are as follows: In addition to being a person <u>known</u> to be sincere and have integrity, your personal attributes, as it pertains to your ability to feel and show <u>fortitude</u>, <u>gratitude</u>, and <u>patience</u>, and to <u>plan</u> and <u>organize</u>, and to <u>trust but verify</u>.

Please remember what usually happens to the "end product" if you "skimp" or "short-change" yourself when applying these ingredients. The results usually turn out different than what you expected. So do not skimp.

Keep in mind that we may not, at all times, be able to be the very best, the #1 in any particular endeavor, <u>BUT</u> we should always show everyone around us the very best version of ourselves. And this is very much okay.

<u>Important Postscript</u>: When you are assimilating your "ingredients," if in making your honest evaluation of yourself and you sense that you may be a little "light" on some of the absolute necessary "ingredients," do not be "stopped in your track"; get busy changing yourself to meet all requirements. It is a challenge worth meeting "head on." Accept the fact that all "ingredients" called for must be present to achieve the results you will be reaching for.

A Young Person Doing Some "Thinking Out Loud"

I have now completed my formal education. Here I am. Okay! What's next?

I can't just stand here. I have to do something. I agree, but what do I want to do?

Well, I do not really know. I am an adolescent now and Mom and Dad are kind of tapering off on telling me what to do. I guess that is a good thing for me, but I do not know that yet.

I have observed a few things while living my daily life in the last few years. I have noticed that if I <u>smile</u> when I meet people, they smile right back at me. I have noticed when people ask me to help them get something done and I do it, and do it well, they react in a very happy way and they say to me, "Thank you," in a way that makes me feel very good to hear. I have noticed that when I do spontaneous things involving myself and other people, such as "holding a door open for someone," "helping someone get up after falling," etc., they respond in a very kind manner.

I have overheard conversations other people have had with each other about "work" and how they are trying to "make ends meet." I did understand that "making ends meet" seems to be a "thing" that does not appear to be all that easy to accomplish. I have learned from my Mom and Dad that "work is of super importance to people. The kind of "work" that I have been accustomed to up to this point is "school work." And although there were times when that work, for me, was difficult to accomplish, I did learn early on with my teachers that all I ever needed to do is figure out what my problem was and <u>ask</u> them and I would have my answer.

Now, this "Mom and Dad" kind of work that is needed to "make ends meet" is different, and I sense that I really need to get a firm handle on exactly what it is, what is means, and why there seems to be so many types and levels of work.

But one thing that will be noticeably different for me now when it looks like I will soon be pretty much on my own, doing my own things – I am only <u>one</u> human being. I used to have Mom and Dad running interference for me, and help me when I needed help. Now, again, I have to do for myself what I learned to do. But what happens when I run up against things that are needed to be done but I do not know anything about it? What happens then?

Well, I guess I have to do it in a manner I used to do it when I did not know about something. I would ask Mom and Dad. But now, on my own, I will not always have Mom and Dad around to ask "What should I do?" I have noticed, however, other "grownups" talk to each other, ask each other questions, and, after completing their conversation, sometimes smile at each other, shake hands, and say thank you, and sometimes say "I owe you one." I think that is how, sometimes, if not most of the time, "adults" go about finding out or learning what they need to do to proceed resolving problems and/or resolving differences between each other that may have been earlier problems. That seems to be a very workable and relatively "easy way" to proceed. But what if I need to ask questions of help from someone and there is no one I know around to ask? What should I do then? I know there are always other people around to ask questions and I remember Mom and Dad always saying "be nice, respectful, and courteous." I suppose if I ask my questions in a proper and respectful manner these other people may give me some helpful answers. (I think this young person is very much on the right rack and will do okay in life.) The reading of this book should be beneficial to human beings of all ages. To all of those human beings who like to be reminded of good things, such as "knowledge."

The More You Observe!

The more you actually see what is happening around us as it concerns people helping people; you should feel a large degree of excitement. To me, it seems like we are becoming more willing and quicker to extend a helping hand to people we see in need. I am hoping this is an omen for good and is giving us some indication as to the future of our world society.

Let us join those who help, to give them help.

Ability – Motivation – Attitude

A human being without knowledge is not worth much!

On the surface, this is a sad and unkind thing to say. But "THINK ABOUT IT!" It is a fact!

Ability is what you are capable of doing. It is what you need to help you to create value for others. The value that you first create that others need will provide you with value in return. The more things you are capable of doing, the more expansive your abilities become, the more valuable as a human being you will become to yourself and others.

Motivation is what you tell yourself are your reasons for activating your abilities on a daily basis. It is your answer to yourself for WHY you are living on this earth in the first place.

Attitude is your mind set when it comes to accepting full responsibility for the fulfillment of all obligations to do the things that you have promised. And your mind set when it comes to your positive and helpful cooperation with all of the people with whom you will be working.

If you ever think about "What can I do for myself to gain more positive values," think about the meaning of the words ABILITY, MOTIVATION, and ATTITUDE. Remember that:

"Ability" represents what you are capable of doing.

Motivation determines what you decide to do.

Attitude determines how well you do what you decided to do.

Always work on increasing your "strength" in each of these areas. The "stronger" you get, the more valuable you become.

319

Waking Up! It is a Blessing!

Every day in order to do the best things for yourself with every "move" you make from the "second" you wake up in the morning is to have and repeat a "MOTTO" to yourself to get your thinking "going" and your most appropriate attitude in "gear."

A "MOTTO" is a maxim, an expression of a general truth, especially as to conduct. It is adopted as expressing one's guiding principles. It is a sentence, phrase, or word attached to or inscribed on anything (perhaps your mind) as appropriate to it.

Such as, perhaps: "Good morning, my world, I am building a good life for myself and my family. I need to carefully choose how to deal beneficially with my personal health, my personal and business finances, and my proper application of my knowledge of good, positive human relations."

If you do this for yourself every morning as you awake, it should help you to "set the stage" for how you should act and behave to obtain the best overall results for yourself.

Remember, nothing ventured, nothing gained. We all know what being good to ourselves and others is all about. We just have to remember to act on that knowledge at every opportunity we are offered.

Our goal in living our lives should not be merely to exist, but to live and be successful. And to do so with all the "gusto" that knowledge will help you achieve.

There is "Strength" in Numbers!

➤ In the number of other human beings who are willing and able to always "have your back."
➤ In the number of other human beings who value the "abilities: you possess to help them accomplish their needs and wants.
➤ In the number of $1.00 bills you can save for yourself and your family.

Remember!

➤ "Positive action speaks louder than positive words."
➤ "Time is only a valuable resource if you do something valuable with it."
➤ "Knowledge is an advantage to you, but <u>ONLY</u> if you learn how to use it in a positive manner."

Motivation for a human being is like
gasoline for the car engine.

Without it you do not go anywhere.

Enjoy life – It does have an expiration date.

"Your Base?"

A "base" is the bottom of anything, considered as its support. It is that on which a thing stands or rests. It is the <u>FOUNDATION</u>.

Your base, your foundation, will be the most important aspect of your productive life.

Once you have provided yourself with a proper foundation that will suit your needs and particular wants, your happy and productive life's journey can begin.

As you enter the formal education phase of your life, you are beginning to lay the first "bricks" to your "foundation." Each level of formal education you complete will add strength to your foundation. The more formal education you attain in the subjects and future work you wish to be involved with, the stronger your "foundation" will become.

Remember! A human being without knowledge is not worth much.

Once your formal education phase has been properly completed, you will start to exercise your initial "Abilities" to make them grow and expand to the point where you will become experienced in <u>your</u> chosen endeavor and will be in a position to create "value" to fill others' needs and wants which will, in return, reward you with "value" that will satisfy your needs and reasonable wants.

Note the meaning of the word, "Ability."

Ability is the power or capacity that you build up within you to enable you to do or act in any relation. It is your competence in any occupation or field of action, from the possession of capacity, skill, means, or other qualifications.

In other words, the more meaningful, valuable work that you can accomplish, the more "value" you will gain for yourself.

Now, when you add to your "Abilities" a good basic knowledge of human relations, as is the gist of this entire book, *Tit4Tat*, you will, if you diligently exercise and use this knowledge, give yourself every available opportunity to be very successful.

Teach Me to Learn

"To <u>TEACH</u> is to impart knowledge of or skill in any meaningful and useful subject. To make it available in a clear and factual manner to ALL who wish to acquire it."

"To <u>LEARN</u> is to ascertain, detect, and discover new knowledge of or skill in any meaningful and useful subject and <u>ADD</u> that to one's store of abilities."

"To <u>ASCERTAIN</u> is to verify facts by inquiry or analysis."

"To <u>DETECT</u> implies becoming aware of something which has been obscure, secret, or concealed."

"To <u>DISCOVER</u> is also used as a synonym of learning in order to suggest that new information acquired is surprising to the learner."

(The American College Dictionary)

"The information shared with all the readers of this book, be it <u>NEW</u> to you or be it a <u>REMINDER</u> to you, allow it to give you an "Aha!" moment and proceed living your good life with good knowledge and much help waiting for you just for the asking.

When you have a well thought out strategy and plan for accomplishing anything meaningful, you are giving yourself the best possible chance for overall personal success.

Are You Yearning for Learning?

To some people, "learning" is a joy to be had every single day of their lives. And the main reason for these feelings of joy is that "learning" provides you with knowledge, and knowledge is what gives you the ability to do things that allows you to be a productive and content member of society. When you feel and know that you are being productive, feeling content is a most wonderful by-product.

Being and feeling as a productive person, in a positive way, is probably the first major link you will have to a long and happy satisfying life.

Consider the meaning of the word "productive": "Having the power of producing, being creative. To produce goods and services having exchangeable value." In our world, being a productive human being, producing, creating things that are needed and wanted by other human beings is the only thing that will allow us, as individuals, to satisfy our own needs and wants. Is this not a good "picture" to always think about every day?

The scary part about this "picture" in your mind should be that without knowledge you cannot become a productive individual. I have a saying in this book that "a human being without knowledge is not worth much." And sadly, this is so true, albeit an unkind thing to say.

Now, the knowledge that each of us, individually, will need to have, to give us a "membership" in a productive society, will be noteworthy.

First, you must always keep in mind and accept with the utmost respect that everything positive that you will attempt to accomplish must involve some effort of other human beings, including yourself. If you "forget" this fact for a "nanosecond" while you are working with others to accomplish your objective/goal, you may end up being less successful.

Once you have made your decision as to what you want to be involved with to be productive, the obvious comes to mind. It is, of course, the specific knowledge needed, based on what you have decided to "do." Here, you should "COMPETE" with yourself every day to become more and more knowledgeable about all you need to know to perform your "specific" work and become the best of the best in performance.

If you try to "sail" through life without a good comprehension of how positive human relations works, for your benefit, you may stumble across many unproductive moments in your life.

So, besides the specific knowledge/experience you will need to be successful in your choice of endeavor – LISTEN! Your overall abilities must include a good basic understanding of how positive human relations works in real life and it must be exercised DAILY.

Know that we can all be whatever we want to be as long as we keep our desires of what we want to be within the realm of reality for us. And that we understand and fully accept that OUR DESTINY IS OURS TO PRODUCE. And it will depend entirely on our personal "abilities" and our strongest desire to do what it takes.

When it comes to each of us, personally, the following is, to my way of thinking, a very important consideration for when you make your decisions about what you want to do to cause you to live a good and productive life.

Remember and accept that your life is all about you and your future family. When we talk about how to become a "productive" human being, the FINAL decision as to what you should focus on when building a good life for yourself is exactly what YOU WANT TO DO – It should be what you are most interested in; what you see as the most enjoyable activity that you want to become involved with and, of course, which will be in DEMAND by other human beings, thereby giving you the opportunity to be well rewarded for your work.

Do all that you can do to always be a sincere friend to all those who wish you well and who are in a position, in life, to help you by "teaching you" and "help guide you" along the way.

Change?

When should the word "change" enter our thinking?

When "change" is being considered, it is usually always to make different all things that are not working to our benefit in a positive sense.

So, we usually change or should think of changing when the things that are happening to us are not making us feel happy and/or satisfied and they continue ceaselessly.

Remember, always keep in mind that when things are not working well, in your favor, there is always some kind of human inconsistency involved. And the inconsistency usually is in the relationship with other human beings. A no-brainer, right? Okay!

Now, if you choose to totally ignore, in any situation, the inconsistency involved there is no need for you to change your thinking on the subject. You just decide to accept any inconsistencies and accompanying consequences and live with it.

However, you do not want to "shoot yourself in the foot" by becoming known to others as an aloof individual. You should never forget and you should always remind yourself, daily, that in this "world" of ours you can never accomplish, by yourself, anything meaningful and worthwhile. You will always be heavily dependent on other human beings to assist you, to help you one way or another to accomplish things that will meet your desires.

Having said this, if or when you want to or need to make certain changes for your exclusive benefits, in your behavioral action toward others – keep reviewing the "Human Relations" section in this book. This section, I believe, will give you sufficient understanding of what needs to be done to accomplish any change you feel is important for you to make.

In light of the foregoing, let us also consider the following questions.

How often do we "take inventory of ourselves?"

What I mean here is simply this. Do we recognize and understand, clearly, how our daily behavior and action toward others can generate positiveness and/or negativeness?

When your "day" seems to carry on in a flawless manner giving you reasons to smile and have feelings of gratitude – do you ever wonder why this is happening? On the other hand, if your "day" turns out to be the opposite of the aforesaid and gives you an experience you would not wish on anyone – do you ever wonder why this is happening?

So what have we here? On "one hand" we have very pleasant and positive happenings and, on the other hand, very unpleasant and negative happenings. Okay, so we have a "mixed bag" of daily happenings. But, do you realize, do you understand that you have had a "hand" in creating these days for yourself? You may be partially responsible or, at times, you could be totally responsible for each "good" or "bad" happening.

What is my point here? Whenever anything happens in your life that is either "good" or "bad" for you, are you at all interested in learning and understanding what the causes or effects are in each instant? What was it that you did; what role did you play that caused "a good thing" to happen to your benefit? When you learn the answer, would you not want to "copy" what you did and cause several more repeats of the "good happening?"

Equally important to you is to learn what you did, what role you played that caused a "bad thing" to happen to your disadvantage. Also, when you learn the answer, in this case, would you not want to Remember what you did and then avoid any future repeats of the "bad happening?"

This is just another instant of "proof" that we each, all of us, have a "job" to do to give us every opportunity to live a good life.

Why Should I Follow Suggestions?

Well, there is only one reasonable answer.

If you are the one and only person, human being, that the entire world is seeking for "knowledge-packed action" advice because you are the "know-it-all guru," then you will not need anyone to provide suggestions to you.

I like to get a "dig" in like that once in a while – it is soothing the frustrations that sometimes comes with trying to find the right "words" to use.

Do not take offense – there is no such living human being as I just described above. We all need suggestions at times to help us move forward in a positive way.

What I am trying to do here as a "teacher" is suggest several "avenues" that you can "walk down" to accomplish many things that can help you to live a good life.

To my way of thinking, it may not be enough to just offer advice on specific things to do that will work for you. But to also offer you several logical common sense <u>reasons</u> why these things will work.

When you understand positive reasons for why things, in general, "works," you can put on your own "thinking cap" and perhaps develop several more positive reasons why it should work for you. Remember, as a human being it seems that the more positive reasons we can give ourselves that what we are about to do will "work" for us – the more enthusiastic we will probably be to get it done. And this is what really counts.

Knowledge alone can make you a very interesting person, but without taking <u>ACTIONS</u> on your knowledge it will not make you a successful person.

An important suggestion that I have benefited by being aware of is you should identify REALITY as it will apply to your own person. We need to learn how to face and accept REALITY.

We have heard so many different "positive" sayings over time, sayings such as (paraphrased):

1. "You can be whatever you want to be!"
2. "If I can do it – anyone can do it!"
3. "You can be all that you can be!"

Assuming a "saying" is intended to include ALL human beings, of these three "sayings," to my way of thinking, only the #3 saying makes any sense in real life.

We talk a lot about "DIFFERENCES" in all of us human beings and how we hope that someday (soon) "differences" in human beings will no longer play an injurious part in the efforts needed to "getting along" and being productive partners for mutual benefits.

However, our "differences" will <u>ALWAYS</u> play a part in how well we can do for ourselves, individually, in living our lives when it comes to "personal productivity."

We cannot all become DOCTORS. We cannot all become PRESIDENT of our great country – USA. We cannot all become SCIENTISTS. We cannot all become MATHEMATICIANS. You all know where I am going with this ranting.

It is a "truism" and it is "reality!" that "we cannot be whatever we want to be." But, "we can be ALL that we can be." More simply put, and in keeping with "reality," our current personal knowledge and abilities will be the directing force of what we can or will be in our respective futures.

Identifying to ourselves our "basket" of knowledge and our abilities to get specific things done well and on time will be a good start for living a good life.

You will learn what your capacity is as a productive human being and what that can do for you – if you pursue your "talent" with gusto.

If you set your goals to take full advantage of your current knowledge and abilities and provide your personal ACTIONS to reaching your goals – you will reach your goals and have that great feeling of satisfaction and contentment. And further, as a result you are to be considered as a successful person in your rank.

THE "BIG" INDIFFERENCE!

What does it mean to be a human being with "indifference" in their attitude toward living "things"?

"Indifference (if you are) means you lack interest in or concern with how 'things' work out in the end. You classify, in your mind, things to be unimportant and of mediocre quality."

"Indifference, unconcern, listlessness, apathy, insensibility all imply lack of feelings. Indifference denotes an absence of feelings or interest, an absence of concern. It is not caring in the face of what might be expected to cause uneasiness or apprehension.

Insensibility denotes an absence of capacity for feeling or of susceptibility to emotional influences."

"Being indifferent is having no feeling, favorable or unfavorable, to some 'thing' or 'person.' Falling short of any standard of excellence. Not making a difference or mattering, either way, as to a person."

(so sayest our dictionary)

To my way of thinking, when you are considered to be indifferent you are like a person "sitting on the fence." You are not <u>here</u> and you are not <u>there</u>. You are, in a manner of speaking, in a space entirely void of matter.

Now I ask of each of us, when we become a "fence sitter," especially as it may concern the fate of other human beings, what positive 'values' do we bring to the table?

If we are all in agreement that our ultimate "PURPOSE" for existing on our earth is to "have happiness and the least amount of suffering," every "feeling" we generate from our soul should be focused on this purpose for all living things. We all deserve the opportunity to "harness" this purpose. However, we should all understand, expect, and accept that we will have to <u>EARN</u> this privilege by assisting in the procurement process.

The "Tit4Tat" concept, when adhered to, can help all of us reach the "goal" line.

If you agree with this thinking – GREAT!

If you disagree – <u>NOT SO GREAT!</u> However, if you are prepared to offer a logical, credible, and humane explanation for assuming the "negative" position – this may help to resolve, favorably, any dissent.

"Hypothetically Speaking"

Think About it!

Here you are, standing by yourself, wondering what to do next. We are always wondering what to do next once we complete what we are now doing.

When you are doing things that bring you feelings of fun and laughter, which we will refer to here as pleasure, it seems to be, many times, spontaneous. It is a natural personal impulse, <u>without</u> effort or premeditation.

However, when it comes to each of us trying to put ourselves in the best "line" or "queue" to accomplish the most for ourselves, while living our lives, we may not always give it sufficient effort or premeditation to provide ourselves with the best opportunities.

If you ever get the feeling that you should perhaps have done more for yourself, put more effort and premeditation into your "value"-driven plans for living your life; it will be very much <u>okay</u> for you to do a re-evaluation and establish whatever changes may be beneficial for you. A good life, to continue to be good, will require periodic adjustments. All potentially positive adjustments should be considered by you.

This scenario albeit "hypothetical," at this moment, could quite possibly turn into reality for many of us.

This book, with its very "common sense" helpful REMINDERS is intended to help you focus your thinking on what most of us know and understand as good, effective "working" knowledge.

Focus!?

Focus is something we should always do much more of. The dictionary's definitions of the word "*focus*" are many, but in the context of this writing the meaning we choose to use is "to concentrate: "to focus on our thoughts."

What happens in your mind when you allow yourself time to "focus" and continue to concentrate as you perform your responsibilities? There is much written by "medical" professionals on "How to focus a wandering mind," but here we will try to make ourselves understand from the simplest point of view what we mean.

<u>Point of Interest</u>: I have read that there was a "study" made that sampled over 2,000 adults during their day-to-day activities and found that 47 percent of the time their minds were not focused on what they were doing. Even more striking, when people's minds were wandering they reported being less Happy.

Now, I am by no stretch of anyone's imagination trying to impersonate a "mind" medical professional to give a "medical" opinion. I will simply try to make it simple to get a useful, practical feeling of what you can experience when you focus, concentrate, keep on thinking about what you are (currently) doing and <u>why</u> you are doing it.

Depending on what kind of work you do during most of your day, "focusing" on your task-at-hand can keep you safer, and doing better and more quality as well as quantity of work. And the end result will garner for you more praise and more happy feelings, including perhaps a few extra dollars in financial reward.

And from your point of view, what you need to do is <u>remind yourself</u> of the importance to you of your job. And tell yourself that all "things," except your "task-at-hand," is put on "<u>HOLD</u>" until you have completed the work. "Multi-tasking" is having many "irons in the fire" at the same time, <u>but only</u> one is expected to be worked by you at a time.

"Thinking" about what you are doing at all times is an absolute necessity for positive success.

Can You "TOP" This?

When referring to your current life situation, "Can you TOP this?" This may be what you are subconsciously thinking every time you tell yourself, "I wish things were 'different' in my life."

When we start to think this way, let us first remind ourselves of this unalterable "fact," which is, and this applies to every human being on our earth, that we are an inescapable integral part of the most potentially productive "do-it-yourself" life culture. Our individual progress and growth of our lives is resulting from our individual development or improvement by education or training, and the enlightenment or refinement resulting from such development.

Now, to answer the pending question, "Can you TOP this?"

The answer is YES! We can make our individual lives BETTER and, then again, still BETTER. Remember, better is better. Also, let us never forget that there is "NO FREE LUNCH" ever. Everything that has great "value" will "cost you!"

The cost to you, in this situation, will be borne by your prudence and very strong desires and clear (to you) definition of what part of your "life" you want to seek betterment for. This is a very important objective – to know, with specificity, what you realistically want to accomplish.

This is the same as getting into your car for a drive. You must be clearly aware of your destinations. And if you are not, it is suggested you do not start driving, get out of your car and determine where you want to go. If you drive and keep on driving without a fixed destination, you are wasting your time and gasoline and wear and tear on your car.

Observe! "Time" is a valuable "commodity." But it is only valuable if you use it to accomplish something of "value."

As you keep on reading this book, the writer is hopeful that you will realize the importance to you of the many obvious "moves" that you can make to help improve your own situations.

A Silly Thought? Maybe! Maybe Not!

How important, to you, is having fun?

Having fun or looking to pick up an opportunity to earn some more money? That question may sometimes cause some confusion for us and sometimes we may make a decision which may not necessarily be in our best interest.

When you find yourself with this kind of dilemma, give the following thought some "thinking time."

First and foremost, you need to keep in mind that without a sufficiently adequate "financial security cushion" in the form of a savings account, you cannot, in all honesty, tell yourself that you are "well off." This "security cushion" is intended to cover yourself and your family's financial needs for a reasonably long time, if you experience a temporary "stop" in your regular income stream. If you have no "cushion," you may experience some family unpleasantness if your financial obligations cannot be met in a timely fashion.

However, living our individual lives is intended to be both pleasant and productive for each of us. So here is the "thought" I was referring to above. When it comes to creating and having "fun" for ourselves, this is something we can plan, execute, and enjoy at any time in a "New York minute." All we need to do is set aside the "time" we will need.

Finding, accepting, and executing an opportunity to earn meaningful rewards or money is not something that "grows on trees" or is always readily available to all of us. Finding meaningful opportunities to earn rewards or money in most instances is not easy to find. Therefore, any such opportunities, as they may present themselves to you, should, in my opinion, <u>NEVER</u> be overlooked in order to make time for fun and other pleasantness for yourself and your family.

See the point? You can always make "fun" a part of your life at any time. But productive "money-making" opportunities are not just sitting on a "shelf" waiting for you to "pick one" when you feel like it.

Just a Thought!

What Do You Do When You Do
Not Know What To Do?

Have you ever pondered this question?

It could pertain to any one of us at any moment. Maybe your answer is "you punt!" Probably, the only thing that may get you is some more time to ponder your "game plan." And, well, it may be what you needed. Time available can become perhaps the most important asset you can have if you know how to effectively use it.

Take any one of us and call him "you."

"You might act as if you know what you are doing "TODAY," but unbeknownst to others you are lost in your own thoughts. Your current lack of direction may be at the root of your confusion. Instead of pretending like you have all the answers now, admit what you do not know so you can focus on what you do know. Revealing your vulnerability is not a sign of weakness; it takes strength to show up as a human, complete with your imperfections. Success will continue to be yours if you remain honest with yourself.

Your answer to yourself to the above "heading" question is simple and uncomplicated. As one human being in the midst of seven billion plus other human beings in our world, you are like all human beings – constantly subjected to uncertainties as to how to proceed and move forward. When this happens, immediately recognize that you are in this position because there was something you did not know. You correct that by simply ASKING FOR HELP.

"Trust **But** Verify"

In order to effectively <u>verify</u> anything that is or will be of significant importance to you, you must be able to actually <u>see</u> it with <u>your own eyes</u> and to <u>understand</u> it with <u>your own mind</u>. You should <u>NEVER</u> rely on "hearsay" based on others' eyes and minds. You have to completely involve yourself. You must hear it "straight from the horse's mouth."

Do not "sell" this advice, "short" or you can end up with the "short end of the stick."

"REALITY"?!

Your "Reality" is what is important to you. Your realistic "Plans" for your future will be your "Ladder" to your success. If you create an unrealistic plan/goal to challenge yourself – it will be like putting up a 4-foot stepladder to try to reach a 40-foot "top." That by itself will not do it for you.

Your "reality" is or will be based solely on your Abilities and Experiences to get things done.

You do not want your initial "plans" to represent the need for "requirements" that go far beyond your current abilities and experiences. If they do, you are admitting into your life a potential "game changer" that we refer to as "frustrations."

"Frustration" is the "culprit" that can choke your desires to continue to try to reach your goals. However, if you remember "times" in your past when you really wanted something and you knew why you wanted that something, and it made much common sense for you to have it – somehow you managed to get it. This is still very much the "ATTITUDE" you must "dress yourself" in every morning as you awake from a good night's sleep. You need to know what your needs and realistic wants are. And you need to have developed a clear and complete understanding of what "steps" you need to take to achieve what you very much want to achieve.

Remember that, in a manner of speaking, we all have a limited amount of time to live on our earth and since our total time is unknown and not guaranteed to us, we should be very "select" when we initiate our plans/goals for how we want to live our lives and for what we want to accomplish. Realizing and accepting that our time is our most valuable asset, let us decide right now to use it wisely.

At the beginning of this section, "Reality," I suggested that the way you will be able to live your life will depend on and be based on your

<u>personal abilities and experiences</u>. In other words, what have you learned to do well that will be of value to other human beings?

You must always keep in mind how the positive Tit4Tat concept works. There are, to my way of thinking, no exceptions. You <u>must first</u> put yourself in a position that enables you to help create value, and do that before you can expect to receive value. In that order. "I give you like for like."

We do not start out living our lives knowing <u>all</u> that we ever need to know and having all the personal experience we need to have in order to provide for <u>all</u> that we will need and want. Having said this, I am wondering if God's "Garden of Eden" would have provided for all this.

It is too late to make any conjectures on that point.

However, as far as our personal knowledge of "things" and our personal experiences in getting things done, we pretty much <u>all</u> start out at the "starting line" with very little.

Differences in our abilities and our experiences between all of us human beings, once we leave the "starting line," begin to "grow." In the beginning, our "parents" will receive the "credit" for how and what they did to enable us to start forming, in our minds, a clear, positive "picture" of what we would all need to personally perform well on this earth together with all other human beings.

Once we leave the "starting line," our parents, our culture, our society, i.e., our environment, that we are exposed to, to my way thinking, play an enormously important role in the outcome of our personal attitude and how we keep on living our lives. Sometimes the results we, as individuals, achieve turn out to be very positive, very good, and very productive; and sometimes, for some of us, less than the foregoing.

<u>Question</u>? Is it fair, you think, to invoke the old saying, "It is what it is" and let's move on? Or should we say, "It is what it is," but if it represents something less than <u>good</u> it does not have to be; it can be changed. I would opt for this last sentence.

We all know and hopefully we all accept that we are very much an integral part of the "Do-it-yourself" life. Therefore, it will be totally up to each of us to learn and decide on which way our lives will turn out. And, of course, there is <u>only</u> one way all of our lives should be lived. The purpose of living our lives should be to be "happy" and consist of as few "sufferings" as humanly possible.

<u>We know</u> that if we keep our "bodies" healthy we will be better off. If we are not in the best of health, we must try to do what we need to do to get healthy.

<u>We know</u> that our personal finances are a strong motivator in deciding how our personal life will play out. We know that if we want a better financial situation for ourselves, we must spend less or earn more, and maintain a happy equilibrium between earning and spending your money.

<u>We know</u> that the subject of good human relations is the "crux," is the decisive point in making our individual lives what God intended them to be.

If we take these noted three "We knows" and do the most positive work on each of them, we should, by all accounts, emerge <u>WINNERS</u>.

Remember this "Axiom" – If <u>you</u> need or want more of anything, <u>you</u> must <u>learn more and do more</u>.

How Should We Face Reality?

(as it concerns living our lives)

Do you feel happy and content with your life to date? When it comes to material "wealth," you know, the "things" you now have, do you feel happy and content?

Perhaps most human beings feel that they need or must have a certain amount, and certain kinds of material things in order to have good feelings. Of course, the other part of having genuine feelings of happiness and contentment (probably more important) will depend on the quality of the relationships with other human beings.

For this scenario, let us say, we are not satisfied with what we have accomplished to date when it comes to either or both human relations and/or material things (aka, personal finance).

Okay! We want more of everything. Then we ask ourselves, "What are we ready, willing, and able to do" for ourselves in order to have better and more good relationships with other human beings? What are we willing to do to gain more material things that will make us feel more satisfied?

Well, we can all say, "I will do whatever it takes as long as I get what I need and want."

Again, if we are willing to deal in this manner with what we perceive we are missing and want, the question now becomes, "Why don't we have it yet?" Can you answer the question Why?

We have dealt with the "mystic" of the question "WHY" several times in this book. And what we have learned is simply this. When something does not go "right" for us, when we have opposition to what we are proposing, when our productive efforts simply stop working in our favor, when other human beings stop liking us – we always wonder what happened, and we should always <u>ASK</u> ourselves this three-letter word

"WHY?" The complete honest answer to this question (in detail) will give you the reasons – it is what it is.

When you put this detailed list of "reasons" in front of you, you can start mitigating all the "negative" reasons, and if you do this successfully you should be able to move forward in a positive sense.

If there are still some reasons you have not been successful in mitigating and you cannot reach an amicable compromise, you may have to forget about whatever was and move on.

This type of scenario, to my way of thinking, will help you to "clarify" any problems however simple or complicated.

The important point here, now, is if you do provide yourself with a complete and honest answer as to "Why" you do not have the things you want, you should be looking at the solutions to obtaining what you want.

Here comes the difficult part – whatever the "solution" suggests are the reasons, you will have to deal with them. Whatever the "solutions" require you to do, you have to do in order to gain what you are missing. Now the question becomes, "are you ready, willing, and able" to do what you need to do? If you are ready and you are able and you "do," you should sooner or later have the things you consider important to you to make you feel happier and content.

You can repeat this scenario each time you are "wanting" for something and you are having difficulty obtaining it.

That was "verbally" a simple answer to a somewhat tougher question. If you want something and you know how to go about getting it in a proper way, it can become yours. This is assuming, of course, that you have been dealing with reality. Meaning, here, that you have the knowledge and ability and a strong desire to obtain it.

However, if you are not "willing to do whatever it takes" or you are not ready and able because of your current knowledge and ability to do it, then whatever you wanted cannot be yours unless someone else makes you a gift of it, or you make a conscious decision and effort to first obtain more knowledge and ability to allow you to proceed.

Listen! Sometimes the toughest thing to do when things do not go "our way," but which may provide you with a "mountain" of pleasant living is to <u>become satisfied with what you already have</u>, but keep on trying for more. Learn more of what you need to know to provide you with the "ability" to get more things done for yourself. Also remember, time is on your side as long as you do smart PLANNING.

Are Some People Obstinate?

(not easily controlled)

When you want to share your thoughts on any subject, especially a subject so universally important as <u>Human Relations</u> and what you can do for yourself to give you opportunities to live a better life, you will try to reach as many "readers" as possible. There is nothing better than starting out with an obvious statement.

The composition of "Readers" of any book is, I think, usually very diversified. You will have Readers who already know the subject well, but they are interested in how others view the subject. You will have Readers who knew a little bit about the subject and who are interested in learning more, and again how others view the subject. You will have Readers who have, perhaps, never thought much about the importance to them and the potentially positive effect of the subject when building a better life and now want to learn as much as they can.

Then you may have a Reader who may be sitting on the proverbial "fence" and who are neither here nor there with their thinking on the subject. These Readers are not too sure of what and how they should believe in a subject like this. As a result, they may develop an antagonistic attitude toward the author. Because they may feel that even though they may not know much at all about the subject, they still "poo poo" much of the thinking on this subject. In other words, they may have acquired the "Know-It-All" syndrome and, as a result, may not accept the potential benefits waiting for them if they would only "Try It!"

The reason for the above "Reader analysis," if you will, is because there are small sections in this book where the author tries to get through an assumed to be wall of resistance by perhaps some readers, and I do not want that "small" part of writing to be in any way considered as an affront to any Reader. All the author is trying to do is his very best to get his thoughts across and understood.

I hope the next few paragraphs will not apply to any of the Readers of this book. But just in case, I will write it.

If I say to you, "You simply have to accept the information covered in this book and work it to your full benefit," some of the Readers will come right back with "I don't have to accept anything from anybody if I don't want to, and nobody is going to tell me what to do." You know what? You would be 100% correct. You do not have to accept anything that someone else suggests you should do to make things easier, more profitable, and better for yourself. You do not even have to try it to see if it would really work.

OK! So where does this stubbornness get you? I would suggest, not very far. Probably, absolutely nowhere.

If or when a situation like this develops, who is the WINNER? Absolutely no one. Certainly not that Reader if he/she will not be sufficiently open-minded to realize and understand that you can only learn about new things from other human beings.

If you know of a person who may have this kind of an attitude about learning new things that could definitely provide them with opportunities to do better for themselves, tell them, "Cut yourself some slack" and "<u>TRY IT!</u>." And when you see how well it will work for you, do not hesitate for a "nanosecond" to show your gratitude by acknowledging your good fortune by simply "paying it forward."

A Very Nutritious "Food for Thought!"

How can you build success for yourself and your family? If we had a good answer to this question, and we reviewed that answer in our minds every morning as we prepare to enter another day of living a good life, it would, no doubt, make each day a little easier for us and probably more productive.

Why don't we consider a thought like this for a start!

Each one of us needs positive daily direction in varying degrees. Clear, positive direction can make every step, every move, and every thought you generate bring you closer to what you desire from living your life. A step, a move, a thought, when focused on an established goal/objective can minimize all possible disruptions and speed up your arrival at your own pre-determined destinations in life. And this requires only one "Act" on your part to get this "Big Ball" rolling, as it were, and that is your decision as to "WHAT DO YOU WANT FROM LIFE?" This "Act" or action on your part is very important to your overall well-being, so carefully think about it, talk about it with your closest "well-wishers" and you make the decisions. Best way to remember what you decided on is to carefully and accurately write it down for "posterity."

Every day you must realize and accept one very large "FACT" – If you don't know in which direction you want to be "heading" with your life, neither you nor anyone else can help you find the way. You will still have a life, but it will not be the life that you decided on. It will be strictly "pot luck." You deserve a well-planned (by you), good life that will meet most, if not all, of your personal, realistic, and positive desires. Your valiant attempt at achieving this is what will make it happen for you.

To be successful with any endeavor, there are no secrets to accomplishing anything that you truly want to accomplish. It is only realistic ideas and good and intelligent work that will be needed from you. Of course, we must always keep in mind the extent and limit of our own abilities when we focus on things that we feel strongly about wanting from our lives. Keeping within reality, for each of us, is very important to help prevent frustrations from building within us. We must accept that the meaning of "reality" can be, and usually is, different to each of us, based on our known abilities.

"Live in the Moment"

How to be "MINDFUL" and "LIVE IN THE MOMENT" should not be difficult to understand. Let's see if we can make clearer what a basic understanding should be. What is our objective?

I am making an assumption here that every reader's objective in living their lives is to have "happiness and the least amount of suffering." This will be our goal. By "living in the moment" should be helpful to all readers in reaching the objective.

To "live in the moment" means being present, conscious, and aware of the present with ALL of our senses, sight, hearing, smell, taste, and touch. Living in the moment, also referred to as mindfulness, is a state of active, open, intentional attention on the present. The idea of being mindful, being present, being more conscious of life as it happens – may seem contradictory to those who are used to sacrificing living for pursuing their goals, but cultivating mindfulness will help you achieve your goals and enjoy life more. It means not dwelling on the past, or being anxious or worrying about the future.

To help us understand better what to "live in the moment" is all about – let's seek the help of some great thinkers and writers.

> "If you have one eye on yesterday (the past) and one eye on tomorrow (the future), you are going to be cockeyed today (the present)" (Anonymous).

> "Do not dwell on the past, do not dream of the future, concentrate the mind on the present moment" (Buddha).

> "Today is the first day of the rest of your life" (Charles Dederich).

> "Children have neither past nor future, they enjoy the present, which very few of us do" (Jeandela Brugere).

> "The best thing about the future is that is comes only one day at the time" (Abraham Lincoln).

349

Each day we have to acknowledge to ourselves what our responsibilities are, to ourselves, and make certain our day, each and every day, is filled with our own activities that satisfy our responsibilities.

"Be!"

Be Mindful, Be Alert, Be Selective in every moment of your life. This will offer you your best opportunities for having your best life possible.

Be useful, Be responsible, Be honorable, Be compassionate in every moment of your life. This will help give all others whose life you will "touch" the best opportunity for their lives to be the best possible.

The combination of the above, in you, makes you a BIG WINNER.

"After years of trying and working hard, I still do not have what I believe I should have. What is the use? I quit right now!"

Have you ever known anyone who may have felt this way and then actually quit "life" as it were?

Someone very young and just starting out in life may look at the "world" and think, "This is a big world, so much good and bad going on, it is so confusing, which way do I turn, what do I need to do to live a good life?"

These are hypothetical questions. But I am not so sure that questions like these are unfounded. These questions may occur with some frequency amongst some of our human brothers and sisters.

When we discover the human beings that may be experiencing having thoughts like these, they should be reminded that – "Starting over again with a clear understanding of what needs to be done to live a better life is not a sign of failure, <u>it is truly a sign of strength and intelligence</u>.

However, the one very important aspect of living a better life is the need <u>to accept</u> the undeniable fact that the "Job" to accomplish it is a "Do it yourself job."

In all that you will plan to do, that you will do, and that you do do, REMEMBER that there will <u>always</u> be another human being besides yourself that you will need to rely on to get the right job done correctly. Ergo understanding the very basics of Human Relations and how to effectively use it will be "your ace up your sleeve."

This book, *Tit4Tat*, hopefully will be your "key" to help you to get to "first base" with many opportunities and then to eventually reach "Home Plate" with your goals.

Between Human Beings

I believe that sometimes when you feel anger, you have the right to show anger. But remember that by being angry <u>NEVER</u> gives you the right to be <u>CRUEL</u>.

REMEMBER

When you get angry, feel frustrated and are at the end of your "fuse," and you clench your fist and want to create your own justice, THINK ABOUT IT! – Then forget about it! – It serves no purpose. And <u>you</u> walk away <u>THE</u> better person without any regrets.

To Gain Anything Worthwhile
Will Always Be a Challenge

Living a good life for any and all of us is an enormous challenge that we should all accept. We should work "intelligently" at thoroughly understanding all the ramifications.

As human beings, we are all on the same team regardless of what religion we follow and practice. When we play the game of "life," we are constantly doing things to each other and for each other. And when we do, we receive in return responses to our words and actions.

As we all know, there are times when the responses from other human beings are exactly "spot on" what we wanted and needed. And it makes our life and feelings, for that moment, much better, much improved. We should immediately "THINK," "What did I do or say to deserve such favorable response?" Then tuck your answer away in the alert part of your memory bank and allow the feelings that you created by whatever you said and did to be repeated daily.

Conversely, there will be times when the responses you receive are quite the opposite of what is noted above. Again, we should immediately "THINK," "What did I do or say that provoked such an unfavorable response?" Also, again tuck your answer away in your alert memory bank and just keep thinking about it, <u>BUT DO NOT REPEAT IT</u>.

You cannot get away from the fact that you are and will forever be the "designated hitter" in your own "game of life." And what you decide to do for yourself to provide yourself with the best possible life is 100% your responsibility and your decision. Choose all your future "moves" well and be good to yourself and to others.

Remember! "You are what you eat." If you eat healthy and steadily exercise your body and mind, you will be and stay healthy. Also remember! "You are what you repeatedly do." If you consistently do honorable, kind, and useful things, you become known as a human being everyone wants to have around.

The privileges to live a good life come with certain responsibilities that need to be fulfilled by each of us. Perhaps we can refer to these responsibilities as the "official game book" that a team coach uses as a solid reference to how to best "play the game." It is very much a Team sport. It is a sport where all human beings are contenders for a playing position and no player remains unchosen.

But who is the coach? Well, unlike the sports games we usually talk about (i.e., football and basketball) where each team has a coach, this is unique. Every human being involved in the "game of life" is their own coach. They will coach themselves with all the help they can earn from their human counterparts. You will understand why I use the word "Earn" as you continue to read this book.

Now, having given my explanation as to who the coach will be, some readers may opt to refer to God as their coach, and that certainly would very much be okay. However, to my way of thinking, I will refer to God as the owner of this very large team.

I believe that God did not create us to give Himself the daily "job" to be our "hand holder." God wants us to live our lives for ourselves. That is one thing, I believe, God has always made very clear, ever since the Adam and Eve debacle. We must live our lives for ourselves, but we will never be by ourselves. God will always be here for each of us to help us find the correct answers to our needs. However, I believe that God, very quickly, comes to the rescue of all who show a sincere desire and dedication to helping themselves, and who believes in the spiritual power. What this means to me is that when you have realistic needs to be met, start working on satisfying those needs in the best way you can, and if you run into any difficulties then you ask God to help you with directions to follow to get you to your goal. There is an amazing feeling that enters your mind and soul when the "owner," our "Father," becomes involved with us. Somehow, your mind, your thinking about your difficulties become much clearer and much more focused that you inevitably find the answers you need to proceed with your life.

To repeat what I said earlier, to be able to live a good life comes with it certain responsibilities, rules that need to be followed, fulfilled by each of us daily. Just like when you are driving a car on public roads, you <u>must</u> follow specific traffic laws, directions all that have been developed for the <u>sole purpose</u> of protecting all human beings involved on the roads. When you follow these directions, you eventually arrive at your destination safe and sound. So it is also with the rules and directions involved with living a good life. These insights were developed over centuries from observing how other human beings react to what and how we do things <u>to</u> each other and <u>for</u> each other. We record in our minds what we did to receive favorable, kind, and useful responses, and we repeat them over and over again. Also, we record similar type information that cause the opposite to happen in response <u>AND</u> if we are smart human beings (which we are), <u>we do not repeat them</u>.

All of these learned directives, rules, etc. are collected into one subject matter which we refer to as "Human Relations."

It is the *Tit4Tat* concept utilized to its fullest positive extent.

ADVICE

("To give counsel to; offer an opinion to, as worthy or expedient to be followed. To recommend as wise, prudent, etc., to give information to.")

Sometimes people and advice do not melt together very well to form a positive. Why is this?

When we receive <u>un</u>solicited advice from others who know us and who have our best interest at heart, and we do not listen carefully to what is being said, we could end up with the "short end of the stick." And we also run the risk of not receiving any future advice.

It is true that sometimes unsolicited advice can be somewhat "loose" and not very useful to your specific situations. If this happens, still listen and then all you need to do is say "thank you for your thoughts," and then do what you wish with it.

Some people give out "advice" very freely because they want to hear themselves talk. They want people to feel that they know about a lot of things even though they may have no clue about what they are saying. When this happens, respond in an appropriate way without being disrespectful and unkind.

Then, of course, there are some people whose advice "you would kill for" and your ears could not be more tuned in.

THINK ABOUT IT!

When we talk about listening to others, we should <u>always</u> anticipate that something worthwhile may be shared that could help us in a very large way. However, what we hear could also amount to what may be related to "gobbledygook."

Let us assume that 50 percent of the time when we listen to others' advice we may benefit very much from it. And 50 percent of the time it could be a total waste of time. Unless you are someone who is convinced that you can always tell which 50 percent you should be listening to before you hear it, you should perhaps listen to ALL and then decide for yourself which advice to keep.

However, at ALL times it is a potentially good thing if ALL your "advisors" feel good about sharing "things" with you, so do not give cause to discourage that feeling.

Always respond with respect and kindness. Simply say with a SMILE, "Thank you for sharing this with me" or "Thank you for your thoughts; I will think about that."

Leave yourself "wide open" for as much help and assistance you can handle.

"Late, Past, and Future"

How do these words relate to each other? Ask yourself this question if you have a concern about your preparedness for your future?

"Is it too "late" to now do for myself what I should have done in my "past" to better prepare myself for my future?"

This world of ours not only revolves around its axis, but the human beings occupying this world can change every "living minute" of their lives. Their outlook on life changes, their feelings change with the changes that occur daily in every aspect of living. Some of the changes that occur within us, to us are, it seems, somewhat automatic and we usually refer to it as "coping with" circumstances. We can tend with the need for change and betterment usually with a degree of success.

I believe any suggested answer to the above question, "Is it too late," is a resounding NO; it will never be too late to "re-define" yourself in a serious move to bring betterment to yourself and your family.

If "things" are going well for you but you want to accomplish more, or if what you have been doing is no longer as productive as it once was, or if you are simply "sick and tired" of continuing what you have been doing, all of these reasons will foster strong feelings for change and betterment.

Now, if and when you make a decision to "change" for the better, your "ways and means" to live your life, you must still make absolutely certain that you are prepared, fully prepared, to cope with, primarily, your personal finances until your betterment objective has been reached and now can be relied on to paying you adequate dividends.

Never throw "Caution to the Wind" when dealing with you and your family's personal well-being. Make sure the "scale" is tipping in your favor.

Well, what is my point here? It is quite simple. Never force yourself to be satisfied with something you are not. Life is too short to disqualify yourself from living a good life that you can be proud of and truly enjoy with your whole family. Reconfigure, alter your plans for the balance of your life for yourself and your family, get all members on board and do whatever it takes to get you there. Remember, tell yourself, "If it is to be, it is up to me because this is a do-it-yourself life."

Think About It!

When disagreements, strong opposition over any significant positive matters occur between human beings – THINK "soothe it, smooth it before you lose it."

One of our objectives, I believe, should be, as we journey through our life, to "ruffle as few feathers" as possible.

Our attitude on our respective parts that many times seems to be, for whatever reason, at "the ready" to demean, disrespect, and antagonize another human being (your opposition) when strong disagreements occur is always for naught. It does not give long-lasting satisfaction, but rather stirs up your own body's operating system with vile "stuff" that will not bode well for your own personal health.

The combination of the choice of words we use, the tone of our voice we project, the sincerity or insincerity that may be showing in our faces can be a deciding factor in how well we can properly mitigate strong disagreements between human beings on any matter. Clear communication, sincere communication, accurate and timely communication are the best remedies I can think of.

Is there any argument for this cause?

We Are Not Alone

Look at our entire world. It is huge! It is so full of useful knowledge. We all need much knowledge in order to function at our best and receive the best returns from our efforts. Not to worry! We have so many highly qualified, knowledgeable people, "teachers," who are ready and willing to help us learn more. All we need to do is decide (we individually must decide) what we want to learn and then start learning.

But first we should strive to become a human being who has some good "baggage." Meaning, we have to provide ourselves with the solid basic knowledge of how to co-exist in a most favorable way with other human beings. When we have learned this and we exercise this knowledge on a daily basis, we will quickly realize the magnitude of "helpful hands" that we are surrounded by.

These other human beings with the available "helpful hands" will "step up to the plate" and cover all those areas of knowledge that we simply cannot have ourselves. All we will have to do is <u>ASK</u>. And when they realize and can see that we are carrying the right "baggage," they will quickly come to our aid.

THINK ABOUT IT! How could we go wrong with becoming totally Human Relations conscious?

Benefits!

"Benefits" – is "anything that is for the good of a person or thing."

Have you ever thought in this way? Whenever we do anything, the reason is to gain some benefit for ourselves. This can be interpreted to be selfish, unselfish, kind, compassionate, and useful.

Here are some examples.

- ➤ We work for the benefit of collecting a paycheck;
- ➤ We exercise because we want the benefits that accrue from being healthy;
- ➤ We eat healthy foods for the same reasons;
- ➤ We are helpful to others because we are kind and want others to feel the same about us;
- ➤ We anticipate others' needs and help prevent difficulties from happening because we are kind, considerate, observant, useful, and hope that others will do the same for us when and if needed.

What are we doing when we do this? We are practicing positive human relations at its very best. And the benefits to us, individually, are that we can be pretty sure of receiving high returns of kindness when we need to be on the receiving end of help. The concept of "Tit4Tat," "I give you like for like" is then in "full bloom." The end result for all concerned is more "Happiness!" This should be a worthwhile pursuit for <u>ALL</u> members of our "world family."

"Consistency"

This word, "consistency," is a word which meaning, if not used or adhered to properly, can wreak havoc with your good life, or when used properly it can help make your life a living "Garden of Eden" in comparison. This is a very important choice for everyone to be guided by for the long run.

The meaning of the word "consistency," in the context of this writing, is "constant adherence to the same principles, course, etc." Meaning, when you decide to start, to begin, to do something, anything that is "known" to be good, healthy, profitable for you and is not on the "instant gratification" time table, it will take "time," as much time as will be needed, and must be accepted and allowed in order to reach the benefits sought.

When you do the right things for yourself, on a consistent basis, you are helping yourself create very good situations for yourself and your future. "Consistency," in a manner of speaking, can be used as the strict "RULE" for achieving and retaining a very healthy and productive life for yourself and your future.

Think consistency when dealing with your personal health, your personal finances, your knowledge of human relations.

Listen! If and when you do the "things" that are not good for you (we all know what they are) on a consistent basis, you are developing for yourself a negative status. Again, herein lies lots of "common sense!"

The noteworthy part of all this is that you are the absolute "Ruler" of the so-called "control stick." You own it! But we sometimes seem to use it so "willy-nilly." We do some things with great consistency that turns out to be the most correct thing we can do to and for ourselves. And then at other times we do the complete opposite. We do things that we "like and enjoy" very much, but they are not things that will be in our best interest in the long run. Why do we do that?

Is this not an interesting phenomenon? We sometimes do that which we should know is not good for us, but for some reason we accept it and keep on doing it. "SMOKING" is one thing that comes to mind among many other things. Why? If you worked on giving yourself a good, clear answer, you would be a "BIG WINNER!" Work on it! It is, after all, your own life.

Why don't you "Think About" this following statement: "Do you believe that the concept of 'consistency' will apply to all those super-talented athletic human beings we know about?" Where do you think they would be "today" if they had not applied and exhibited great, consistent attitudes and actions in their ongoing very rigorous training? And what about all other highly successful professional human beings?

It is applying all the good you possess, all your knowledge on a very consistent basis that will "land" you on the success "Mark."

Remember to Remember

Remember what the dentist used to tell the children who did not want to brush their teeth on a regular basis? He/she would tell them: "You don't have to brush all of your teeth; brush only those that you want to keep." Get it!

Well, when we talk about what we as individual human beings need to do to gain the most from living our lives; we should accept without any questions the following scenario:

> "Good and positive Human Relations for ALL, dictates, suggests, and respectfully requests that we are respectful, sincere, honest, and kind to each other in our daily lives."

But, like "brushing your teeth," you don't have to be this way to everybody from the human race. What? I am not kidding! You only have to be respectful, sincere, honest, and kind to those human beings whom you need to rely on for your future well-being. And if you can identify who those human beings are now and will be in your future, you have it made. You will know exactly to whom you should direct your niceties. I would expect you now to interrupt me by loudly proclaiming that "I am nuts!" You could tell me that although you may know at this very moment who the human beings are that you need to rely on, but "how am I supposed to look into my future and decide, at this moment, whom I need to rely on for my future well-being?" Look! You pose a good question! Sure, we have already determined that our individual lives are a "do-it-yourself project." You and only you can decide how this question should be answered. Ponder! Ponder! Ponder! Have you come up with an answer yet?

I feel certain that you will come up with the correct answer. However, I will still tell you what my answer is.

Answer:

You will <u>only</u> have to show and be respectful, sincere, honest, and kind to those human beings whom you need to rely on your entire life for:

> ➤ Your health
> ➤ Your loving relationship with your family
> ➤ Your financial well-being
> ➤ Your future opportunities
> ➤ Your "employer" who pays you
> ➤ Your colleagues
> ➤ Your friends
> ➤ Your neighbors
> ➤ Your doctor
> ➤ Your policeman
> ➤ Your fireman
> ➤ Your minister, for all your invisible support
> ➤ Your automobile mechanics
> ➤ Etc.

Look at the many different human beings you would need to rely on. I think it would be safe to suggest that the human beings you will need to rely on now and into your future will be <u>Every Human Being</u> that touches your life in one way or another.

Are We Late?

Late for what? For joining the millions of human beings who already profess their satisfactions of accepting that living our lives is truly a "do-it-yourself project" <u>AND</u> that learning to understand and accept that each and every human being on our earth is different from one another and that is very much okay.

These two "mega thoughts" represent, to my way of thinking, two "milestones" that many of us have reached. What we are now faced with is continuing to diligently working on communicating, sincerely, with the balance of our human brothers and sisters, our reasons for accepting these two "mega thoughts!"

The thought of accepting that the results from our individual lives do represent a "do-it-yourself project" is, in my opinion, a "NO BRAINER." Because if we do not accept that and do, in a positive way, for ourselves what we need to do – Who will do it?

Do not ask what our "world" can do for <u>you</u>. Ask what <u>you</u> can do for <u>our</u> "world" and for yourself, and in the process try to help those human brothers and sisters who may not be able to help themselves. That is the idea behind the true sense of "working" within the "do-it-yourself" concept of living a good life.

Accepting differences in all human beings and treating each other as absolute true equals in the eye of our "MAKER" is a critical ingredient in what it will take to form the human bond essential in "getting along." Once we "get along" with each other by doing for each other, those things that will build genuine trust within all of us, we may never again take a "war-like" attitude and action against each other.

I answer (the heading question) are we late? No, we are not late. It is never too late to do whatever it takes to accomplish lasting niceties for other human beings, including yourself.

But you wonder as you move on in life, how long will it take for everybody to "get it"?

When we say we should <u>ALL</u> accept differences in each other, why should it be so difficult for <u>ALL</u> of us to get on "the same train and take the ride together?"

Sometimes we, individually, have a very strong "comfort zone" that is often an almost inescapable position to be in. I believe our individual "comfort zone" is made up of at least two (2) important personal attributes. One is a lack of understanding why and what specific differences exist in all of us. And, two, is the insurmountable (in some cases) selfishness within us. We simply do not want to change our personal situations. We do not want to chance compromising what we already know we have and what we understand.

When it comes to wanting and trying to understand "others," it is almost a "*fait accompli*" immediately before anything happens. It triggers a selfish thought. "Why should I understand you?" "You should make every attempt to understand me first." How insurmountable is this scenario?

What is a "diplomat" to do? Well, a good, experienced diplomat would probably say, "I want my mommy." And if that does not work, he would try to reach an initial agreement to have an "all inclusive" sincere dialogue with his oppositions with the sole and expressed purpose of reaching a mutual understanding of each other's reasons for "living." If this works, we should now have reached a mutual, honest, and complete understanding of each other's <u>real</u> reasons for existing in this world of ours.

Now we can start, call it, the follow-up dialogue by offering and accepting, and accepting and offering what should be mutually acceptable and rewarding "stuff" for each side. Remember, if there is "something" "on the table" that cannot be fairly interpreted as mutually beneficial – "forget about it"; it should not be there. However, sometimes a negative response of "I don't want it" may be attributed to not having a clear, factual understanding of what that "something" really means to all concerned. How "something" could or will be mutually beneficial may need a few more words of honest advice. Try it! That is how we learn to be convinced of things we may not be totally familiar with.

This ain't easy! Who said it was?

We cannot afford, nor can it ever become acceptable to employ the "instant gratification" phenomenon to anything mutually worthwhile that we need to accomplish.

More than ever, "TODAY," the need for "Diplomacy at Work" is totally required for any degree of meaningful success. This means, to my way of thinking, that we have to compromise our "selfish positions." We have to declare, figuratively, "here is one for you" and "here is one for me" in equal meaningful value and in fair and realistic proportions.

This is so that "fairness" will be in "vogue" for all to truly enjoy in a way and manner totally to the liking of each of us individually. In other words, you will not, unless you choose to, have to enjoy living your life in accordance with "my" will. Would that not be a "humdinger?"

"The Terrestrial Vault"

Home of the Largest Human Family Ever Known

Total Membership – 7 Billion Plus

It is a fact that we are all brought forth by birth into this tremendous family with such immense diversity in all aspects of living a life.

Our biggest problem that seems to have existed since time immemorial and still has not been sufficiently neutralized is that we, as one large family, do not like any of our "foreign" siblings. Except we, of course, like ourselves (meaning I) very much since we (meaning I) are perfect in every way imaginable. (I trust you will read this sentence and clearly notice its misplaced humor).

What mechanism did God install in our brain that is preventing us from being and acting as a "traditional family" usually should? Such as sharing love and enthusiasm for each other and engaging in and striving for living a life filled with happiness and as little suffering as possible.

We do not seem to want or we do not try very hard to understand each other and our respective motives or reasons for wanting to live our lives the way we each do. And until we do, we cannot possibly, in my opinion, try to change, to any degree (compromise), our ways of living in order to try to accommodate "difference."

I believe that if all of us in the basic tenet of our mutual beliefs are on the "same page" when it concerns true positive human relations, such as "live and let live," then there should never have to be any significant negative discourse between any of us.

We should all accept that the "old adage" of "live and let live" means exactly what it says. "Let live" has to include doing absolutely nothing that will hinder or prevent any human being from living a positive good and healthy life.

Perception is Reality

Your perception of something is your reality!

The way you see things, the way you hear things, and the way you think, and the way you understand what is happening, this becomes your reality. Other human being's perception of you should be of utmost importance to you.

Albert Einstein has been quoted as saying, "Reality is merely an illusion, albeit a very persistent one."

Douglas Adams has been quoted as saying, "Everything you see or hear or experience in any way at all is specific to you. You create a universe by perceiving it, so everything in the universe you perceive is specific to you."

Most of us probably have, at one time or another, used the phrase, "Perception is Reality." What do we mean when using this phrase?

An illusion is something that deceives by producing a false impression. An illusion is a false mental image or conception which may be a misinterpretation of a real appearance or may be something imagined. It may be pleasing, harmless, or even useful.

When it comes to having a perception of something, such as your perception of (the way you view) another human being or vice versa, another human being's perception of you, what, if anything, should we be concerned about?

Again, you need to give this question some serious thought. Now, you wonder why? Think about it! The way we humans view each other and the work that we do will be the legacy we will leave behind. Every interaction we have with other human beings, both personally and professionally, leave an impression. As we go about conducting our lives, your life, humans make judgments about our character, our appearance, and our abilities.

And as we live on, we <u>leave paper trails</u> depicting to some degree our life's history, our behavior from things like resumes, credit reports, e-mails, and sometimes the many goofy things we can do through the Internet. This can lead anyone to draw/form conclusions about who we are.

So, perhaps some readers may say, "So What!" Well, I say, "<u>LISTEN!</u>" Another human being's perception of you can <u>make or break</u> your future opportunities to do better for yourself. This would be especially true if this other human being is someone you need to rely on for your own betterment.

Remember the quote I used earlier in this book from the Ziggy cartoon?

> "Your <u>present</u> will be determined by your <u>past</u>.
> Therefore, in the <u>future</u> you should be very careful what
> you do in your past."

Perception is indeed REALITY. In today's world, business or personal CHARACTER and INTEGRITY as well as suitable ABILITIES will, if these qualities are good and present, help pave a smooth road for you to a good life. However, if these qualities ARE NOT good and present, it may pave a very bumpy, pot hole-riddled road to a LESS than good life. Be very much aware of how others perceive you.

If we all believe that perception is reality, then it is extremely important for all of us to lead with authenticity. Being an authentic human being means to be reliable and trustworthy. When you lead with authenticity, you are showing the quality of <u>transparency</u>, <u>reliability</u>, and <u>genuineness</u>. When it comes to personal and business relationships, we must spend a lot more time building the <u>I like you</u>, <u>I know you</u>, and <u>I trust you</u> factors, and we must earn it through patience.

What human beings perceive is usually what they believe, and it is based on what they <u>see</u>, <u>hear</u>, and <u>think</u>. So make certain you develop an appropriate <u>IMAGE</u> of yourself and be certain never to tarnish your image.

It is Good for Us to Recognize Our WISDOM

If we would stop, for a short while, what we were planning on doing and THINK again before we went any further, how would our personal lives turn out?

Think about the <u>TIME</u> it takes to build things of value to us. Think about the <u>TIME</u> it takes to completely destroy things of value to us.

Think about any kind of value, especially ideal social values that you personally want to achieve. As a for instance, let us consider your <u>REPUTATION</u>. "Reputation" is the word which refers to the position a person occupies or the standing that he/she has in the opinion (mind) of others in respect to accomplishments, integrity, and the like. In our world of high interdependency, what could be more helpful to each of us than a stellar reputation?

Winston Churchill reportedly said, "to <u>build</u> may have to be the slow 'laborious task' of years. To <u>destroy</u> can be the thoughtless act of a single day."

Listen! I am suggesting that the most valuable possessions a human being can "own" in their entire life and which should be considered the foundations of everything civil and positive and is what we should work to build on every single day of our lives is our <u>REPUTATION</u>. Note, it is not money.

Think about it! <u>As an example</u>, "You fully understand how enjoying a stellar reputation can truly benefit you and, therefore, over the past, say, 25 years you have added, on a consistent basis each day, total positiveness to what others think of you. Then one day, in one 24-hour period of your life, you are the <u>CAUSE</u> of a most reprehensible deed affecting others, and that will be judged by others as totally inexcusable. The net results to you and your life's stellar reputation could mean something like "ANNIHILATION" of a good portion, if not in total, of all positive future opportunities you could have had to live a good life.

Remember this saying! Make certain you fully understand its intended meaning. "Your <u>present</u> will be determined by your <u>PAST</u>. Therefore, in the <u>future</u> you should be very careful what you do in your <u>PAST</u>."

Think some more about this situation.

When things, in general, are going well for you and most things seem to be going your way, you feel elated, happy, and satisfied. Those are great feelings to have. These are feelings you should always try to generate for yourself and your family all the time.

However, contrary feelings do sometimes enter our lives and then we wonder what happened. When things happen in your life that are not "happiness"-producing moments, if you immediately try to learn the reasons why unhappy things happen, you could probably "fix it" and turn a frown into a smile.

Well, this book, *Tit4Tat*, I believe can put you back on the right track that can lead you to more consistent happiness and satisfaction each and every day of the rest of your life. All it will take from your end is "all you got." And if you bet "all you got" on a pretty sure thing, you can become a BIG WINNER!

Are You a Good "SERVANT"?

Being a good "SERVANT" paves your way for a very good life. The definition of the word "Servant," one of many, but the one most appropriate for the context of this book is *"a person in the service of another."*

As you read this book, you will no doubt have the feelings and understanding that each of us human beings, in our world of seven-plus billion human beings, because of our growing interdependence on each other, are each other's "SERVANT."

Perhaps we should use the word "SERVANT" in a more "symbolic" way. After all, think about it. There is very little that we can accomplish in our lives without the input, help, advice, work, etc. by others. Everything we do, everything we accomplish is never without a "helping hand" from some other human being. Think about it and you will understand where I am coming from.

The more people we serve and the more people who are willing to serve us will make for a very "profitable" life for all of us, in every respect.

Old Saying!

Adherence to which will equal positive results.

There is a very old saying that I feel certain you have heard many times before, but do you really think about what it means?

The saying is, "You don't bite the hand that feeds you." Please, really think about it. I hope you all get it.

It is so easy to remember this "saying." And if you keep reminding yourself of its "deep" meaning whenever you work with others and for others for personal gains, you will, I am sure, want to adhere to this sage advice for the benefit of yourself and others.

Remember what human beings respond best to. It is another human being who is known to be useful, responsible, honorable, compassionate, disciplined, and who has a positive attitude coupled with integrity.

That sounds like a real "mouthful," right? And in today's "world," it is the one combination that will help propel you to success and happiness.

Easy Question!

Here is an easy question for each of us to remember. However, your "honest" answer to yourself will, in my opinion, play an important pivotal role for you in how well you will be living a good and successful life.

Does trying to please others <u>FIRST</u>, please you?

If it does, I believe you will be "home free" and do well after reading this book.

If trying to please others FIRST does not necessarily please you, then you need to try to learn something about yourself as to <u>why</u> it does not please you.

The reasons for concern, I believe, should be because "pleasing" others <u>first</u> is a very important ingredient to possess in our "mental make-up" needed for providing ourselves with a long, good, and productive life.

When you realize what significant positive impact this kind of thinking can have for each of us, "putting others first," you will no doubt recognize the enormous <u>LOGIC</u> behind it. It is another attribute of true COMMON SENSE.

Yes We Can!

We can make our own lives more pleasant and more productive and sometimes the same for our "opposition" if we become more tolerable and, to a degree, more condescending toward other human being's perceived short-comings. We should be more tolerable of others, especially in situations that could not or would not change our own lives for the worse. Let us not "stand on ceremony" just for spite; it will probably not serve any purpose other than adding "fuel to the fire" if there are already glowing embers present.

THINK ABOUT IT! Figuratively speaking, if we want "fire"/dissention amongst ourselves, by all means add lots of "dry, seasoned wood" to an already smoldering "fire" situation. However, if you are concerned about not causing a "conflagration," do whatever you can think of to put out the "fire" completely and immediately. Do not ever wait or hold out for your "opposition" to commence any "mending" steps – you take the lead and you will be the better human being for doing so. And many times your, perhaps, fierce opposition will become a friend rather than a foe. And should that not be every human being's objective/goal – to make "enemies" friends?

Do consider this fact! At all times when you show your positive, noble, self-assertive side of your humanity, you are, in essence, in my opinion, showing your intelligence to all who are watching. By following and adhering to the above type of thinking and action, you are exercising your eclectic ways to the best results.

Can We Talk?

Conversation is communication, and communication between two or more human beings to be most effective should always be conversation.

Do not sell this concept short. Why? Well, THINK ABOUT IT! The word "conversation" means "having informal interchange of thoughts by spoken words." The word "writing" still means having a conversation, but one decides to commit one's thoughts to writing. Writing does not allow for immediate questioning of or clarity of what is said, as in the spoken word. Nor will we have the "advantage" of "voice" and "personal demeanor" which, many times, will help to reach a more complete understanding of a conversation.

When you interchange your thoughts with someone else, you are in effect "letting your hair down," meaning you are revealing your feelings on specific matters to that someone else. The main reason for having any interchange of thoughts is to do just that – to let someone else know, very clearly, how you feel about any specific matter.

Is this important? Well, it depends. Sometimes, perhaps a lot of times, the "matters" involved could be in the context of our daily lives referred to as "minutia." And minutia, to my way of thinking, can be any "transfer of thoughts that are, in essence, "meaningless" and offer nothing to change our lives one way or the other. This effect I would call not important.

However, the next type of "transfer of thought" is of high importance to the persons transferring a thought and equally important to the person receiving the thought. This would be transfer of thoughts that deal with feelings of happiness and unhappiness, feelings of hurt and alleged deception, sharp disagreements of anything meaningful, etc. In other words, "thoughts," if not understood clearly by both the giver and receiver of the thoughts, can lead to continued misunderstandings and potential destruction of an otherwise good life.

Do You Ever Make MISTAKES?
Cause Blunders and "Screw-Ups"?

When you are the cause for anything like the above happenings, your "saving grace" could be your good reputation. What do I mean?

Well, think about it! If you cause a mistake, blunder, or "screw-up," and you are known as a person who is kind, thoughtful, useful, and honest, others are usually very quick to "forgive and forget." Why is that?

Well, again, think about it! How would you personally deal with something like this if someone you liked and respected caused some mishap to your "life?" Would you not immediately extend an "olive branch" and tell them, "It's okay, we will fix it." I believe that is very close to reality.

Criticism and Opposition

In a democracy, CRITICISM and OPPOSITION, to very meaningful, important, and serious matters seem to flow freely without sufficient forethought. Also, it seems to be tolerated and accepted as "constitutional" and believed to be indispensable.

To criticize anything and to be in opposition of anything can be a "POSITIVE" if it is rendered with sincerity and not with malevolence to unfairly gain an "upper hand."

In addition, since the word "criticism" means "the act of passing judgment as to the merits of anything," criticism should <u>ONLY</u> be leveled at someone with the sole intent and sincerity to HELP that someone.

However, the "Human Right" to cause "criticism" and to be in "opposition" to things should <u>ONLY</u> be exercised in the name of "positive progress" for the benefit of the large majority implied. And should always be accompanied with a reasonable "come back" showing credible and descriptive reasons for any and all disagreements.

Keep the following in mind, always, that a response to any proposal of significance should never be just "I don't like it." If you cannot <u>add</u> anything positive to the "cause" in question, don't get involved. And do not speak just to hear yourself talk. That would be wasting valuable time.

"Open Mic" (Microphone) Syndrome

If you are a person known to be of strong moral fiber and integrity, and it is of great importance to you that others continue to feel that way about you, be very much aware of the "Open Mic" Syndrome. Don't "feed" it.

Our "Hi Tech" industry can do many good things for all of us, on "one hand." But it is the other "hand" you should be aware of. Know how easy it has become to observe and to listen to individuals living their daily lives even if they are literally "miles" away from the electronic culprit doing the listening and observing.

Be careful, be aware, be smart, use your intelligence, never talk or write about anyone or anything in a derogatory manner. It is the safest and best way to maintain your integrity intact. You will never know when you will unknowingly be "on stage." Besides, "talking" about anyone or anything in a "derogatory" manner does not give you any advantages, but possibly many disadvantages.

Now having said this, it does not mean that you cannot properly criticize someone or something, BUT always keep in mind that there is only one rational or valid reason or purpose for criticizing anything or anyone and that is to help make something better. And all criticism offered with this purpose in mind should never, in my opinion, be made through a "third" party, but instead always made face-to-face in privacy with the person you tend to try to help. Also, before you propose any criticism, make certain that you have all "your ducks in a row," that you have sufficient knowledge about each situation that allows you to feel sufficiently strong that your criticism should or could help.

If you do not have sufficient knowledge and you are only out to "blow your own horn," "don't open your mouth." But instead, if you feel like it, offer to help work with the situation to make it better.

The above thoughts are based on the "facts" that all too often we hear others say things, believing that no one else is listening, that should never have been uttered from "the lips" of people who are held in high esteem and integrity.

Wow! Did you really say that about me?

Peace of Mind

"Peace of mind is a state of mental and emotional calmness, happiness, and freedom, with no worries, fears, or stress" (our dictionary).

"It is possible to divide every kind of happiness and suffering into two main categories: mental and physical. Of the two, it is the MIND that exerts the greatest influence on most of us. The mind registers every event, no matter how small. Hence, we should devote our most serious efforts to bringing about mental peace" (The Dalai Lama).

The description of "peace of mind" by our dictionary is no doubt based on a vision of a "Utopian" environment, which is something the entire world should strive to achieve. However, I believe we can all agree that our ability and aptitude (the medicine required) to filling this prescription is a long way off from "FDA's" approval.

However, to my way of thinking, there are many things we, as mere mortals, can do to help ourselves move closer to filling this prescription. Think about it! Let's talk.

Having "peace of mind" is the quality needed to live our lives the way our creator intended for all of us to live. So the closer we can help ourselves get to the "peace of mind" feeling, the better we will be able to live our lives.

Let's think out loud! What things happen in our daily lives that can cause us to not have peace of mind?

We are being reminded of three (3) distinct categories of life-fulfilling needs. These are all very personal needs and where our individual attitudes will play a significant role in improving our chances to accommodate ourselves. It is <u>Personal Health</u>, <u>Personal Finance</u>, and our relationships with other human beings, aka <u>Human Relations</u>.

Now, what can happen within these three (3) categories that can "Royally" disjoin our lives if we, individually, do not "spring" to the rescue? None of the tactics that I will suggest we should employ in our correction mode is by any stretch of our imagination "Rocket Science."

It is just plain, clear thinking about human miscalculations when it comes to living our lives.

When you sense that something is not right with the way your life, at any particular moment, is playing out before your eyes find an opportunity to stop what you are doing, and take a few moments and just "let go," clear your mind. And, then rewind your memory as far back as you need to, to realize when something was starting to go "South." Clearly identify what you understand was happening in your life (good idea to write it down). Then put on your "Reasoning hat" and provide yourself with some honest, straight, and simple explanation of <u>why</u> you believe what happened, happened. Now, once you have reached this point the answers you will need to make your situation better should be right in front of your eyes. Now, deal with it and cause yourself to feel better. Do whatever you need to do to add to your "peace of mind." So many times in order to solve a "problem" that we may have had a hand in creating, all we have to do is to think about identifying it, put it on the "table" for all involved to see and understand, and then get your "mending machine" and fix it all. The only time you will not, in my opinion, be successful in solving your own problem in this manner is if you are stubborn and have no flexibility.

Your "mending machine," as I choose to call it, is simply your understanding that the "problem" needs to be resolved in order for all involved to achieve more peace of mind. And you are a "Diplomat" who recognizes that the intent of Diplomacy is compromise. And, at times, an apology may be in order. As it were, your positive attitude toward resolving an important matter for the good of all is your "mending machine."

When you think about it from a pure, logical human relations point of view, PEACE is always available albeit at a price. A price that we have to rationalize, negotiate, and reach agreement on and then fully accept with no thoughts of vengeance attached.

Tolerance!

"Tolerance is giving to every other human being every right that you claim for yourself."

(Robert Green Ingersoll)

Listen!

Everywhere you go and in all that you want to accomplish – keep adding "new partners" to help you smooth the "road."

Life is not meant to go at it alone.

Creative Visualizations

What is this, and how can it help you to attain the best life possible for yourself and your family?

When you visualize something, you are forming a mental image or picture of that something. To have a good life, you first have to determine what "having a good life" means to you. You have to clearly identify, to yourself, what you want to have happen in your life that you will be happy and content with calling a "good life!"

The process you go through in identifying what you want to do with your life should be an interesting and very pleasant undertaking. You THINK, you DETERMINE, and you PLAN. Then you visualize your whole scenario, your goals. And when you visualize your goals, you begin to live the life you are planning to achieve. From that moment, all your decisions and all your actions will begin to lead you toward what you are visualizing. This "move" on your part will relax your mind and reduce any fear or concern you may have had about your future. Because now you already know, in your mind, that you are on the "road" that will lead you to where you want to be.

And now, all you need to keep on remembering and exercising is the CONSISTENCY required in properly dealing with all positive matters. Your goals. This will bring you to the DESTINATION YOU decided on.

"Trust and Security"

You may only get <u>one chance</u> to convey the feelings of trust and security to another human being.

The word "KEY" is also an important word for all of us to understand. What does the word mean as it relates to Human Relations?

A "key" has always been a tool used to open things. "Key" = means of attaining, understanding, solving (the "key" to solving a problem). The more keys you have access to give you more opportunities to enter through more "closed doors." The right "key" helps you reach, achieve, or accomplish "things." The right "key" helps you understand many things needed to solve problems.

Think about it! Connecting in positive ways with other human beings require special "keys" of understanding.

To my way of thinking, the two most valuable "keys" that any human being can possess is the "security key" and the "trust key," held together on the same key chain.

<u>Security</u> – "The feeling of freedom from danger and risk. The feeling of freedom from apprehension or doubt. The feeling of confidence."

<u>Trust</u> – "The feeling of being able to rely on the integrity and justice of another human being. The feeling of confidence in the ability or intentions of another human being to do what he/she agrees to do."

Think about this! The human beings you meet and that you want to connect with, if you know that they are providing these two important "keys" and always used them in tandem, would it not be a "piece of cake" for you to make the connection?

This "key carrying" scenario is <u>REAL</u> in <u>REAL LIFE</u>. You and I and everyone else who want the best life for us cannot or should not leave home without possessing and being <u>KNOWN</u> to always provide these two "keys." Trust and Security are the only things that can and will solidify a positive relationship with other human beings.

A positive relationship with other human beings is the absolute best way for all of us to create a successful good life for ourselves. We will all do ourselves a great deed by always adhering to these facts.

Courtesy

Oh! Courtesy. Oh! Courtesy. Where art thou!

Oh! Courtesy. We need more of the pleasant feelings you help to create.

The "Tit4Tat" concept works all the time. Where is the proof? Ah! The proof, the undeniable proof. Everybody must have proof; if they don't, nothing happens, right? Well. Okay. The undeniable proof to each of us that the "Tit4Tat" concept works is found in the most trustworthy place that we can all accept as "IT." It is in <u>YOU</u>, in <u>ME</u>, in <u>EVERYBODY</u>. Understand the Tit4Tat concept, <u>Live it in reality</u> and you will have all the proof you want of how well it works.

To be courteous may be one of the easiest ways and very effective ways to bring a degree of pleasantness to everyone you make contact with. It is easy to accomplish and it will not cause a financial drain on us.

For those of us who always remember to exercise courtesy when the opportunity is there, we salute you and thank you for making the recipients of your actions feel better.

For those of us who do not remember until the opportunity to show courtesy has passed, we suggest that we try to "slow down" a bit so that we do not ruin the opportunity in the future.

Showing courtesy is easy and simple. And courtesy is having excellence of manners and behavior and politeness. When we read books like this one, it is a forgone conclusion that we possess these qualifications.

The bottom line is: exercising courtesy is "Totally" an integral part of using the "Tit4Tat" concept – "I give you like for like" and <u>I will be the first to show it.</u>

Smile, thank you, you are welcome, have a nice day, good to see you again, let me help you with that, how are you, etc. – <u>Keep adding to this</u>

<u>list</u>. These are words that usually bring a smile to a recipient's face and a feel-good feeling.

Holding a door for someone, showing an "After you, please" attitude to someone, "Don't unnecessarily use your car horn" when driving, "you first" attitude at stop signs when driving a car, "stop or slow down" for people crossing a street when driving a car. Promote helpfulness, convenience, and safety at every opportunity you come across. This could be referred to both as an unselfish way and a selfish way to behave – I think you know what I mean.

A nice <u>SMILE</u> is the best and most favorable introduction you can provide to anyone you meet – old friends, new friends, and total strangers. A sincere smile from you, or a return smile when you receive it from someone else, seems to remove many perceived or perhaps expected barriers to a spontaneous meeting. A smile seems to contain the ingredients to a more positive encounter.

So, remember the "weapon" you possess when meeting anyone – SMILE. If not convinced, think about all those times in the past when you have met people who may have been the first ones to crack a smile for you.

How Should We Dress?

<u>Your Answer</u>: "Any way I want!?

<u>Consideration</u>: Clothes do not "make" the person, <u>BUT</u> plays an important and sometimes a deciding role in <u>introducing</u> the person.

This is one time, of many times, we have to show consideration for others, especially if we are seeking their assistance.

How to Argue

Having an argument with someone is like any negotiating session over a very sensitive subject.

You use tact and you remain tactful.

You use meaningful words to accurately describe your point of view.

You maintain a respectful demeanor.

Remember! You are having a discussion, not a "fight."

Remember! "Compromise" is not a dirty word; it is the essence of diplomacy.

Consistency and Persistency (Twin Brothers)

Being consistent and persistent when performing positive "niceties" to others (including you) is very much a deciding factor in getting positive results in return.

When you begin to work on your "good life" and you begin to seek "help" and "information" from your fellow human beings, and you begin to receive what you need, do realize what is happening. It is the "Tit4Tat" concept at work in real time.

Always remember, you must be the FIRST to provide someone with a positive "good" before you can expect to receive a positive "good" in return.

Also consider this – if you do not receive a distinct positive "good" in return, do not be discouraged or upset. You probably gave some "good" to another human being who has not been accustomed to receiving much "good" and, therefore, you probably "shocked" the heck out of the person. However, you keep on being the FIRST person to be giving the "good." This is where the (twin brothers) "consistency" and "persistency" approach will eventually pay you a return with "good." Believe me, it will be very much worth your efforts when the "good" start flowing your way.

Being Organized Give You Feelings of Success

I do not have time to be organized! WOW! The reason you do not have time to be organized is <u>only</u> because you are not organized.

Try the "10 minute" organizing effort!

First, sit yourself down and decide to just "WASTE" 10 minutes of time. Just sit quietly by yourself for one 10-minute period (time yourself). During this 10-minute period, think about each minute that passes. You should have a feeling that each minute, even though it is only 60 seconds, is a lot of time when you are just sitting around.

Now think about the various things that you usually find yourself needing to do to get things done so that you can move on with living a good life each and every day.

Being organized, whether it is operating your home or operating a business, is all about having a clear picture in your mind of the <u>important</u> things that all need to be completed in order for you to fulfill your obligations, your responsibilities.

Once you have a clear and complete "picture" of what you are responsible for to complete, you prioritize each and every item of work. You tell yourself, based on each item's "importance" that FIRST, this item, Second, this item, etc. until you have all of your responsibilities accounted for. Then you start with the first item, complete it, and move on to the second item, complete it, etc.

Now let us get back to my "10-minute" organizing effort. Everything we do will have to use up some of our time. However, if we learn to realize and remember that many things, especially around and in our home, does not necessarily take much time to actually get done. Usually when we complain and become frustrated with that "everything," mostly stuff that seems to give us that "clutter" feeling, never seems to get done and just piles up. If we realize that so much of this type of "work" can be done, corrected, in just 10 minutes, we probably will feel less frustration and much better.

Why not give it a try?!

Independent?

Do we want to be independent?

Can we be independent and still have the ability to live a good and productive life?

Here is a partial description of what an independent person would be subjected to. Think about it as you read it, and then ask yourself if it would be your best choice for living your life.

> "Being independent means: not being influenced by others in matters of opinion, conduct, etc.; thinking or acting for oneself; not subject to another's authority or jurisdiction; free; not influenced by the thought or action of others; not dependent; not depending or contingent on something else for existence; not relying on another or others for aid or support; declining others' aid or support; refusing to be under obligations to others."

What do you think? Do you believe it would be possible to be an immovable independent human being and still be able to live a good and productive life? One reason why I decided to write a little bit on this subject is that, at times, I have met people who act and behave toward others as if they truly believed that they are totally independent and therefore can do whatever they feel like doing or saying. I do not know, but perhaps an accurate way to describe such a person is with the word "ARROGANT."

Being free to choose your actions and behavior based on what you know to be good, positive, and productive is not a description of an indendent person. It is a description of a person who is living in a free and democratic environment.

Also, how could we "think" that we could literally stay away from listening to and learning from others of things that would perhaps otherwise "go way over our heads" and leaving us destined to go on living our lives unbeknownst of what others know that can help our lives become better and better?

No! Let us be and remain independent only as to how we guide our own lives through the "thick and thin" with honesty and compassion toward ourselves and all others with whom we come in contact during our lives.

Do this and you will feel very good about it!

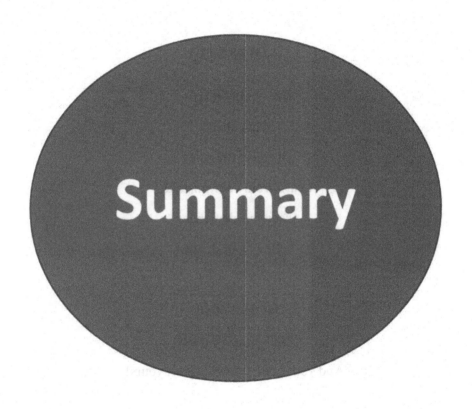

Summary

Always try

Use common sense

Plan ahead

Respect the rules

Learn from your mistakes

Face the challenges

Follow your dreams

But most of all –

Believe in yourself

And your good life will be all yours!

SUMMARY

I am hopeful that you enjoyed reading about these reminders and that your personal life will greatly benefit by their application.

Keep in mind that there are essentially four (4) things that you cannot get back:

- ✓ The "stone" after it is thrown.
- ✓ The word after it is said.
- ✓ The opportunity after it is missed.
- ✓ The time after it is gone.

You know the saying, "If you build it, they will come." I believe that this saying may be a reference to Noah's Ark, when God directed Noah to build the ark and to put the animals on it. Noah asked God how he would get the animals and God told Noah – "If you build it, they will come."

Bring that saying forward to now, the 21st century. How do you think we can use that same saying today to clarify and make a very important "point" as it concerns each of our personal lives?

Well, let us think about it this way – you are one regular human being (the "raw material") and you attach to yourself specialized finishing material which will turn you into a special human being of increased value to yourself and others. The specialized material would be effective knowledge and your actions covering <u>human relations</u>, <u>personal finance</u>, <u>planning</u>, <u>health</u>, and <u>spiritual nourishment</u>. Now you have built yourself into a very valuable human commodity and when other human beings learn about your existence "<u>THEY</u> will come." You will be the beneficiary of very positive SELF REALIZATION, the fulfillment of your potential capacities.

Do you agree? "If you <u>LISTEN</u> and <u>WATCH</u>, you can hear and see, very clearly, how more and more each day our human brothers and sisters turn to each other with "helping hands" and with lots of compassion whenever there are important needs to be met. To me, that spells <u>HOPE</u> in large bright letters.

In the author's humble opinion, this book and its intent can clearly help move all the readers in the same direction.

And, as an aside, to our <u>LEADERS</u> in whom we place our trust and well-being – <u>LISTEN</u> to what your constituency need and want, according to their <u>RIGHTS</u> as human beings. Do not assume you know, make certain you know, and this should be your only objective as their servant – to help them reach their goals. Do not digress for a nanosecond. And do not even think "WAR!"

Once you have <u>prepared</u> yourself for living a good "do-it-yourself" life and you feel confident in challenging productive endeavors, take <u>your</u> meaning and understanding of the following two words – **MOTIVATION** and **DISCIPLINE** – and join them together as your self-consciousness <u>MOTTO</u>. Know that forgetting, even for a brief moment, the reasons and the rules <u>you decided</u> to follow, to help yourself, may upset your good life.

Your **MOTIVATION** – Always keep thinking of <u>your reasons</u>, <u>your incentive</u> for persuading yourself to proceed with your (any) project.

Your **DISCIPLINE** – Always act <u>with consistency</u> in accordance with the rules <u>you have</u> established for reaching your objective.

Know and accept that the TEACHER will not recruit a class; instead, the students will seek a teacher. Do not wait around for the opportunity to learn. Decide what you want to know and go find someone who knows it.

Keep on remembering this too! Realize and accept that we cannot accomplish in "one day" all the meaningful "things" we need and want to do for ourselves and humanity. However, personal feelings of <u>self-satisfaction</u> in the most noble sense may be the single most important feeling we should diligently work to achieve for ourselves. <u>PLANNING</u>, therefore, in our lives, becomes an all-important endeavor on our respective parts to achieve the most with our time for all good causes.

Now when you have completed the reading of this book, you no doubt realize how much we all need to do for ourselves and for others in order to live a good life.

We have a lot to offer each other as it concerns the "nutritious fodder" needed by all to live a good life. And there are human differences that we need to find an effective way to understand and deal with.

How can we, <u>ALL OF US</u>, properly deal with certain human differences which, if they remain not clearly understood, usually produce nothing of real <u>mutual</u> benefit?

Remember this? – "It is my way or the highway!"

This is an old covetous saying that should never, in my opinion, be employed when the proverbial wisdom of "live and let live" is most definitely involved with any "difference" looking for an amicable settlement.

If you truly do not like and cannot live with what someone is trying to impose on your current lifestyle, do not just respond with something like "I don't like it" or "I believe you are totally off the track." Instead, respond with more intelligence, with something specific from your side that may improve favorably upon what has been suggested. Remember and accept that the words "live and let live" mean just that – you live your life in a manner that pleases you and does not hinder in any way, shape, or form others to live their lives in a manner that pleases them. However, there is one <u>caveat</u> that <u>all</u> must adhere to which is a very simple and very obvious one – you do not "step on the toes" of others "intentionally."

Do show, at every opportunity, your human elegance, your gracefully refined attributes toward all living things, including yourself.

During your life's existence you may, at times, feel stubbornness, insensitiveness, selfishness. These are attributes that all of us possess in varying degrees. If these attributes cannot be obliterated or substantially "downsized" in their negativeness, "both sides," in any attempt at equalization, will continue to live in disharmony.

To give yourself the most opportunities to live your life successfully and dealing with your personal financial situations, your positive relationship with other human beings – "FIND A NEED AND FILL IT."

Helping to fill others' needs <u>first</u> will cause your activities to greatly influence your abilities to satisfy your own personal needs. Remember "Tit4Tat." And for everyone's sake – <u>do not ever succumb; do not ever yield to GREED</u>. GREED will always, without exception, distort your positive power of reasoning. A simple definition of greed is "to have more than is necessary."

Be yourself and effect change if you so desire.

We are all subjected to "problems" which can be emotional, financial, or both.

If you feel overwhelmed – simplify your life; review in your mind what you really want to do.

You have to monitor your life, your efforts, constantly to make certain you stay on the right "track" that you have decided on.

As a self-protector, we must be, in our own minds and for our own protection, the "policeman," the "fireman," the "medical alert connection," the "driving instructor," the "lookout" for human miscalculations.

As you complete your reading of this book, "take your own temperature!" Meaning, give some serious thought to your own personal situation. Ask yourself, "where am I today with my progress for living the best life I can give myself and my family? Am I due for some changes that will bring me faster and closer to realizing my goals?" Remember the suggestion regarding <u>CHANGE</u> that can give you a new NORM and a much improved life.

Let us not forget that we are all "works in progress." And let us not mistakenly think that we are finished.

When anger rises, think of the consequences.

The obvious – when we get ready to do something, anything, you have already decided <u>WHY</u> you will be doing it. This <u>WHY?</u> is your reason for doing it. Now, for any of us human beings to truly benefit from our efforts to do something, especially with the absolute limit of 24 hours in our day to do it – we should make certain, in our minds, that what we are about to start and complete will <u>ADD</u> a meaningful result, totally relevant to the well-being and happiness for our family. If it is not going to add something meaningful to your life – Why would you even bother to do it? The reason for this statement is an effort to cause us to truly focus the time we have on this earth to <u>ONLY</u> pay attention to positive maneuvers on our respective parts that will boost our chances for living a good and healthy life.

What we all need to be keenly aware of to start every day of our remaining days on this earth, and may there be countless days, is a **<u>CLEAN MIND</u>** – meaning your mind should be filled with **<u>CLEAR, POSITIVE, KIND</u>**, and **<u>CONSTRUCTIVE</u>** thoughts that are all geared toward fulfilling your daily responsibilities needed to reach your absolute goals. Your mind needs to be filled with something, so what you fill your mind with are these thoughts and then the accompanied necessary **<u>ACTION</u>** by you, which together will culminate in a highly profitable day for you. This is the kind of thinking that will, day after day, help you achieve satisfaction and peace of mind – the daily end results everyone wants.

Ability is a general word for mental power, native or acquired, enabling one to do things well. How can we give ourselves an "edge" that will give us a more clear and a more convincing feeling that our desired success in life will become attainable? Become a serious, sincere student of <u>LEARNING</u>. Pack your brain full of knowledge in your field of interest.

Certainly not the least of the many things we need to accomplish to reach our goals – <u>BUT</u> a very important point of knowledge. If things do not work out like you expect it to work out, **<u>you owe it to yourself to learn "why."</u>**

A strong feeling of satisfaction with yourself for who you are and what you have done to date is a wonderful feeling to enjoy. If you are blessed with this feeling now, be ever more thankful. But remember to "STAY HUNGRY"; it increases your desires to accomplish more.

If for some reason your personal feelings for your accomplishments to date have not reached your self-imposed level of satisfaction, remember that "Rome was not built in one day." And the word <u>CHANGE</u> was invented for all of us, when needed, to do things differently in order to achieve our goals. Make some appropriate changes to your *modus operandi*. "Yesterday" is gone and "tomorrow" is the first day of your future.

Remember that <u>words</u> of encouragement and kindness are important to everyone. And <u>actions</u> based on the words is equally, if not more, important. Pay close attention to what people say and pay **closer** attention to what they do. Do they mean what they say?

Do the best you can and then do a little more.

When the <u>LIGHT</u> is bright and steady we can all see more clearly.

<u>LIGHT</u> to us human beings is <u>KNOWLEDGE</u>.

<u>DARE</u> to see another point of view.

<u>TOGETHER</u> we will have every opportunity to resolve negative, injurious differences.

There can be a new beginning for each of us every future minute that blesses our lives.

GO FOR "THE WHOLE 9 YARDS."

INCREASE YOUR FACE VALUE

SMILE

"Y O L O"

You only live once!

Make it the best "once" you ever did!

Do not put yourself in a position of being VULNERABLE – strengthen ALL aspects of yourself and your life – do not permit, by your demeanor, anyone to assume that you have weakness they can exploit.

PROGRESS is powered from within

What you end up with, at any stage of your life, you will have provided for yourself. BUT NEVER FORGET that the assistance you will need and that you can receive from other human beings should be considered by you as one of the greatest assets you can always count on for your own provisions. Do not be short-sighted; think and plan for your long term.

Always remember and accept that DIFFERENCES in human beings is a very normal happening. A human difference can function as either a joiner or dis-joiner of people. Differences will always be with us. We should try to understand why a specific difference, from our own point of view, exists in another human being, and accept it or not accept it.

If we accept a difference or not accept a difference in another human being, in either situation there is, to my way of thinking, one inescapable responsibility we must ALL accept and provide for, which is to always GIVE respect and kindness (a non-hostile attitude). "If we cannot end our differences, at least we can help make the world safe for diversity" (John F. Kennedy).

There is, in my opinion, nothing "etched in stone" that would dictate that we must "LIKE" everyone on this earth. BUT we must RESPECT and HONOR the FACT that ALL OF US (excluding EVIL) have all the same RIGHTS to live a constructive and secure life that we claim for ourselves. If we, any of us, go against this observation with our personal action, WE ARE WRONG!

In this big world that we live in, there will always be human beings who have much less than we have, and there will be those who have much more than we have. So what do we do, those of us who are stuck in the middle? Well, we can do the things that may always be beneficial to us – we can do whatever we can do to help those who have much less than we have. And we can do whatever we can to be useful and respectful to those who have much more than we have, and the result for us may be a "trickle down" effect of some of the good stuff that we could use.

Note that a "disservice" is a non-desirable service and is something you do not want to impose on yourself. In my humble opinion, if you do not, at the least, try to get a good sense of what these REMINDERS can help you to accomplish, you will be providing yourself with a disservice.

Remember that everything you say or do will effect certain consequences for you. Everything you say or do that is considered GOOD! or considered BAD! by others will create either good results or bad results for you. "Do unto others what you would want others to do to you," then you will, I believe, always have someone to "have your back."

Remember when you "feed" something, you are providing that something with the requisite materials for development, maintenance, or operation. By "feeding" something, it will become more plentiful for you. So, make certain that you "feed" only that which you want to become more plentiful. Make it very clear to yourself what kind of thinking and actions by you will be the best for you in reaching and benefiting from your PLANS for a good future.

Learn how and accept that living your daily life "below" your means will allow you to have peace of mind and something left for "tomorrow," and tomorrow will be more important to you than yesterday.

For everything you will participate in doing during your productive lifetime – keep in mind the human life supporting "things" that must continue to be available, with uninterrupted certainty, to ALL human beings, and then make certain that you wholeheartedly support and do your part in the essential maintenance of all such "things." I am referring, at this moment, to clean healthy air to breathe, clean healthy water to drink, an adequate supply of healthy food to eat, and a natural environment that can sustain itself and reconstruct itself, as needed, and not be subjected to a continuous human display of senseless destruction.

Always remember that we are learning how to prepare ourselves to live a good life and to be a "magnate" for good opportunities in a "do-it-yourself" life. Educate yourself for what <u>YOU</u> want to do.

"DARE TO SEE ANOTHER POINT OF VIEW."

I wish you the very best.

Sincerely,

Grandfather

The end of this book hopefully will be the beginning of many more "POSITIVES" for you.

May God Bless All of You!